Let me start with a not altogether surprising confession:

I'm a bit of a coward.

If I were ever asked to join the Army, I'd be the first one to sign up. For postal duties. In a remote field in Scotland.

Fortunately, no one's asking this overweight petrolhead to head for the nearest sand dune and start brandishing an SA80. Because we've already got the best soldiers in the world and they do an incredible job. And *Real Heroes* will show you exactly how they do it – 24 hours a day, 365 days a year.

I've lost my lunch in an F15 fighter jet and been scared witless on a jet-powered snowmobile, which turned out to be so biblically fast I thought my insides had, briefly, become my outsides. For an ordinary bloke like me, these were truly terrifying experiences. But they were nothing compared to the realities of life on the Afghanistan front line for our troops.

Real Heroes gives a fascinating insight into their tough military world. It reveals the extraordinary courage it takes to disarm a roadside bomb. The detailed planning and execution of special operations to breach Taliban strongholds. And the compelling drama of a 12-man SAS operation to avenge the death of their British comrades killed by IED booby traps.

These are the heart-stopping stories of real men and women fighting a very real war. None more so than Lance Corporal Matt Croucher, the Royal Marine reservist who hurled himself on top of a grenade to save his pals. Matt Croucher's bravery shows why we should all be in awe of our Armed Forces.

That's why I'm so proud that the people of this country have dug deep and raised millions for the Help for Heroes charity.

By buying this book, you've done your bit to swell those coffers, too.

It may not seem the most heroic act in the world.

It doesn't compare with surviving a Taliban bomb blast.

But it will help make a real difference to the life of someone who has.

REAL HEROES

ALL-ACTION TRUE STORIES FROM THE FRONT-LINE!

Harper Press

HarperPress
An imprint of HarperCollinsPublishers
77–85 Fulham Palace Road
Hammersmith, London W6 8JB
www.harpercollins.co.uk

Visit our authors' blog: www.fifthestate.co.uk
Like this book? www.bookarmy.co.uk

First published by HarperPress in 2009

1

A catalogue record for this book
is available from the British Library

ISBN 978-0-00-734874-9

Designed by seagulls.net

Printed and bound in Germany by Mohn Media

FOREWORD

I have witnessed first-hand the bravery and professionalism of our country's Armed Forces in Afghanistan.

© SKY 1/TIGER ASPECT

This book gives a gripping insight into what life is like on the front line, where the troops face death on a daily basis.

In the Taliban, British troops are confronted by determined enemies who are continually changing their tactics.

The Afghan climate is an enemy, too. As a country, Afghanistan has the greatest extremes of temperature on the planet, making the fight even harder. In the height of summer it can hit 50 degrees C, but in the depths of winter it drops to subzero temperatures, creating harsh fighting conditions all year round.

Many servicemen and women are away from home for more than six months at a time, which has an impact not only on their lives, but also on the lives of the loved ones they leave behind.

That's why it is so important for us to try to understand the acts of courage this band of brave young men and women perform on a daily basis.

It is far too easy to get detached from what is really happening in Afghanistan, 3,500 miles from home – when the death of a soldier is no longer headline news.

I have the greatest respect for the men and women of our Armed Forces, and though they may be thousands of miles away, I hope this book brings you closer to understanding the valuable job they are doing on our behalf.

© GETTY

THE WAR IN AFGHANISTAN FROM 2001: A HISTORY

By Robert Kellaway and Tom Newton Dunn

The devastating act of terrorism on 11 September 2001 left the world holding its breath. How would America respond to the atrocities that turned New York's Twin Towers into a mountain of ash and killed more than 2,900 people?

The answer came 26 days later, as the United States launched Operation Enduring Freedom in Afghanistan. The mission was to hunt down 9/11 mastermind Osama bin Laden and free the country from the Taliban who harboured him.

Prime Minister Tony Blair vowed that Britain would stand 'shoulder to shoulder' with the United States. As a result, British forces have fought from day one of the war that has raged for eight years and continues to this day.

On 7 October 2001 two British hunter-killer submarines came to periscope depth in the Arabian Sea off the coast of Pakistan. The nuclear boats HMS *Trafalgar* and HMS *Triumph* launched a barrage of Tomahawk land attack (cruise) missiles (TLAM). The GPS guided-weapons flew across Pakistan before smashing several 455-kg warheads into a Taliban training camp in rural Afghanistan.

The missiles were among the first shots in a deadly opening bombardment targeting 30 key sites across the country. This grew into a massive aerial bombing campaign that allowed the Afghan Northern Alliance, led by warlord general Rashid Dostum, to attack the Taliban. Backed by US special forces, the Alliance stormed the holy city of Mazar-i-Sharif and charged south to Kabul, driving the Taliban out on 12 November 2001. The Northern Alliance took control of the capital's strategically vital Bagram air base the same day.

Explosions rock Taliban positions in Tora Bora.

Afghans celebrated as the religious hardliners fled. Life under the Taliban had brought misery to many ordinary people. Music, dancing and even kite-flying were banned as sinful pleasures. Teachers were murdered, women were barred from public life and strict gender rules were enforced.

Four days later, on 16 November 2001, a C130 Hercules aircraft loaded with 100 elite British commandos

Canadian Light Infantry in the mountains of Tora Bora.

© GETTY

from C Squadron, the Special Boat Service, touched down. The Alliance was furious. No one told them of the SBS mission and it was only through luck that they had not fired on the aircraft. The SBS – with its motto 'By strength and guile' – ignored the hostile welcome and set about securing the base and setting up effective air-traffic control. Bagram immediately became a headquarters for British special forces, and within days two full SAS squadrons – 120 troopers, half the elite force's fighting strength – were planning a raid deep into enemy territory.

The SAS commanding officer, a dashing colonel, was to personally lead A and G Squadrons on Operation Trent to destroy an al-Qaeda opium storage plant in lawless Helmand province. The target was 970 km away in mountains close to the border with Pakistan and defended by 60 to 100 hostile Afghans guarding opium worth up to £50 million.

A team of eight HALO (high altitude low opening) SAS skydivers parachuted into the desert at night to set up a landing strip 160 km from the target. Two waves of six US Hercules aircraft dropped the two SAS squadrons and more than 30 vehicles into the desert. The SAS then stormed the opium plant in broad daylight, winning a Distinguished Service Order, two Conspicuous Gallantry Crosses and two Military Crosses. One trooper was seriously injured in the fight, the biggest battle fought by the 'Who Dares Wins' Regiment since the Second World War.

On 25 November 2001, eight SBS commandos were called in after 300 Taliban prisoners of war – including the American Talibani John Walker Lindh – rioted and seized the armoury at the Qala-i-Jangi fortress near Mazar-i-Sharif. The SBS team fought for seven days to put down the rebellion, during which CIA interrogator Johnny Spann was murdered.

A Canadian soldier explores a Tora Bora cave.

Just 86 of the 300 Taliban prisoners survived the battle.

In December 2001, 12 SBS commandos were hot on the heels of bin Laden as they helped US forces assault the mountainous Tora Bora cave system close to the Khyber Pass. The SBS played a key role guiding US forces and calling in airstrikes as al-Qaeda fought a desperate rearguard action. The SBS commandos captured and cleared countless enemy positions but were unable to stop al-Qaeda from retreating across the border into Pakistan.

In March 2002, Royal Marines from 45 Commando joined US Navy Seals and 101st Airborne in Operation Anaconda, an attack on Taliban commanders in the Shahi-Kot Valley. The mission went badly from the start. Two US Chinooks were shot down by rocket-propelled grenades as they assaulted the heavily defended Takur Ghar mountaintop. Navy Seal Neil Roberts fell off the tail ramp of the first Chinook as it was hit. He was captured and killed by enemy forces. The US suffered eight deaths and 72 casualties in the two-week mission. The Marines of 45 Commando, based in Arbroath, were then ordered on four search-and-destroy missions to seek out al-Qaeda and Taliban forces. However, they were criticized by American commanders after they discovered weapons caches but failed to contact enemy fighters.

Eventually, operations in Afghanistan began to tail off as US President George Bush and Tony Blair turned their attentions towards Iraq. From 2003 to 2005, British forces in Afghanistan fell to as few as 300, working as part of NATO's International Security Assistance Force (ISAF) around Kabul. As war raged in Iraq, the Taliban regrouped and re-armed around Kandahar and Helmand province in southern Afghanistan.

In response, six RAF Harriers flying bombing missions from the US base at Kandahar Airfield were the main British weapon taking the fight to the Taliban.

In the spring of 2006, that all changed with the arrival in Helmand of 3,150 crack troops from 16 Air Assault Brigade on a mission codenamed Operation Herrick IV. The troops' job was to protect a massive reconstruction effort in southern Afghanistan that the ISAF hoped would win over Taliban supporters. The British plan was to create a 'development triangle' centred around Helmand's capital Lashkar Gah that would deliver new prosperity to locals. This triangle was then expected to spread like an 'inkspot' across the map, winning support away from the Taliban, who had little to offer in comparison.

The plan looked so good that in February 2006, Defence Secretary John Reid said that he hoped British forces might not have to fire a shot in anger.

But the reality on the ground was different when the troops arrived. The Afghan government, led by President Hamid Karzai, demanded that troops move into the Taliban's mountain strongholds in the north of the province. British commanders granted his wish and troops from 3 Para, 2 Royal Gurkha Rifles and 1 Royal Irish Regiment were stationed in platoon houses in Sangin, Now Zad and Musa Qaleh.

Within days, fighting erupted as British troops attempted to recover a downed, unmanned spy plane close to Sangin town. As night fell, the patrol of four wagons was pinned down by a hail of AK-47 and rocket-propelled grenade (RPG) fire and surrounded by enemy fighters. Captain Jim Philippson, 29, helped to lead a quick reaction force (QRF) out of Robinson forward operating base to rescue the pinned patrol. But he was shot dead when the QRF itself was ambushed and Philippson thus became the first British soldier killed in combat with the Taliban on 11 June 2006.

The incident sparked a wave of violence as the Taliban vowed to force British troops out of their territory. The platoon houses were besieged as desperate fighting ensued.

In August 2006, Corporal Bryan Budd, 29, of A Company, 3 Para, was leading a patrol

Corporal Bryan Budd in Sangin.

to protect a group of engineers working close to the platoon house in Sangin. Bryan spotted four Taliban approaching to attack through a cornfield and led a flanking manoeuvre to ambush them. His patrol came under heavy fire; one of his men was hit in the shoulder and another in the nose. The father of two young daughters immediately charged the enemy in the cornfield and killed two Taliban fighters before being shot dead himself. It later emerged that Budd had been hit by friendly fire, but his outstanding courage won him a posthumous Victoria Cross.

On 2 September 2006, disaster struck when a fuel leak aboard an RAF Nimrod surveillance aircraft caused a catastrophic fire. The aircraft crashed into the desert near Kandahar. The resulting loss of 14 lives made it the worst incident since the Falklands conflict in 1982.

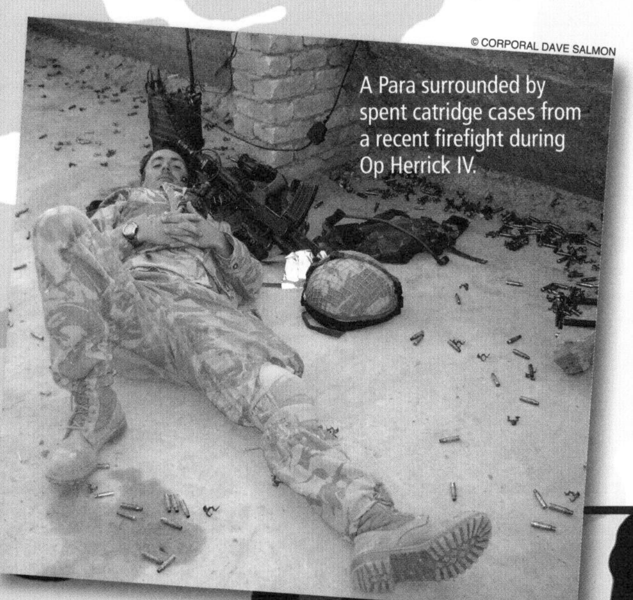

A Para surrounded by spent catridge cases from a recent firefight during Op Herrick IV.

In November 2006 the Paras were replaced in Helmand by the Royal Marines of 3 Commando Brigade on a new campaign, Operation Herrick V. Their aim was to give the Taliban no relief in fighting during the winter months.

On 15 January 2007, two Apache helicopters completed one of the most daring rescue missions in the history of warfare. Royal Marines from Zulu Company, 45 Commando, had retreated, following a disastrous attack on the Taliban stronghold of Jugroom Fort in Garmsir.

In an instance of friendly fire, Lieutenant Corporal Mathew Ford was fatally wounded, and four more of his colleagues were injured. The Marines retreated, only to discover that they had left Mathew Ford behind.

In an unflinching show of bravery, the crew of two Apache helicopters strapped four volunteer heroes – three Marines and a Royal Engineer – to the sides of the aircraft and flew low level at 80 km/h (50 mph) to the scene of the fight. Under heavy fire, they landed at Jugroom Fort, recovered Mathew's body and flew out the way they had come.

Two Distinguished Flying Crosses and three Military Crosses were awarded to the helicopter crews and the engineer involved in the rescue.

In April 2007, 12 Mechanised Brigade arrived with the Royal Anglians, determined to push out from the platoon houses and into the fertile 'green zone' of cultivated land along Helmand river.

On 8 September 2007, Captain Simon Cupples, 25, of A Company, 2nd Battalion, the Mercian Regiment, won the Conspicuous Gallantry Cross after an eight-hour night battle with the Taliban near Darvīshān in Garmsir. During the battle, Private John Botha was shot and killed, Private Luke Cole was shot in the leg and stomach and Private Sam Cooper was shot in the head. Simon Cupples braved enemy fire five times in a bid to find Botha and he and his men successfully recovered Cole and Cooper, who both survived their wounds. The Mercians were awarded three Military Crosses and two Mentions in Dispatches for their courage that night, making the battle one of the most highly decorated in the Afghan war.

In December 2007, during Operation Herrick VII, the decision was taken to recapture Mūsá Qal'eh from the Taliban, who had occupied the town for nine months following a British deal to withdraw. More than 2,000 British and Afghan troops under the command of 52 Infantry Brigade set up a cordon around the town, while a US Combat Air Brigade pounded Taliban positions in the town. After three days of ferocious street fighting, Mūsá Qal'eh was back under British control.

In February 2008, it emerged that Prince Harry had spent ten weeks calling in airstrikes on the Taliban as a Forward Air Controller in the region.

A Para demonstrates the 'thousand yard stare' after a tough contact.

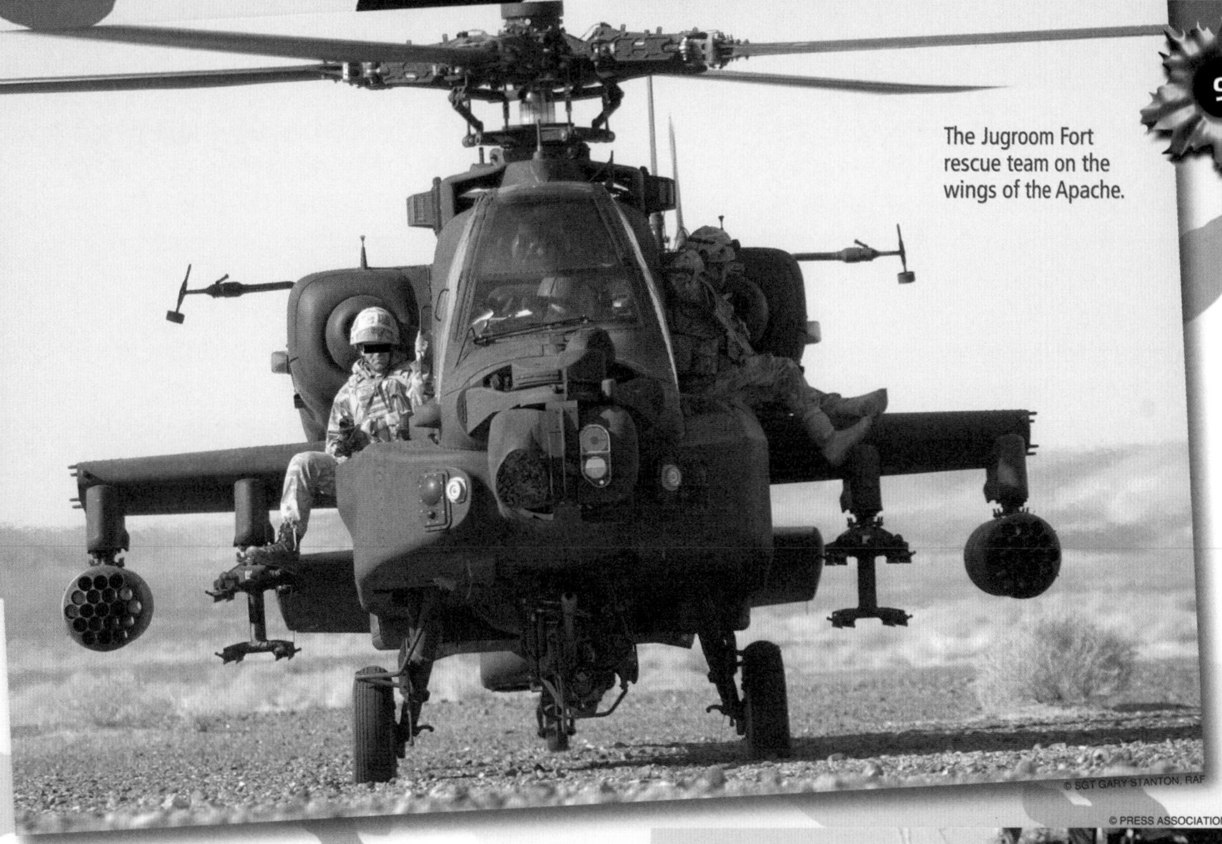

The Jugroom Fort rescue team on the wings of the Apache.

© SGT GARY STANTON, RAF

© PRESS ASSOCIATION

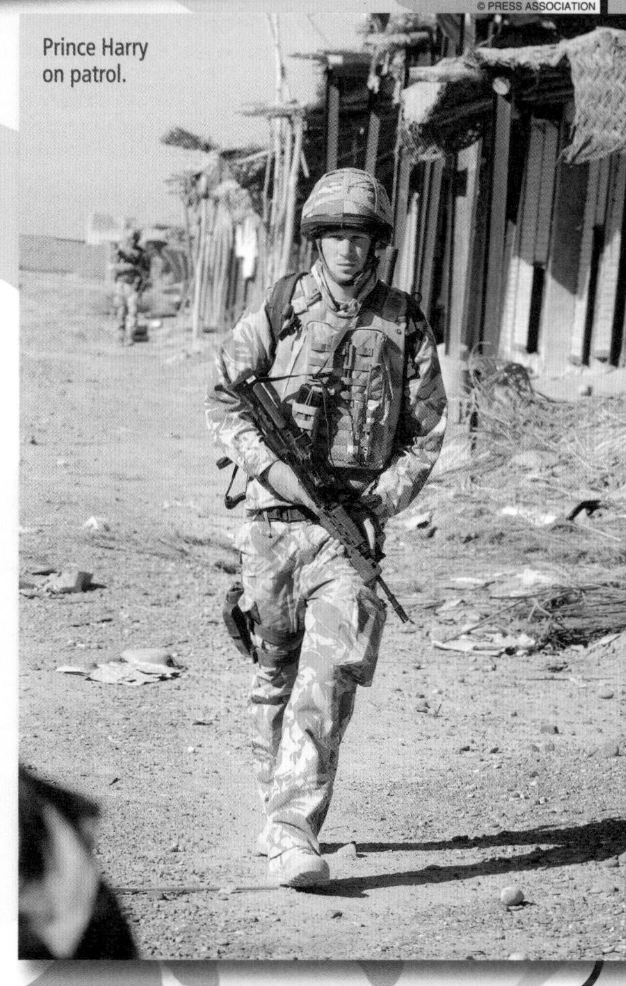

Prince Harry on patrol.

In one incident near the end of his tour, he came under 107 mm rocket fire as he directed a Chinook helicopter into a landing site to pick up casualties near Mūsá Qal'eh.

In the spring of 2008, 16 Air Assault Brigade returned, now on Operation Herrick VIII.

In August 2008, a platoon of 30 troops at Mūsá Qal'eh held out for nine days against 400 Taliban fighters in a battle dubbed the siege of Roshan Tower. The stranded platoon, from A Company, 2nd Battalion, the Princess of Wales's Royal Regiment, known as the Tigers – endured up to 55 mortar rounds hammering their position every day. Their position was the size of a tennis court at the base of the 40-m-tall Roshan communications mast and was too exposed for reinforcements to help. Around 100 enemy insurgents were killed. Miraculously, just one member of the platoon was injured, by shrapnel from a blast.

But the airborne troops' main victory during their six-month tour did not occur until September 2008. In an astonishingly audacious plan, British forces outwitted the

Taliban with a daring double bluff, delivering a massive 200-tonne turbine, split into seven sections, through 160 km of hostile territory to the Kajakī dam. Two hundred soldiers from 2 Para, backed by 400 Afghan troops and heavy air support, created a 'dummy' convoy along Highway 611. The troops fought a series of battles, killing up to 250 insurgents in actions that were ultimately a diversion for the real thing. Meanwhile, the 200-vehicle *real* convoy was travelling along a secret route identified by the Parachute Regiment's elite Pathfinder Platoon.

Engineers strengthened existing roads and built more from scratch to get the convoy to the dam, where it arrived under cover of darkness. Once fully operational, the turbine will provide electricity for 1.5 million people.

By October 2008, the Royal Marines of 3 Commando had once again relieved the Paras – arriving to a baptism by fire during their very first week. A mob of 600 Taliban fighters simultaneously attacked from three sides of the city, but were repelled by British and Afghan forces, who called in devastating air support, killing 60 insurgents.

The battle was close, and the Marines resolved to prevent any repeat attempt by denying the Taliban their nearby stronghold. Their response was Operation Sond Chara – meaning Red Dagger in the Pashto language and named after the 3 Commando Brigade shoulder patch. More than 1,500 Marines, backed by Afghan, Danish and Estonian forces, stormed the neighbouring district of Nād-e'Ali. Between 7 December and Christmas Day, troops covered up to 60 km, clearing trench systems and compounds, at times just 30 m from enemy fighters. Rain poured down on the troops as they slept rough between fire fights. The drenched clay soil turned into a muddy bog reminiscent of the First World War. The mission killed 100 Taliban, captured drugs worth £2 million, destroyed a bomb-making factory and seized the district from Taliban control. Four Royal Marines and one Rifleman were killed during the fierce fighting.

But an even bigger fight still needed to be won before the people of Helmand could celebrate their new freedom to vote in the Afghan presidential elections of 2009.

June 2009 saw the next formation to take over, 19 Light Brigade, launch Operation Panther's Claw, the bloodiest offensive thus

The Kajaki dam convoy, 200 vehicles strong.

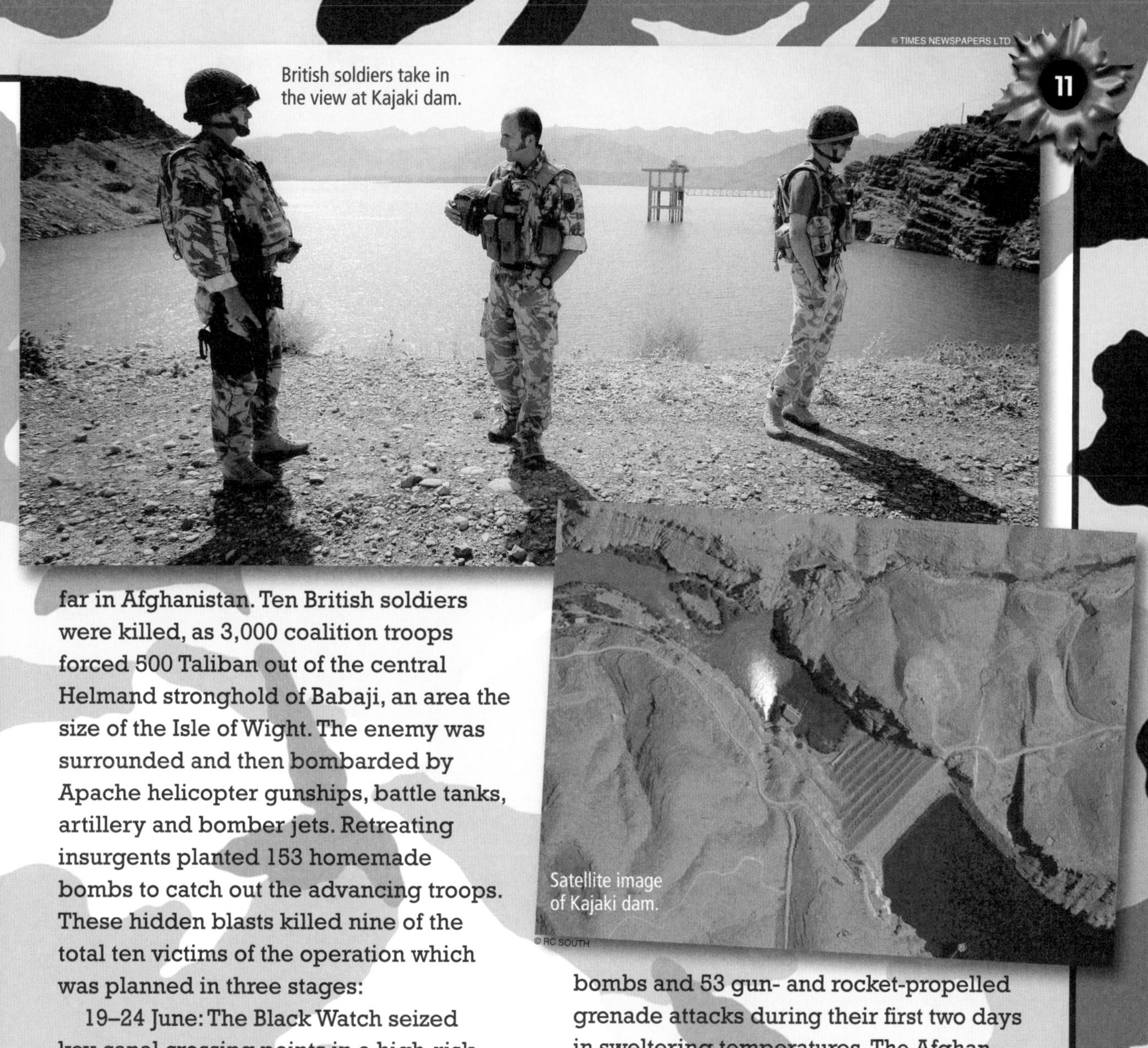
British soldiers take in the view at Kajaki dam.

Satellite image of Kajaki dam.

far in Afghanistan. Ten British soldiers were killed, as 3,000 coalition troops forced 500 Taliban out of the central Helmand stronghold of Babaji, an area the size of the Isle of Wight. The enemy was surrounded and then bombarded by Apache helicopter gunships, battle tanks, artillery and bomber jets. Retreating insurgents planted 153 homemade bombs to catch out the advancing troops. These hidden blasts killed nine of the total ten victims of the operation which was planned in three stages:

19–24 June: The Black Watch seized key canal crossing points in a high-risk airborne assault with RAF and US Chinook helicopters over northern Babaji, cutting off the Taliban's escape.

25 June–1 July: The Welsh Guards set up a long block on the western edge of Babaji, fighting through enemy-held ground to seize 14 more canal crossings. Commanding Officer Lieutenant Colonel Rupert Thorneloe was killed on the last day of this stage of the assault as he travelled in a Viking to meet officers.

2–26 July: A powerful armoured column, led by the Light Dragoons and backed by Danish battle tanks, pushed west into Babaji. The Dragoons were targeted by 55 dug-in bombs and 53 gun- and rocket-propelled grenade attacks during their first two days in sweltering temperatures. The Afghan summer sun made the ground so hot that soldiers could not lie flat for cover as they were being shot at.

The operation was declared a victory when the Taliban's battered final line of defence collapsed. Dressed as women in burqas, desperate Taliban fighters launched homemade rafts onto canals in a bid to escape.

In October 2009, a new force – 11 Light Brigade – arrived to pit their might and courage against this ever-determined enemy.

The fight for Helmand goes on, as another band of Heroes emerges…

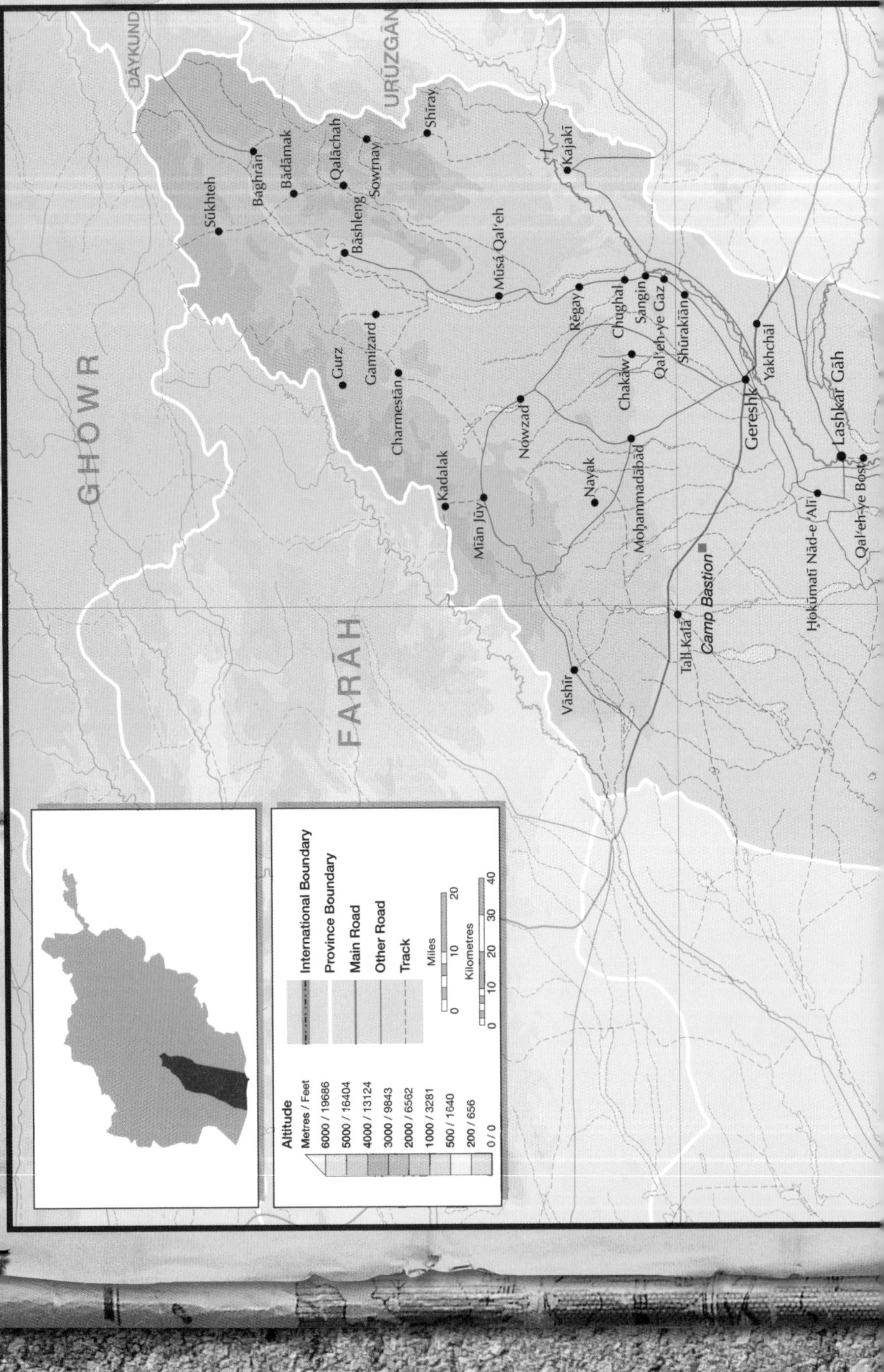

Altitude
Metres / Feet
6000 / 19686
5000 / 16404
4000 / 13124
3000 / 9843
2000 / 6562
1000 / 3281
500 / 1640
200 / 656
0 / 0
International Boundary
Province Boundary
Main Road
Other Road
Track
Miles
0 10 20
Kilometres
0 10 20 30 40
GHOWR
FARĀH
DAYKUND
URŪZGĀN
Sūkhteh
Baghrān
Bādāmak
Qalāchah
Bāshleng
Sowrnay
Shīray
Gurz
Gamīzard
Charmestān
Kadalak
Mīān Jūy
Nowzad
Mūsá Qal'eh
Kajakī
Vāshīr
Nayak
Rēgay
Chughal
Chakāw
Sangin
Moḩammadābād
Qal'eh-ye Gaz
Shūrakīān
Tall Kalā
Camp Bastion
Gereshk
Yakhchāl
Ḩokūmatī Nād-e 'Alī
Lashkar Gāh
Qal'eh-ye Bost

HELMAND PROVINCE

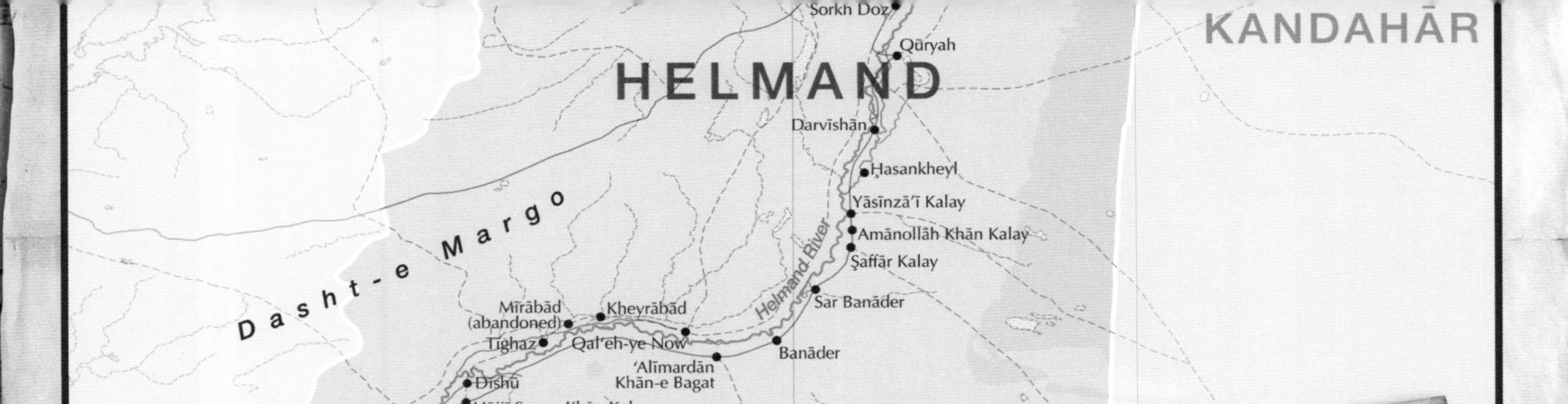

KANDAHĀR

HELMAND

Sorkh Doz
Qūryah
Darvīshān
Hasankheyl
Yāsīnzā'ī Kalay
Amānollāh Khān Kalay
Şaffār Kalay
Sar Banāder
Helmand River
Banāder
'Alīmardān Khān-e Bagat
Kheyrābād
Qal'eh-ye Now
Mīrābād (abandoned)
Tīghaz
Dishū
Ḥājjī Sarvar Khān Kalay
Khvājeh 'Alī 'Olyā
Khvājeh 'Alī Sehyakah
Khvājeh 'Alī Soflā
Landay
Dasht-e Margo

PAKIST

Degrees Longitude East of Greenwich 64

© ED MACY

The Helmand River stretches through the hilly landscape around the dangerous 'Green Zone'.

TORA BORA

THE FORBIDDING TORA BORA MOUNTAIN RANGE SEEMS AS REMOTE FROM NEW YORK AS THE MOON. AND YET IT WAS HERE, IN 2001, THAT OSAMA BIN LADEN WAS BELIEVED TO BE HIDING FOLLOWING THE ATTACK ON THE TWIN TOWERS AND THE SUBSEQUENT NATO INVASION OF AFGHANISTAN.

ON THE RUN FROM THE INVADING FORCE, THE MASTERMIND OF THE DEVASTATING 9/11 ATTACKS THAT KILLED NEARLY 3,000 INNOCENT PEOPLE HAS RETREATED TO A COMPLEX OF CAVES SCATTERED ACROSS THE RUGGED LANDSCAPE.

TRACKING BIN LADEN AND HIS FIGHTERS DOWN WILL BE LIKE SEARCHING FOR A NEEDLE IN A VERY HIGH HAYSTACK... BUT THE ALLIED FORCES ARE DETERMINED TO BRING HIM TO JUSTICE.

A SURRENDER DEADLINE COMES... AND GOES. THE AL-QAEDA FIGHTERS' LAST CHANCE AT A PEACEFUL SURRENDER HAS PASSED. ALL TOO SOON THE PEACE OF THE MOUNTAINSIDE IS SHATTERED. AS THE COALITION FORCES LAUNCH THEIR ATTACK, THE ONCE QUIET LANDSCAPE ERUPTS...

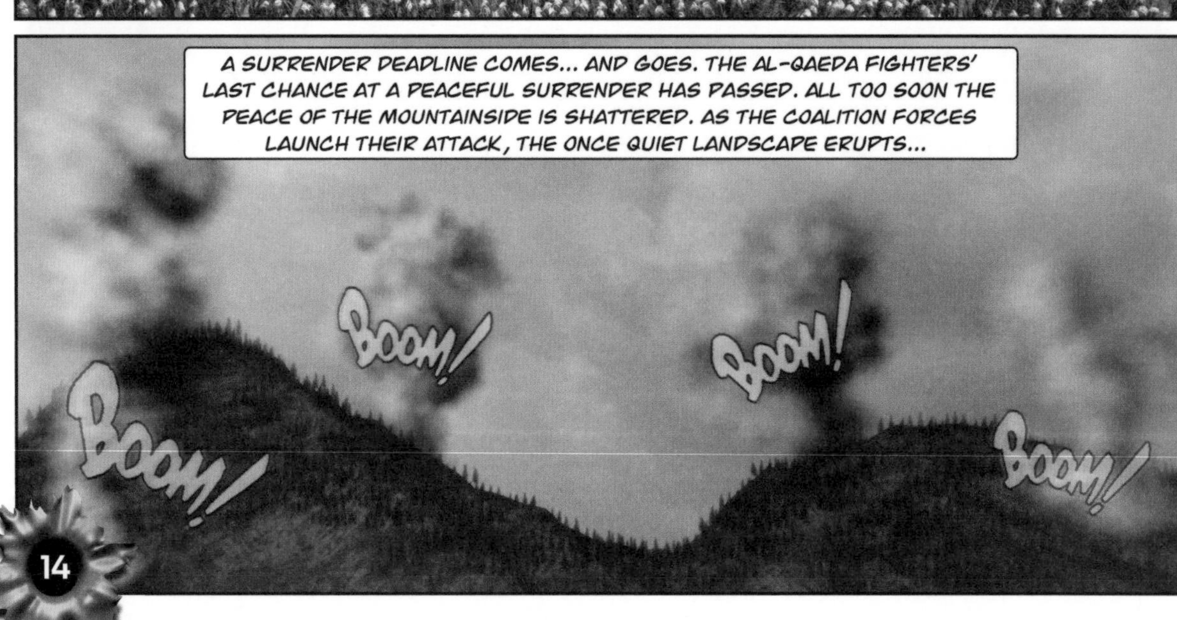

THE EMPTY AFGHAN SKIES ARE RENT BY THE SCREAMING SOUND OF 85 WARPLANES.
THE MIGHTY B-52 POUNDS THE LANDSCAPE, SMASHING THE MOUNTAIN PEAKS AND SHAKING THE NETWORK OF CAVES THEY CONCEAL.
THIS IS SIXPACK, PREPARING TO FIRE. WE'RE ABOVE TARGET. BOMBS AWAY.

AS THE DUST FROM THE WITHERING AERIAL BOMBARDMENT BEGINS TO SETTLE, A CRACK TEAM OF ELITE SPECIAL FORCES ARE MUSTERED TO MOVE IN... **THE MISSION:** TO RECONNOITRE THE TERRITORY, TO SEARCH OUT AND DESTROY ANY TALIBAN OR AL-QAEDA BASES, AND TO PREVENT ANY ENEMY ESCAPING OVER THE BORDER TO PAKISTAN.

AND THEY WON'T BE WORKING ALONE. THE AFGHAN NORTHERN ALLIANCE ARE FIERCELY ANTI-TALIBAN AND WILL BE FIGHTING ALONGSIDE COALITION TROOPS.

AFTER YEARS OF CRUEL, REPRESSIVE TALIBAN CONTROL, THIS IS THEIR CHANCE TO TAKE BACK THEIR COUNTRY - A CHANCE THEY'RE WILLING TO FIGHT FOR.

AS WINTER SETTLES ONTO THE LANDSCAPE, THE AFGHAN FIGHTERS STRUGGLE ACROSS THE BRUTAL TERRAIN. THE SCALE OF THE MISSION SEEMS DAUNTINGLY EPIC, AS THE MEDIA ISSUES DIRE WARNINGS ABOUT THE COMPLEXITY AND EXTENT OF THE CAVE NETWORK.

WITH THE CIA AND SPECIAL FORCES, THE NORTHERN ALLIANCE BEGINS THE SLOW, PAINSTAKING PROCESS OF CLEARING THE 30 KNOWN CAVES.
NOTHING...

EACH AND EVERY ONE MUST BE SEARCHED FOR ANY AMMO, WEAPONS, INTELLIGENCE OR ENEMY PRESENCE.
NO, NOTHING...

IT SOON BECOMES APPARENT THAT THE COMPLEX IS MUCH LESS SOPHISTICATED THAN WAS FEARED. THERE IS NO UNDERGROUND NETWORK, NO HIGH-TECH EQUIPMENT...
DAMMIT, STILL NOTHING! THEY'VE GOT TO BE HERE SOMEWHERE!
...JUST COLD, DANK CAVE AFTER COLD, DANK CAVE.

HANG ON, LOOK AT THIS! PILES AND PILES OF AMMO!
THAT MEANS THEY'RE NEAR BY! QUICK, CALL IT IN!

NOW THAT THE HIDEOUT HAS BEEN IDENTIFIED, THE REAL BATTLE BEGINS. AS SOON AS THE FIND IS CONFIRMED, A BRITISH CHINOOK SWOOPS LOW BETWEEN THE PEAKS WITH A BELLYFUL OF CRACK SAS TROOPS.
HOLD STEADY, LADS, WE'RE COMING IN TO LANDING. THIS COULD BE A BIT BUMPY...

THE SAS TROOPS DEPLOY RAPIDLY ON THE GROUND. THEY NEED TO BE IN POSITION BEFORE **PHASE II** OF THE OPERATION KICKS OFF...

I HAVE EYES ON AL-QAEDA FIGHTERS – THERE ARE FOUR, MAYBE FIVE OF THEM. CUT-OFFS, CONFIRM THAT YOU ARE IN POSITION?

CUT-OFF TEAM 1, IN POSITION!
CUT-OFF TEAM 2, IN POSITION!
ALL TEAMS IN POSITION! HARRIER, YOU ARE GOOD TO FIRE!
KKKRAAACCK!
BANG ON TARGET! GREAT WORK HARRIER! CUT-OFFS, STAND BY, THEY'LL BE HEADING YOUR WAY...

AS SMOKE FROM THE AIRCRAFTS' BOMBS FILLS THE VALLEYS, THE AL-QAEDA FIGHTERS MAKE A DESPERATE BREAK FOR FREEDOM – AND RUN RIGHT INTO THE WAITING TROOPERS...
ROGER THAT, TEAM LEADER! WE CAN SEE THEM NOW!
HERE THEY COME, LADS! DON'T LET THEM THROUGH!

BUT NO SOONER IS ONE SKIRMISH WON THAN WORD COMES IN THAT THERE ARE MORE AL-QAEDA FIGHTERS MOVING AMONG A DIFFERENT SET OF CAVES.
WIZARD, DO YOU READ ME? WE NEED FIREPOWER AT THESE COORDINATES!
PATROL, THIS IS WIZARD. ROGER THAT REQUEST - I'M ON MY WAY.
ANOTHER CRIPPLING AIR STRIKE HITS THE MOUNTAINSIDE...

FIGHTERS STRUGGLE THROUGH THE SMOKE AND CONFUSION, DESPERATE TO ESCAPE WITH THEIR LIVES...

...BUT THERE'S NO WAY OUT.
THEY'RE COMING AT US! FIRE!

THE BATTLE CONTINUES NIGHT AND DAY. THERE IS NO RESPITE FOR THE CORNERED AL-QAEDA FORCES, WHO TRY TO FLEE ALONG HIGH MOUNTAIN PASSES UNDER COVER OF DARKNESS.

NOTHING MOVES UP HERE AT NIGHT BUT THE BAD GUYS. SO I'M AFRAID YOUR LUCK JUST RAN OUT, MATE.
PFFT!

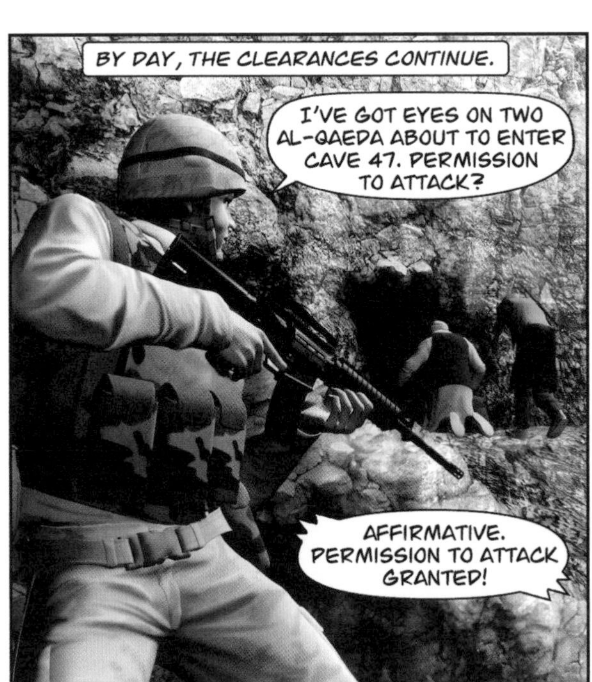
BY DAY, THE CLEARANCES CONTINUE.
I'VE GOT EYES ON TWO AL-QAEDA ABOUT TO ENTER CAVE 47. PERMISSION TO ATTACK?
AFFIRMATIVE. PERMISSION TO ATTACK GRANTED!

OPEN FIRE!
HNH-!
NUMBER 2'S STILL ALIVE - KEEP FIRING!

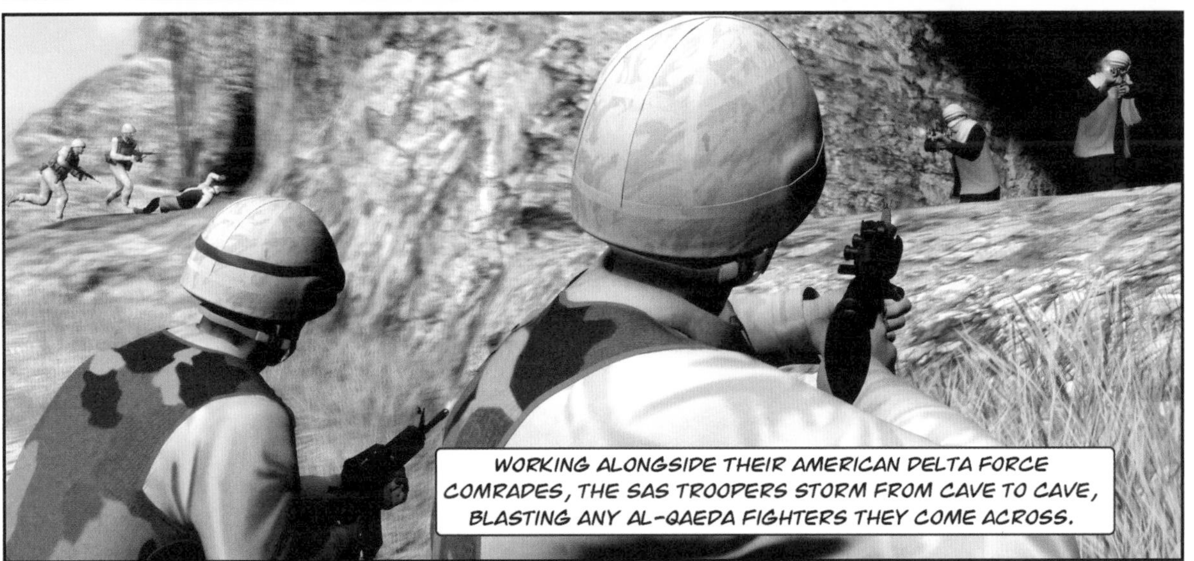
WORKING ALONGSIDE THEIR AMERICAN DELTA FORCE COMRADES, THE SAS TROOPERS STORM FROM CAVE TO CAVE, BLASTING ANY AL-QAEDA FIGHTERS THEY COME ACROSS.

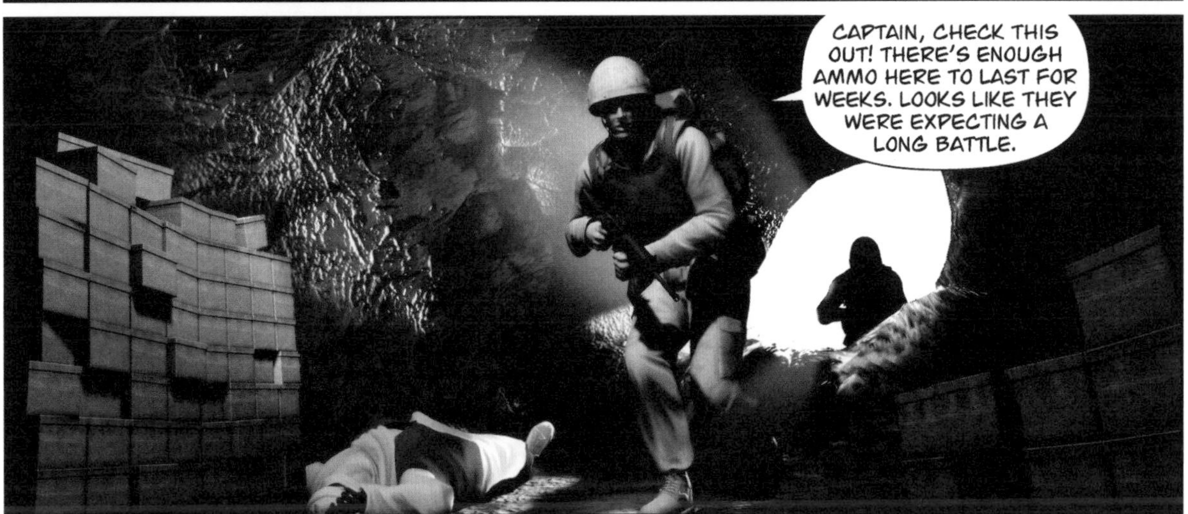
CAPTAIN, CHECK THIS OUT! THERE'S ENOUGH AMMO HERE TO LAST FOR WEEKS. LOOKS LIKE THEY WERE EXPECTING A LONG BATTLE.

HANG ON, THERE'S MORE – MAPS, LAPTOPS...
NO BIN LADEN, BUT IT LOOKS LIKE WE GOT THEIR HQ!

QE
161765 5
NAVY
THE ALLIED FORCES ARE WINNING. BUT WITH THE MASTERMIND BEHIND THE TWIN TOWER BOMBINGS STILL AT LARGE, THE SEARCH CONTINUES. THE AMERICANS THROW EVERYTHING THEY HAVE AT THE HUNT, FROM THE MIGHTY P-3 ORION PATROL AIRCRAFT...

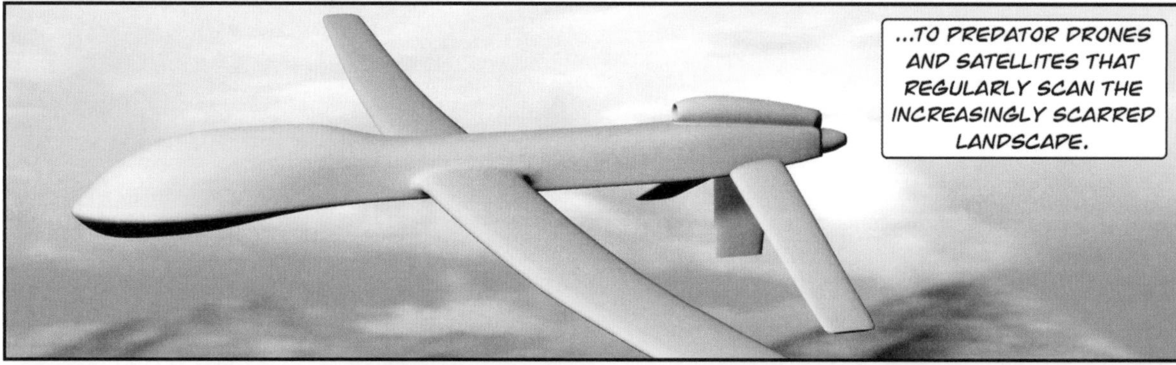
...TO PREDATOR DRONES AND SATELLITES THAT REGULARLY SCAN THE INCREASINGLY SCARRED LANDSCAPE.

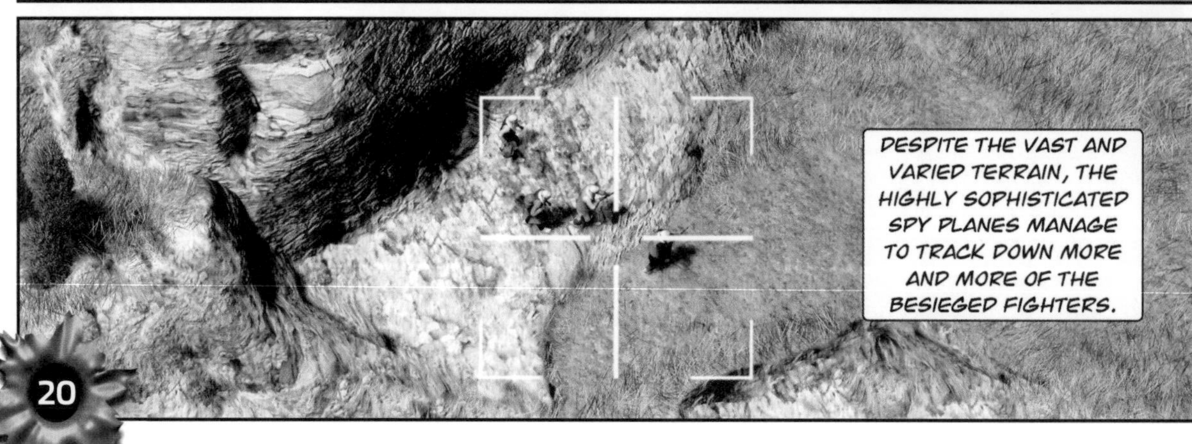
DESPITE THE VAST AND VARIED TERRAIN, THE HIGHLY SOPHISTICATED SPY PLANES MANAGE TO TRACK DOWN MORE AND MORE OF THE BESIEGED FIGHTERS.

TIPPED OFF BY THE ALL-SEEING DRONES, BRITISH TROOPS PREPARE A FURTHER ASSAULT ON A KNOWN HIDEOUT.

22 SAS SQUADRON GET THE CALL AND ARE RAPIDLY READY TO DEPLOY. AS THE FIRST RAYS OF DAYLIGHT STRETCH ACROSS THE SILENT LANDSCAPE, THEY HIT THE GROUND AND MOVE QUICKLY INTO POSITION.

FINGERS ON TRIGGERS, LADS - THERE ARE A LOT OF THEM AND THEIR BACKS ARE AGAINST THE WALL, SO THEY'RE GOING TO BE DESPERATE.

RIGHT, THAT'S THE CAVE ENTRANCE - IT'S GOING TO BE A SQUEEZE. TORCHES ON! AND KEEP YOUR EYES PEELED! READY...?

ATTACK!
GAARRGH!!
GAAAHHH!!

OUTSIDE THE CAVE ENTRANCE, THE REMAINING MEN FROM THE SQUADRON KEEP BEADY-EYED WATCH.
THEY'RE IN! GOOD SHOW, LADS!
I'LL COVER THE NORTH EXIT, YOU COVER THE SOUTH! THEY'RE NOT GETTING OUT OF THIS ONE...

THAT'S ANOTHER ONE CLEARED, SIR! WE GOT NEARLY ALL OF THEM.
TWO RAN OFF TO THE NORTH BUT WE KNOW WHERE THEY'RE HEADING – THEY WON'T GET FAR.
IT'S A SCENE THAT'S BEING REPEATED ACROSS THE WHOLE MOUNTAIN RANGE, AS BRITISH AND AMERICAN SPECIAL FORCES THROW THEMSELVES IN DANGER'S WAY, BRINGING THE FIGHT TO AL-QAEDA IN CAVE AFTER CAVE.

WATCH IT, DANNY, HE'S STILL MOVING! KEEP FIRING!

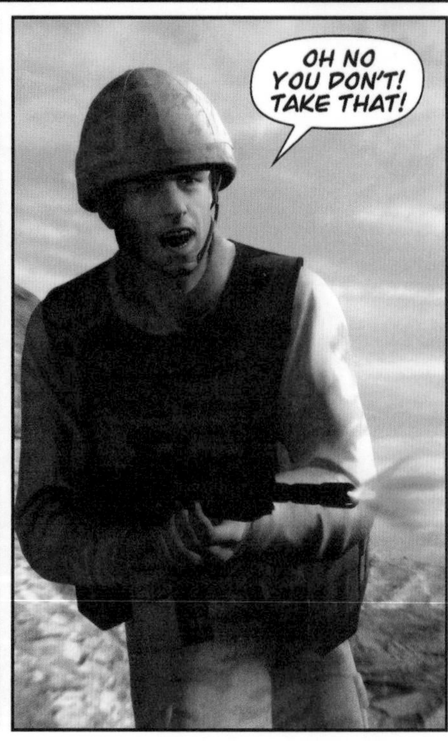
OH NO YOU DON'T! TAKE THAT!

IN YET ANOTHER PART OF THE MOUNTAIN RANGE, A SEPARATE TEAM CHARGE A GLOOMY CAVE ENTRANCE WHEN, FROM WITHIN THE DARKNESS...
...AN AK-47 OPENS FIRE.
@?$%*!! TAKE COVER, TAKE COVER!

A SOLDIER IS HIT!
URGH!
MAN DOWN! WE NEED TO GET HIM OUT OF HERE!

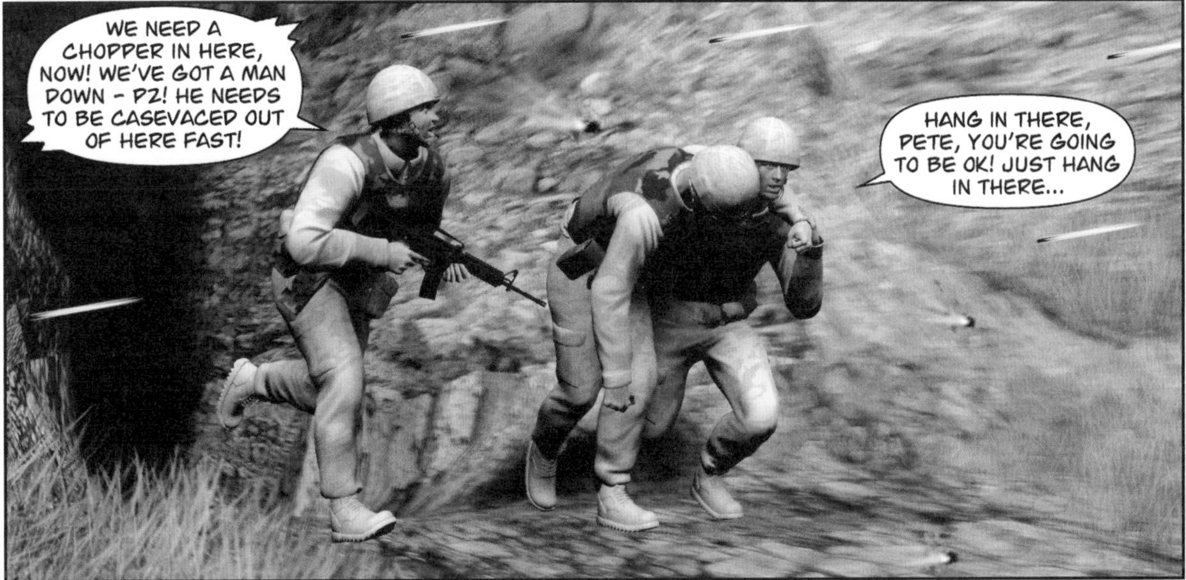
WE NEED A CHOPPER IN HERE, NOW! WE'VE GOT A MAN DOWN – P2! HE NEEDS TO BE CASEVACED OUT OF HERE FAST!
HANG IN THERE, PETE, YOU'RE GOING TO BE OK! JUST HANG IN THERE...

I'VE GOT YOU COVERED! JUST GET HIM THE HELL OUT OF HERE!
AARGH!

HOLD ON, MATE. ARE YOU OK?
YEAH...NO... I DON'T KNOW. IT HURTS LIKE HELL. WHERE'S THE ?$%@& CHOPPER?!

WHILE THE MEN GUARD THEIR FALLEN COMRADE, THE BATTLE FOR THE CAVE RAGES BEHIND THEM.
GROUND FORCE, THIS IS HQ. WE'RE SCRAMBLING THE CHOPPERS BUT IT'S TOO HOT TO LAND. WE NEED TO KNOW HOW LONG YOU CAN HOLD OUT. REPEAT, CONFIRM HOW LONG YOU CAN HOLD OUT!
CHK!
CHK!
CHK!

IN THE DARKNESS OF THE CAVE, THE TROOPERS FIRE CERAMIC BULLETS, SPECIALLY DESIGNED SO THAT THEY WON'T RICOCHET OFF THE CAVE WALLS.
DAMMIT, THERE'S MORE OF THEM! WE'RE OUTNUMBERED!
JUST KEEP FIRING!
WE NEED REINFORCEMENTS! THERE ARE TOO MANY OF THEM!

?$%@&!! I'M HIT!

WITH TWO MEN DOWN, OUTNUMBERED AND OUTFLANKED, THE TIDE HAS TURNED AGAINST THE SAS.
HANG IN THERE, LADS! I'VE CALLED FOR REINFORCEMENTS – THEY'RE ON THEIR WAY!
THEY'D BETTER BLOODY WELL HURRY! WE'RE ALMOST OUT OF AMMO!

AT LAST, THE CHOPPERS ARRIVE – THE 'LITTLE BIRDS' A WELCOME SIGHT FOR THE EXHAUSTED TROOPS ON THE GROUND.
GROUND FORCE, THIS IS DELTA 39. SORRY WE'RE LATE TO THE PARTY.
THEY CIRCLE THE FIREFIGHT, LOOKING FOR A VANTAGE POINT WHERE THEY CAN SAFELY LAND THE EXTRA TROOPS.

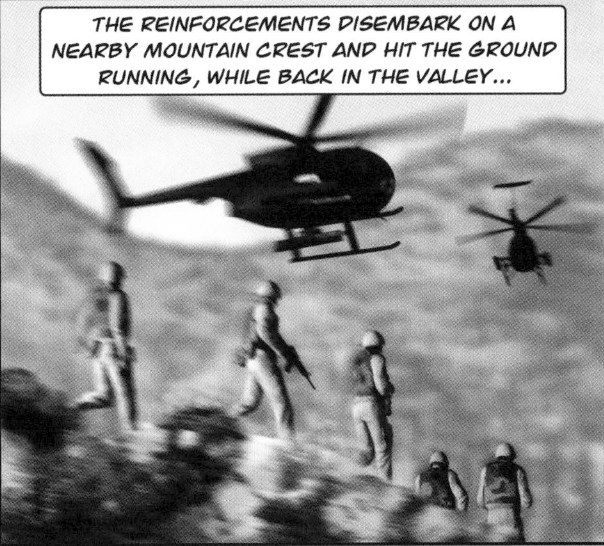
THE REINFORCEMENTS DISEMBARK ON A NEARBY MOUNTAIN CREST AND HIT THE GROUND RUNNING, WHILE BACK IN THE VALLEY...

...TWO MORE CHOPPERS ARRIVE AND LET LOOSE WITH THEIR ROCKETS, BLASTING THE AL-QAEDA FIGHTERS FROM THE SAFETY OF THE CAVE.
ALL WEAPONS FIRE!
WHSH!
WHSH!

BUT THE BATTLE ISN'T OVER YET, AS THE TROOPS SUMMON THEIR STRENGTH FOR A FINAL CLASH. THE SOUND OF BULLETS ECHOES OFF THE STEEP VALLEY WALLS AS FIERCE MAN-TO-MAN FIGHTING RAGES ALONG THE NARROW RAVINE.
CHK! CHK! CHK!
CHK! CHK! CHK!
CHK! CHK! CHK! CHK!
CHK! CHK! CHK! CHK!
WE'VE GOT THEM ON THE RUN, LADS! KEEP AT THEM!

UNTIL AT LAST, 4 1/2 EXHAUSTING HOURS LATER, QUIET DESCENDS ONCE MORE.
THAT'S THE LAST OF THEM, BOSS!
NOT QUITE! I THINK YOU'D BETTER COME IN HERE, SIR. THERE'S A FEW OF THEM STILL HIDING OUT BUT THEY'RE PRETTY BASHED UP. NOT MUCH FIGHT LEFT IN THEM, I DON'T RECKON.

WOUNDED FIGHTERS AREN'T THE ONLY FINDS HIDDEN DEEP WITHIN THE CAVES.
BOSS! GET A LOOK AT THIS! IT'S ANOTHER AMMO STASH!

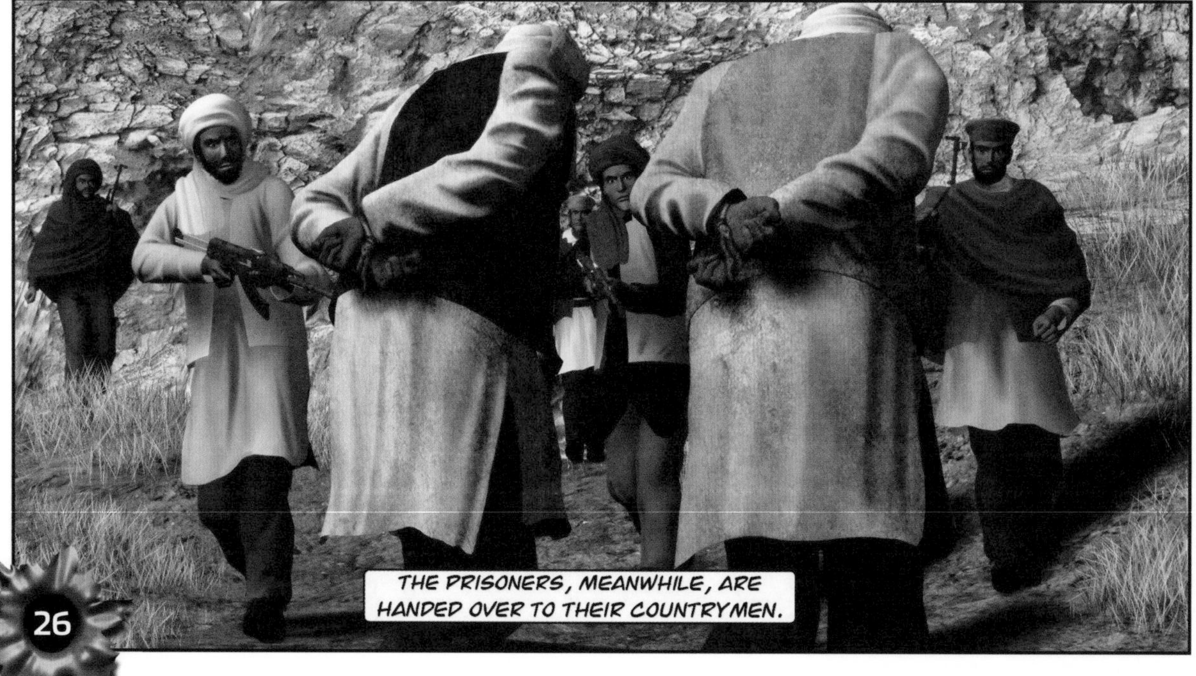
THE PRISONERS, MEANWHILE, ARE HANDED OVER TO THEIR COUNTRYMEN.

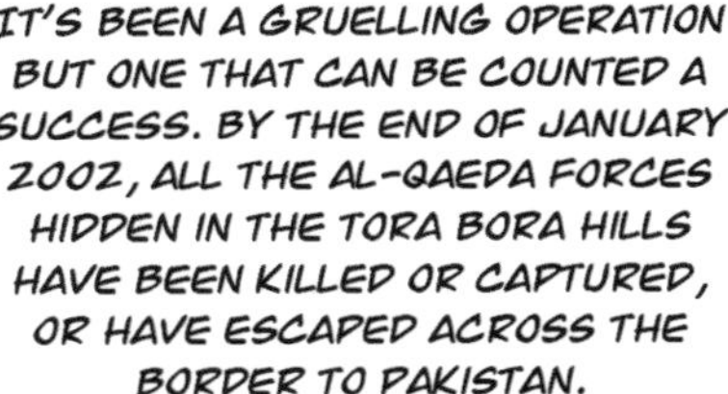

IT'S BEEN A GRUELLING OPERATION BUT ONE THAT CAN BE COUNTED A SUCCESS. BY THE END OF JANUARY 2002, ALL THE AL-QAEDA FORCES HIDDEN IN THE TORA BORA HILLS HAVE BEEN KILLED OR CAPTURED, OR HAVE ESCAPED ACROSS THE BORDER TO PAKISTAN.

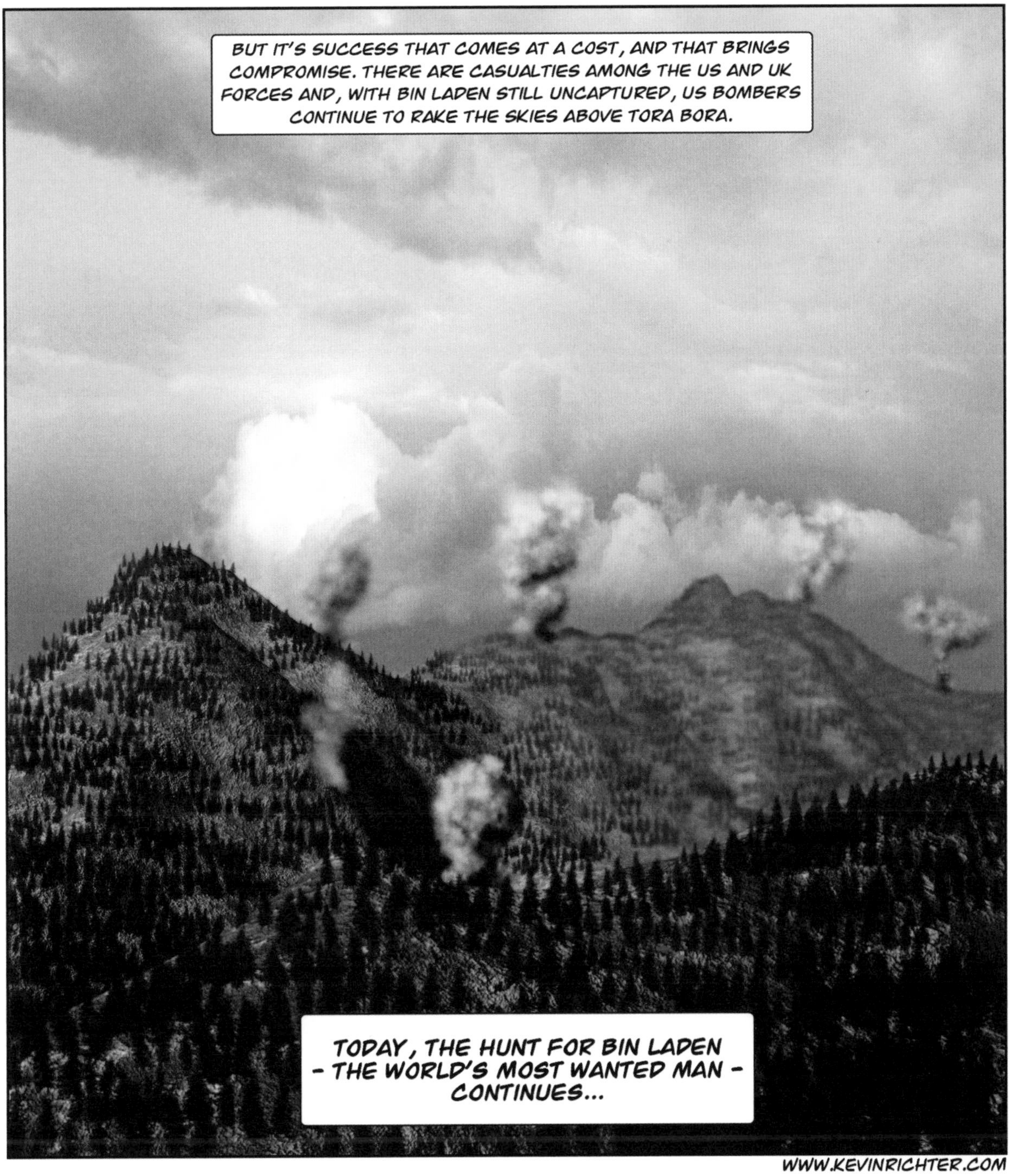

BUT IT'S SUCCESS THAT COMES AT A COST, AND THAT BRINGS COMPROMISE. THERE ARE CASUALTIES AMONG THE US AND UK FORCES AND, WITH BIN LADEN STILL UNCAPTURED, US BOMBERS CONTINUE TO RAKE THE SKIES ABOVE TORA BORA.

TODAY, THE HUNT FOR BIN LADEN - THE WORLD'S MOST WANTED MAN - CONTINUES...

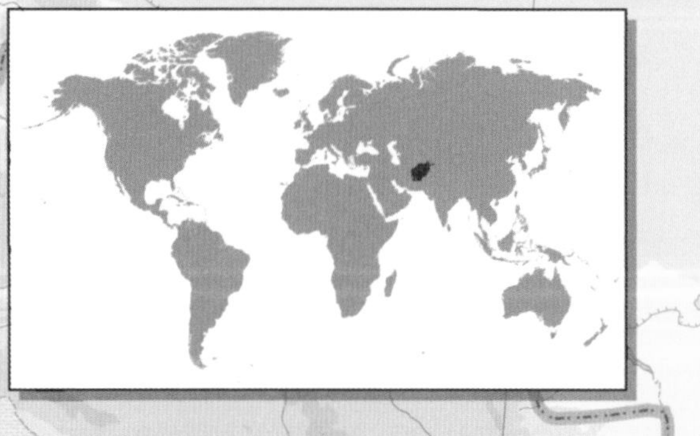

AFGHANISTAN

Conventional long form: Islamic Republic of Afghanistan
Conventional short form: Afghanistan
Local long form: *Jomhuri-ye Eslami-ye Afghanestan*
Local short form: Afghanestan
Formerly called: Republic of Afghanistan

Flag: Three equal vertical stripes of black, red and green, with the national emblem in white centred on the red band. The central emblem shows a mosque and minaret with flags on either side. Below the mosque are numerals for the solar year 1298 (1919 in the Gregorian calendar, the year of Afghan independence from the UK). The image is bordered by a circle consisting of sheaves of wheat on the left and right, and in the upper centre is an Arabic inscription of the *Shahada* (the Muslim creed). Below this are rays of the rising sun over the *Takbir* (an Arabic expression meaning 'God is great'). At lower centre is a scroll bearing the word 'Afghanistan'.

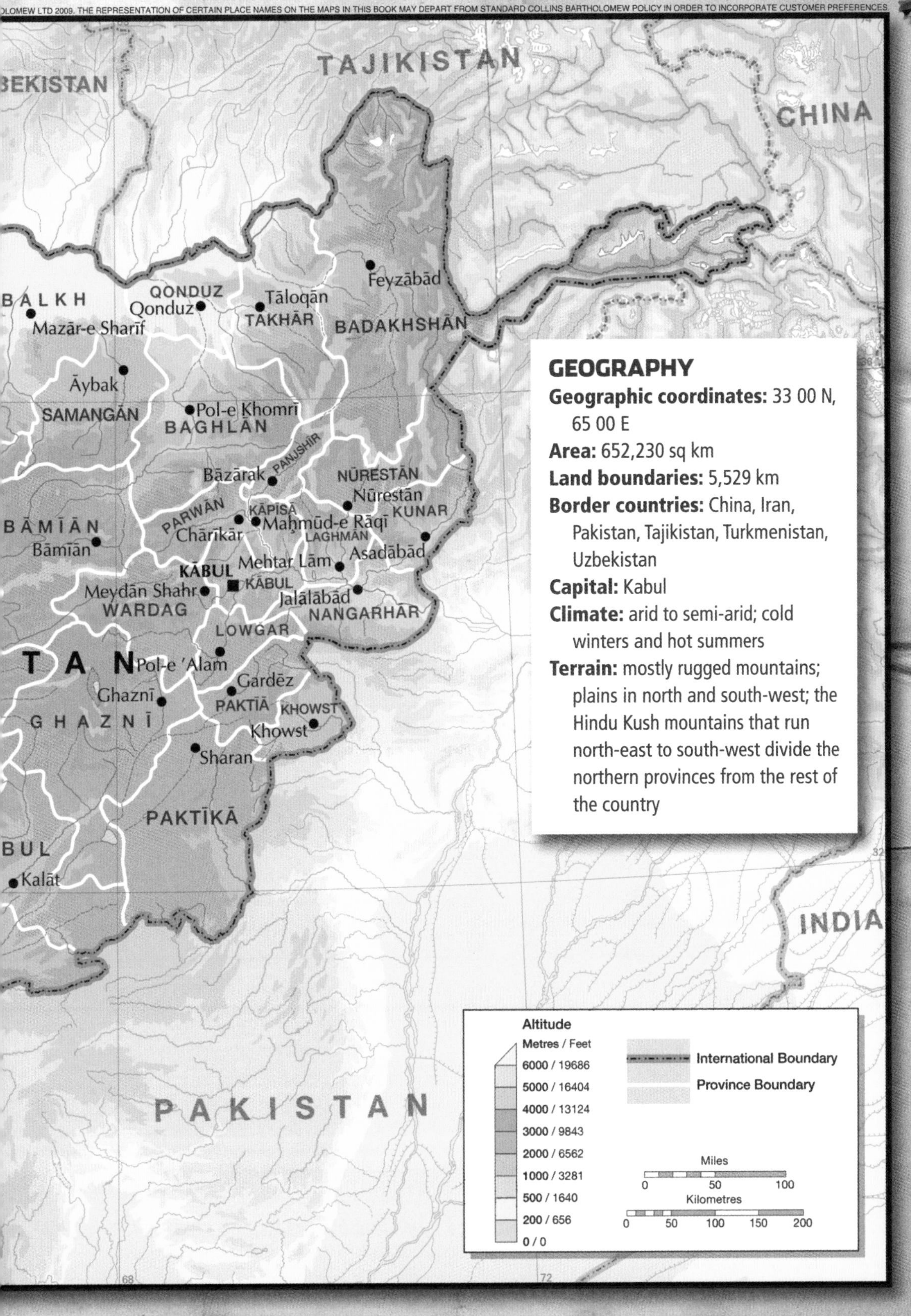

GEOGRAPHY

Geographic coordinates: 33 00 N, 65 00 E

Area: 652,230 sq km

Land boundaries: 5,529 km

Border countries: China, Iran, Pakistan, Tajikistan, Turkmenistan, Uzbekistan

Capital: Kabul

Climate: arid to semi-arid; cold winters and hot summers

Terrain: mostly rugged mountains; plains in north and south-west; the Hindu Kush mountains that run north-east to south-west divide the northern provinces from the rest of the country

AFGHANISTAN By Ben Brown

Afghanistan is one of the most beautiful countries on earth, but also one of the most brutal. It is a place of wild extremes: you can suffer frostbite in the savage cold of winter temperatures as low as –25 degrees Celsius, and heatstroke in the scorching 50-degree summers. Many believe that it is Afghanistan's harsh climate and terrain that have helped breed generations of determined warriors, and also made it such a difficult place for foreign invaders to occupy. There are vast deserts, but much of the country is made up of soaring mountains, including the famous Hindu Kush, while the rugged terrain along the Pakistani border has often made it easy for Taliban and al-Qaeda fighters to hide and to slip away from NATO troops.

A young anti-Taliban fighter overlooks his homeland from a hilltop perch.

DEMOGRAPHICS

Population: 33,609,937 (July 2009 estimate)
Median age: 17.6 years
0–14 years: 44.5%
15–64 years: 53%
65 years and over: 2.4%
Birth rate: 45.46 births/1,000 population
Death rate: 19.18 deaths/1,000 population
Life expectancy at birth: 44.64 years
Ethnic groups: Pashtun 42%, Tajik 27%, Hazara 9%, Uzbek 9%, Aimak 4%, Turkmen 3%, Baloch 2%, other 4%
Religion: Sunni Muslim 80%, Shia Muslim 19%, other 1%
Languages: Afghan Persian or Dari (official) 50%, Pashto (official) 35%, Turkic languages (primarily Uzbek and Turkmen) 11%, 30 minor languages (primarily Balochi and Pashai) 4%, high level of bilingualism
Literacy: 28.1%
male: 43.1%
female: 12.6% (2000 estimate)

Afghanistan is completely landlocked, and shares its borders with six other countries – one reason it has been at the centre of so much war for centuries. It is also among the poorest nations in the world. Afghans farm and grow crops in only a small area of the country – about 12 per cent of the total landmass. In many places, life seems feudal, almost medieval, and people can only expect to live – on average – until their mid-forties.

Almost all Afghans are Muslim, but they come from many different ethnic groups – an amazing patchwork quilt of them. By far the biggest group is the Pashtun, who make up more than 40 per cent of the population and live mainly to the south of the Hindu Kush. They have ruled the country for long periods of its history, and most of the

WHAT IS *PASHTUNWALI*?

Pashtunwali, meaning 'the way of the Pashtuns', is fundamental to Pashtun identity and is an unwritten social code of honour, or *izzat*. *Pashtunwali* is defined by ideals of chivalry, hospitality, specific gender roles and council. Known as *ghayrat* or *nang* in Pashto, the notion of chivalry is based on honourable and courageous actions in battle. An important rule of chivalry is the defence of honour against shame. Under this code of conduct, an insult must be 'answered', or acted on. The notion of hospitality, or *melmastia*, includes feeding strangers and friends, giving gifts and defending any guests. According to *pashtunwali*, for honour to be upheld Pashtuns must also defend the rules of the gendered order, called *purdah* or *namus*. The rules of *purdah* vary from community to community – in stricter communities, women may only leave the house completely veiled, whereas in more liberal communities women do not veil their faces at all. The *jirga*, or council, is the legislative authority in *Pashtunwali*. To participate in the council, Pashtuns must be known for their honour. Often *jirga* are all male, although, on occasion, some women have been known to participate.

Taliban come from this group. There are many Pashtun in Pakistan as well, which is why there are close links between the Taliban and parts of Pakistan. The Pashtun speak Pashto and have an ancient code of conduct and honour called *pashtunwali*. Further north, there are different ethnic groups, including the Tajiks, who have long been rivals of the Pashtun. There are also the Hazaras, Uzbeks and Turkmens, among others. All these ethnic groups are subdivided into hundreds of tribes and clans, based on family ties that date back generations. These divisions mean that Afghanistan is an extremely difficult country to rule: different warlords and tribal leaders sometimes even switch sides in times of conflict, often for money. It can be tricky knowing who is your friend, and who is your enemy.

Afghanistan's rugged landscape makes it a beautiful – but difficult – place to live.

Lush green fields stand in vibrant contrast to Afghanistan's deserts.

LEARN PASHTO

Good communication with locals is essential in Afghanistan. Usually British troops rely on interpreters, but just in case, all British Armed Forces in Afghanistan are issued with this 'Pashto Survival Card'.

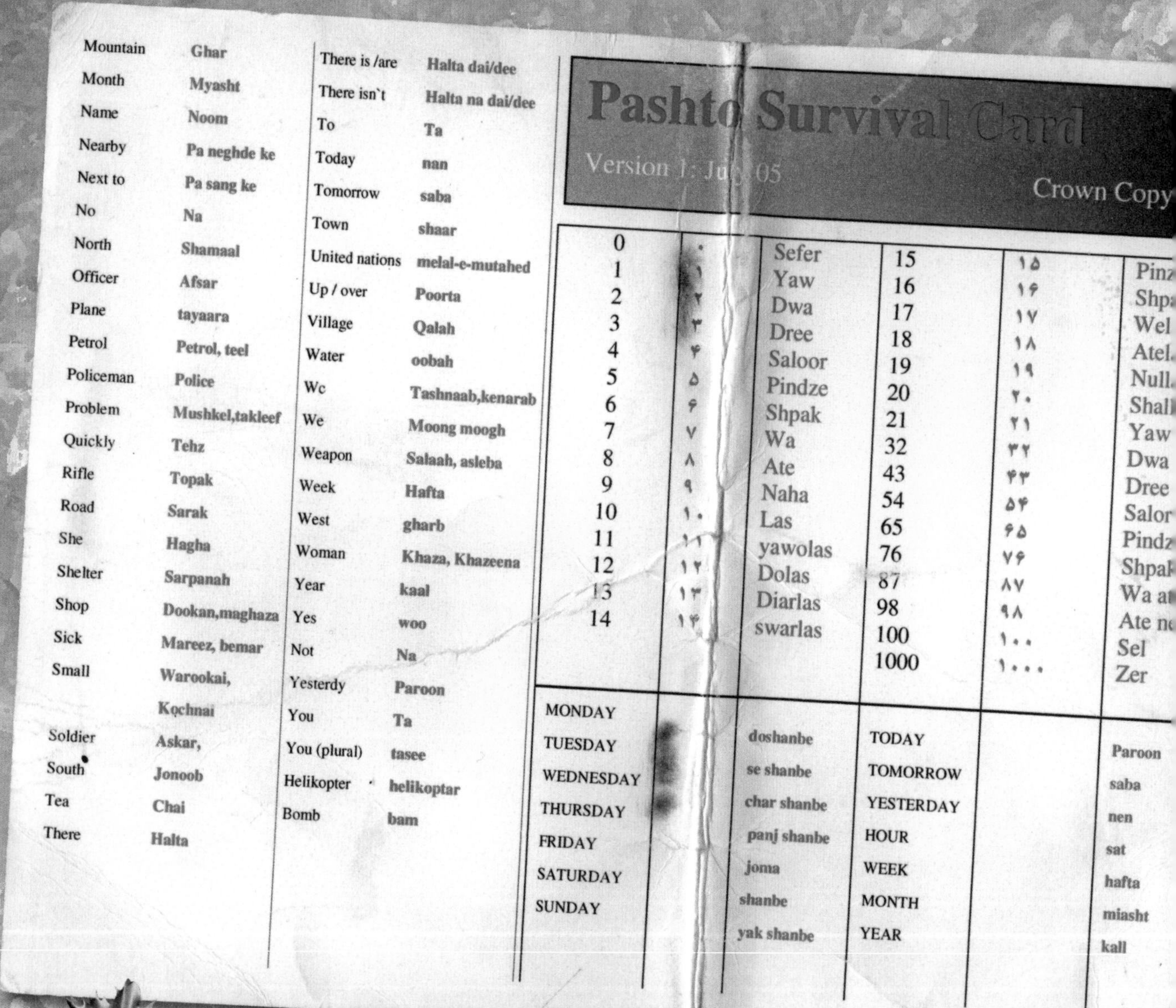

Mountain	Ghar
Month	Myasht
Name	Noom
Nearby	Pa neghde ke
Next to	Pa sang ke
No	Na
North	Shamaal
Officer	Afsar
Plane	tayaara
Petrol	Petrol, teel
Policeman	Police
Problem	Mushkel,takleef
Quickly	Tehz
Rifle	Topak
Road	Sarak
She	Hagha
Shelter	Sarpanah
Shop	Dookan,maghaza
Sick	Mareez, bemar
Small	Warookai, Kochnai
Soldier	Askar,
South	Jonoob
Tea	Chai
There	Halta

There is /are	Halta dai/dee
There isn't	Halta na dai/dee
To	Ta
Today	nan
Tomorrow	saba
Town	shaar
United nations	melal-e-mutahed
Up / over	Poorta
Village	Qalah
Water	oobah
Wc	Tashnaab,kenarab
We	Moong moogh
Weapon	Salaah, asleba
Week	Hafta
West	gharb
Woman	Khaza, Khazeena
Year	kaal
Yes	woo
Not	Na
Yesterdy	Paroon
You	Ta
You (plural)	tasee
Helikopter	helikoptar
Bomb	bam

Pashto Survival Card

Version 1: July 05

Crown Copy

0	٠	Sefer	15	١٥	Pinz
1	١	Yaw	16	١٦	Shp
2	٢	Dwa	17	١٧	Wel
3	٣	Dree	18	١٨	Atel
4	۴	Saloor	19	١٩	Null
5	۵	Pindze	20	٢٠	Shal
6	۶	Shpak	21	٢١	Yaw
7	٧	Wa	32	٣٢	Dwa
8	٨	Ate	43	۴٣	Dree
9	٩	Naha	54	۵۴	Salor
10	١٠	Las	65	۶۵	Pindz
11	١١	yawolas	76	٧۶	Shpak
12	١٢	Dolas	87	٨٧	Wa a
13	١٣	Diarlas	98	٩٨	Ate n
14	١۴	swarlas	100	١٠٠	Sel
			1000	١٠٠٠	Zer

MONDAY	doshanbe	TODAY		Paroon
TUESDAY	se shanbe	TOMORROW		saba
WEDNESDAY	char shanbe	YESTERDAY		nen
THURSDAY	panj shanbe	HOUR		sat
FRIDAY	joma	WEEK		hafta
SATURDAY	shanbe	MONTH		miasht
SUNDAY	yak shanbe	YEAR		kall

PAMPHLETS COURTESY OF THE MUSEUM OF ARMY FLYING

COMMANDS AND QUESTIONS

RING ME	ma ta rawra
OME HERE	dalta rasha
ON'NT RESIST	moqawemat mekawa
EAT	wukhra
GETDOWN	kata sha
GET UP	walar sha
GO AWAY	za
HANDS UP	lasoona jig ka
HOW MUCH?	soomra?
HOW MANY	tso?
LOOK	wagoora
MOVE	harakat woka
ONE AT A TIME	yaw yaw(ba nawbat sara)
PUT	kshegda
RETURN	berta rawagarza
TELL ME	mata wowaya
SIT	kshena (keena)
STOP-stops a man	wadarega
STOP-stops a car	wadarawa
	tasleem sha
	wakhla
	wachawa
	leg wadrega
	sa?
	cheeree? Koom?
	sook?
	walee?
	se wakht?
	sa rang? sa raqam?
lights	cheraghoona gul ka
onnet/	bonat khlas ka
e	mashin gul ka
our	jiboona da teshkra
car	motar wadrawa
f the car	da motar na rawawza
your ID	tazkera de rata wakhaya
ER	khatar

DO YOU HAVE...?	ayaa ta laré?
DO YOU KNOW...?	ayaa ta pohegé?
DO YOU NEED HELP?	komak ta zarootat laré?
DO YOU WANT...?	ta ghwaré?
DON'T BE AFRAID	ma weréga, ma daréga(q=berégha)
I DON'T KNOW	za na pohegam
I DON'T SPEAK DARI	za dari na pohegam
I DON'T SPEAK PASHTO	za pakto (pashto) na pohegom
WE WILL HELP YOU	moong ta sara komak kawo
WHAT IS YOUR NAME?	sta noom sa dai?
WHO IS IN CHARGE?	masool sook dai?
HELP ME !	masara komak wokrai
I'M FROM BRITAIN	za da englistan yam
MY NAME IS...	zma noom.....dai
WHAT S YOUR NAME?	sta noom sa dai?

GREETINGS

HELLO	salaam
REPLY	wa alaikum assalaam
GOOD MORNING	sahar pakhair
REPLY	sahar pakhair
HI	salaam
THANKS	manana
REPLY	qaabel da tashakor na dai
WELCOME	kha raghlee
HOW ARE YOU?	senga yee?
FINE THANKS	kha yam manana
GOOD BYE	da khodai pa amaan
REPLY	pa makha de kha
SEE YOU SOON	tar bia leedalo

Key to Pronunciation

-kh- as in `loch`	-H- strong and breathy `h`
-dh- as in `that`	-T- S-DH- all strong sounds
-sh- as in `shoot`	-gh- a`growl' in the throat
-th- as in `think`	-ch- as in `cheese`

-A- no equivalent, `aah` sound made in back of throat

BAD	kharab
BANDAGE	bandaaj
BIG	ghat, loy
BOY	halak
	doodai
CAR	motar
PHARMACY	dawakhaana
CIVILIAN	mulki
CLOTHING	kalee,jameh
COFFEE	qahwa
DAY	wraz
DESERT	dashta, sahra dashta
DOCTOR	daktar
DOWN	kshata (khkata), teet
EAST	sharq,khateez
ENEMY	doshman, dokhman
EXCELLENT	deer kha, deer aala
FAR	lare
FOOD	doday, khwara
FRIEND	malgaray,dost
FROM	da,la
GIRL	njalai,njalkai
GOOD	kha
GROUND	zmaka
HE	hagha
HELP	komak, mrasta
HERE	dalta,pa de zai ke
HOSPITAL	rooghtoon, shafakhaana
HOUR	saat,geenta
HOUSE	koor
I	za
LATER	wroosta
MAN	sarai
MAP	naqsha
MARKET	market, baazar
MEDICINE	dawa,daroo
MOSQUE	joomat,masjed

© CAPTAIN IAN McLEISH

Communication with ordinary Afghans is vital to reconstruction efforts, and to winning the locals' trust.

Pashto, although spoken throughout only 35 per cent of Afghanistan, is the country's official language and is spoken by over 30 million people throughout Afghanistan and north-west Pakistan.

If you find yourself in a tight spot, some of these words and phrases could avoid a lot of problems.

KIT

© TIMES NEWSPAPERS LTD

A soldier's desert kit, LEFT, and regular personal kit, BELOW.

© TIMES NEWSPAPERS

The standard-issue kit given to British Army infantry soldiers makes them among the best equipped troops in the world. Most items of kit are purely functional, such as boots, helmets and weapons, with safety the main concern. However, some items are also seen as fashion accessories, or, like the solar-power monkey, as a way of making life back at the base a bit more fun.

Troops deployed to Afghanistan are given a Mark 6 helmet and standard-issue goggles.

The helmet can repel 7.62 mm AK-47 rounds from 100 metres away.

The ballistic goggles have three types of lens: dark, clear or yellow tinted.

Soldiers also get ear defenders which are moulded to the shape of the ear channel.

These still allow the soldiers to hear conversations around them and over their radios, but they block out the supersonic sounds of gunfire to guard against long-term hearing damage.

But the biggest life-saver of British troops fighting against the Taliban is their Osprey body armour.

This includes a fragmentation jacket with ballistic plates designed to stop armour-piercing rounds, and it covers the entire torso.

It also includes the capability to add side ballistic plates to provide further protection.

There are detachable collars and epaulettes to protect the neck, upper arms and armpit area from blast fragments.

An Army source said: 'I saw a guy who was hit by a 12.7 mm round from a heavy machine gun. He went down and broke a few ribs, but he got up again and it was the Osprey that saved him.'

Even the non-protective clothing the troops wear is high-tech.

It is made of lightweight material, for example microfibre fast-wicking

Paras' boots, lined up and ready for action.

© TIMES NEWSPAPERS LTD

T-shirts and socks, which pull moisture away from the skin. Because of the sweltering conditions in Afghanistan, the soldiers sweat a lot and this clothing ensures that chafing isn't an additional concern in battle.

Boots are very important for soldiers, as they spend the day on their feet, and they can choose from several makes of boot to ensure that they have the right pair for comfort.

When it comes to weapons, the main gun is the SA80 Mk2 assault rifle, fitted with a telescopic sight and a magazine of thirty rounds. The rifle is British-made and is deadly accurate up to 300 metres, firing 5.56 mm bullets at a muzzle velocity of 940 metres per second.

Troops can also fix a bayonet to the end for close-combat fighting.

For shooting at close quarters, the Sig Sauer P226 is the firearm of choice. It is the new standard-issue pistol for all British forces, replacing the older Browning. The P226 can fire a 9 mm bullet accurately up to 50 metres, from a magazine holding up to fifteen rounds. A standard ten-round magazine can be fired in less than three seconds.

Troops can adapt their kit to ensure that they have everything they need while on the battlefield.

One of the most unusual added pieces of kit is a solar-power monkey which can be attached to their clothes. The monkey soaks up the sun's heat while the troops are out on patrols. They can then use the energy in the tiny device to charge up gadgets like iPods once they return to the base.

The Army source added: 'If you look at what an infantry soldier goes on the ground with now, it is better than it has ever been and it's getting better still. The reason we have so many wounded soldiers now is that fifteen to twenty years ago, they wouldn't have survived. And they owe it to the kit.'

By Andy Crick

Major Mike Shervington of 2 Para, kitted up and and on patrol in Kajakī.

A HEAVY LOAD

Troops on patrol in Afghanistan carry huge rucksacks known as Bergens. When full, this giant camouflaged bag weighs about 30 kg and contains all the vital supplies troops need.

The two items troops simply can't live without are ammunition and water. Therefore, all troops on patrol carry a minimum of 300 rounds. With temperatures reaching 50 degrees C at the height of summer, troops also carry up to 6 litres of water every time they deploy.

Depending on the specific mission, troops will be issued with a combination of hot and cold meal ration packs, enough for two to three meals per day, with dishes ranging from beef stew to peaches in chocolate sauce. Basic cooking equipment such as pots, pans and a stove are shared out among platoons. Boiled sweets and biscuits keep troops going during the day.

In addition to the absolute essentials, a full Bergen will also include a complete change of clothes, a few spare pairs of pants and socks and basic toiletries such as toothbrushes, toothpaste and talcum powder. In the freezing Afghan winter, when temperatures drop below zero, troops also carry a lightweight sleeping bag and a shelter sheet to sleep under, which doubles as a stretcher.

Finally, squaddies always carry a supply of batteries for the patrol radio to make sure they don't lose all-important communications.

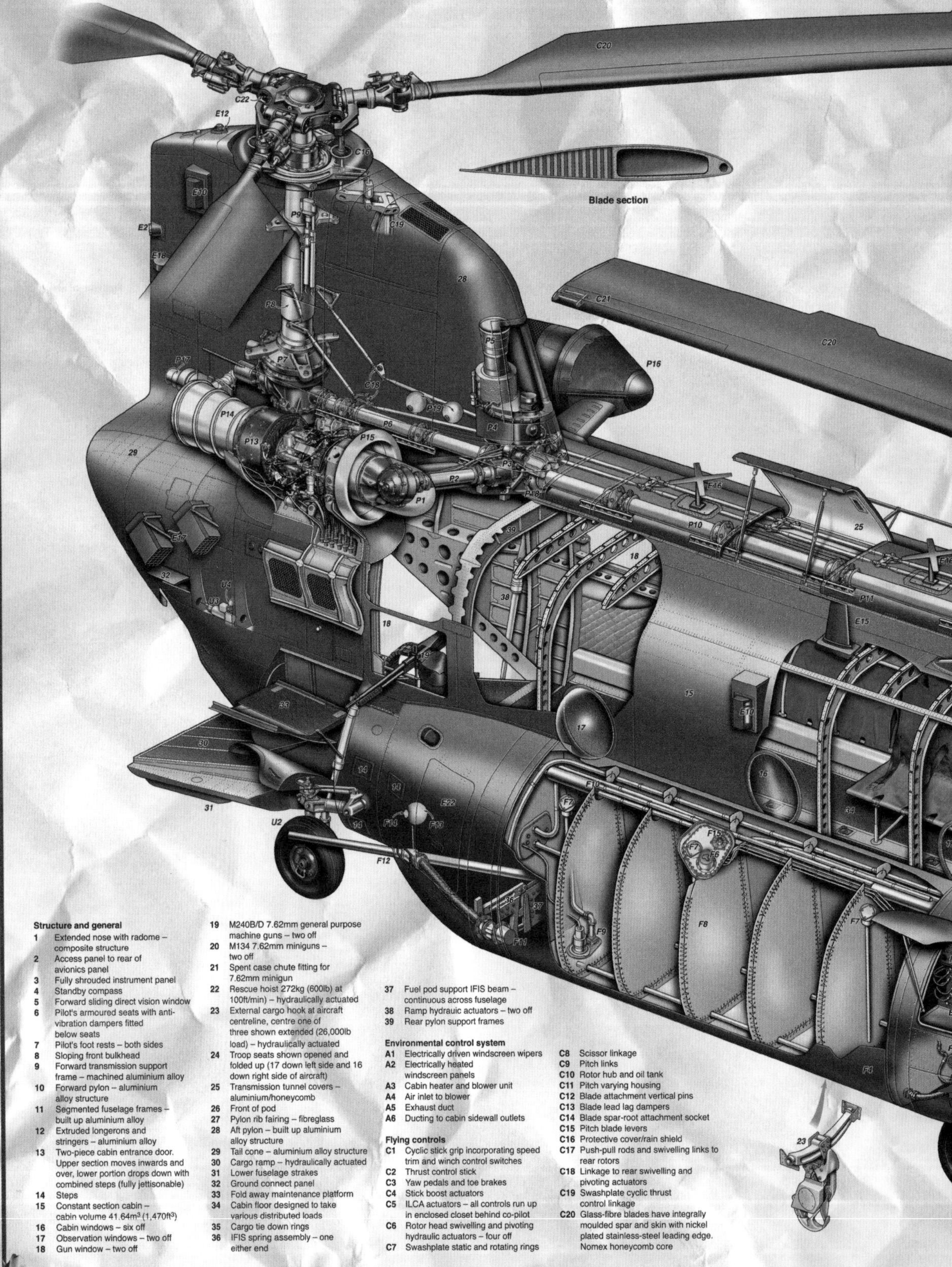

Structure and general

1 Extended nose with radome – composite structure
2 Access panel to rear of avionics panel
3 Fully shrouded instrument panel
4 Standby compass
5 Forward sliding direct vision window
6 Pilot's armoured seats with anti-vibration dampers fitted below seats
7 Pilot's foot rests – both sides
8 Sloping front bulkhead
9 Forward transmission support frame – machined aluminium alloy
10 Forward pylon – aluminium alloy structure
11 Segmented fuselage frames – built up aluminium alloy
12 Extruded longerons and stringers – aluminium alloy
13 Two-piece cabin entrance door. Upper section moves inwards and over, lower portion drops down with combined steps (fully jettisonable)
14 Steps
15 Constant section cabin – cabin volume 41.64m^3 (1,470ft^3)
16 Cabin windows – six off
17 Observation windows – two off
18 Gun window – two off
19 M240B/D 7.62mm general purpose machine guns – two off
20 M134 7.62mm miniguns – two off
21 Spent case chute fitting for 7.62mm minigun
22 Rescue hoist 272kg (600lb) at 100ft/min) – hydraulically actuated
23 External cargo hook at aircraft centreline, centre one of three shown extended (26,000lb load) – hydraulically actuated
24 Troop seats shown opened and folded up (17 down left side and 16 down right side of aircraft)
25 Transmission tunnel covers – aluminium/honeycomb
26 Front of pod
27 Pylon rib fairing – fibreglass
28 Aft pylon – built up aluminium alloy structure
29 Tail cone – aluminium alloy structure
30 Cargo ramp – hydraulically actuated
31 Lower fuselage strakes
32 Ground connect panel
33 Fold away maintenance platform
34 Cabin floor designed to take various distributed loads
35 Cargo tie down rings
36 IFIS spring assembly – one either end
37 Fuel pod support IFIS beam – continuous across fuselage
38 Ramp hydrauic actuators – two off
39 Rear pylon support frames

Environmental control system

A1 Electrically driven windscreen wipers
A2 Electrically heated windscreen panels
A3 Cabin heater and blower unit
A4 Air inlet to blower
A5 Exhaust duct
A6 Ducting to cabin sidewall outlets

Flying controls

C1 Cyclic stick grip incorporating speed trim and winch control switches
C2 Thrust control stick
C3 Yaw pedals and toe brakes
C4 Stick boost actuators
C5 ILCA actuators – all controls run up in enclosed closet behind co-pilot
C6 Rotor head swivelling and pivoting hydraulic actuators – four off
C7 Swashplate static and rotating rings
C8 Scissor linkage
C9 Pitch links
C10 Rotor hub and oil tank
C11 Pitch varying housing
C12 Blade attachment vertical pins
C13 Blade lead lag dampers
C14 Blade spar-root attachment socket
C15 Pitch blade levers
C16 Protective cover/rain shield
C17 Push-pull rods and swivelling links to rear rotors
C18 Linkage to rear swivelling and pivoting actuators
C19 Swashplate cyclic thrust control linkage
C20 Glass-fibre blades have integrally moulded spar and skin with nickel plated stainless-steel leading edge. Nomex honeycomb core

CHINOOK CH47

STARBOARD VIEW

C21 Tip tracking balancing weights and cover plate
C22 Horizontal hinge pins

Instrument panel
D1 Multifunction displays
D2 Master caution indicators
D3 ESIS (electronic situation indication system)
D4 Inclinometer displays
D5 Radar warning indicator
D6 Digital clock
D7 HPRT faults, battery low
D8 Fire handles
D9 Radar altimeter dimming
D10 MFCU – two-off
D11 Radar altimeter indicator
D12 Stick position indicator
D13 CDU
D14 AFCS contol panel
D15 Misc switch panel
D16 Volume and dimming controls

Avionics and electrical
E1 Electrically heated pitot tubes – two off
E2 AN/APR-39A(V)1 pulsed radar warning antenna
E3 Multi-mode radar
E4 FLIR
E5 AIM/APX-118(V) IFF transponder antenna
E6 AN/ARN-147 GS antenna
E7 Forward AN/ALQ-136(V)2 receive antenna
E8 AN/AAR-47 missile warning sensor
E9 OAT gauge
E10 AN/AVR-2 laser warning sensors
E11 ARX-3000 ELT antenna
E12 Upper rotating beacon
E13 Refuelling lights
E14 EGI GPS antenna – two off
E15 AN/ARC-201(D) and AN/ARC-186 VHP AM/FM antenna
E16 AN/ARC-231(V)(C) SATCOM antennas – two off
E17 Chaff pods – both sides
E18 AN/APR-44(V)3 radar warning antenna – both sides
E19 Yaw sensor ports – four off
E20 AN/ARC-220(V)2 HF antenna
E21 Forward avionics bay
E22 Rear avionics bay
E23 IR strobe lights – three off

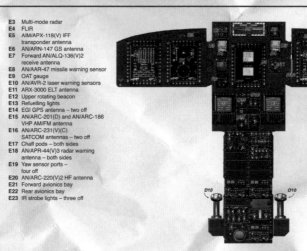

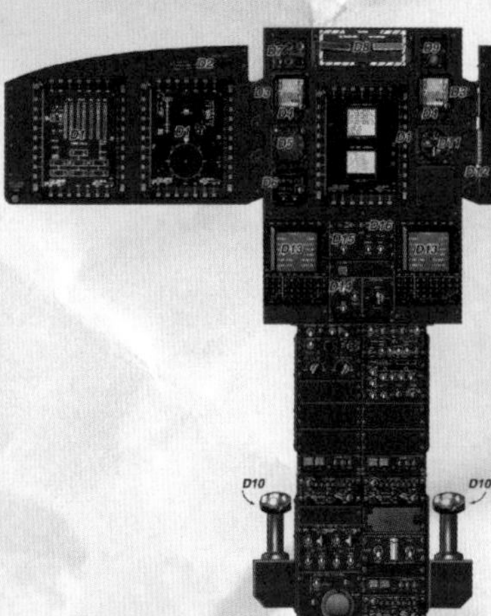
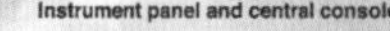

Instrument panel and central console

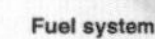

Fuel system
F1 In flight refueling probe – length 8.97m
F2 Transfer hose
F3 Fuel transfer manifold
F4 External fuel pods, Kevlar skin with Nomex honeycomb core
F5 Single-point pressure refuelling nozzle
F6 Gravity fuel filler
F7 Fuel quantity probes
F8 Internal baffles in fuel cell
F9 Booster pump – two per tank
F10 Tank venting lines
F11 Fuel jettison valve
F12 Fuel jettison tube – pneumatically extended
F13 Pneumatic reservoir for fuel jettison tube
F14 Fuel jettison bottle pressure gauge
F15 Fuel level control valve
F16 Refuelling control processor

Powerplant and transmission
P1 Engine transmission gearbox
P2 Engine drive torque shaft
P3 Engine combiner gearbox
P4 Combiner gearbox oil tank
P5 Combiner gearbox cooling fan
P6 Synchronising shaft to rear gearbox
P7 Rear transmission gearbox with accessory gearbox on rear face driving hydraulic pump and generator
P8 Vertical drive shaft to rear rotor
P9 Drive shaft thrust bearing
P10 Forward drive-synchronising shaft – seamless aluminium alloy tubes, dynamically balanced
P11 Drive-shaft shock-absorbing support mountings
P12 Forward transmission gearbox
P13 Honeywell T55-GA-714A engine
P14 Canted tailpipe assembly
P15 Engine inlet
P16 Bypass screen assembly
P17 Auxiliary power unit
P18 Rotor brake
P19 Fire suppression system reservoirs

Undercarriage and hydraulics
U1 Front fixed undercarriage with single disc three-pad brake unit
U2 Rear fully steerable undercarriage – steering through 360 degrees on right leg only. Single disc three pad brake unit
U3 EPUSHA pump
U4 Manual utility hydraulic pump

Reprinted from Flight International

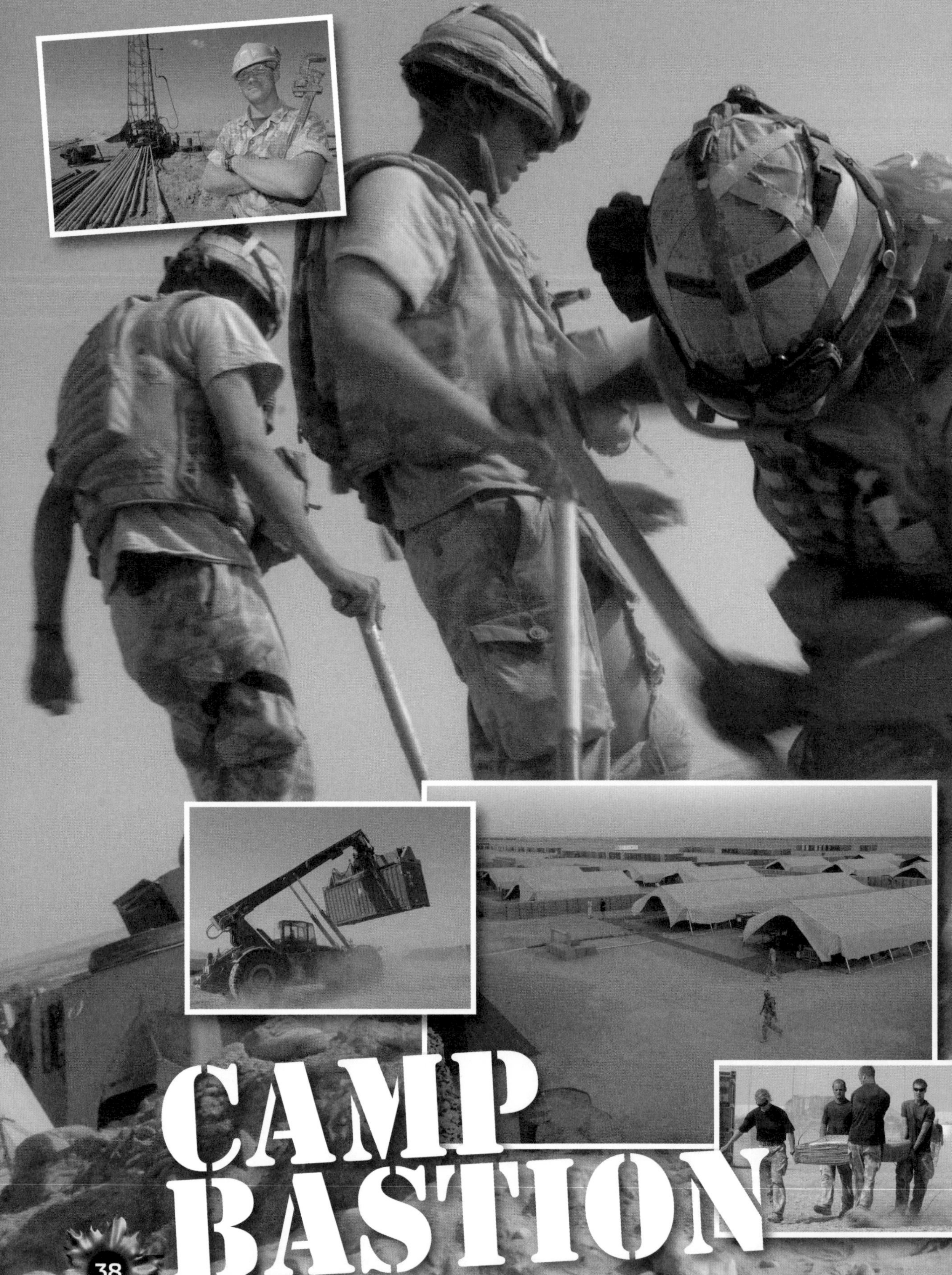

CAMP BASTION

Camp Bastion is the largest British overseas military camp built since World War II.

Located north-west of Lashkar Gāh, the capital of Helmand Province, it is set in a remote desert far from any towns or villages.

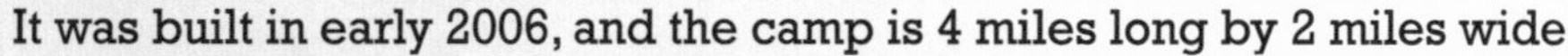

It was built in early 2006, and the camp is 4 miles long by 2 miles wide.

There are currently 14,500 people based at Camp Bastion; of those, 4,800 are British troops, 9,000 are American troops and 700 are civilians.

These soldiers and workers are protected from Taliban rocket attacks by the heavily fortified walls surrounding the camp.

These sturdy walls are made up of thousands of semi-permanent sandbag barriers made by the British company, Hesco.

The giant industrial-sized sandbags have a collapsible wire-mesh frame, which can be erected and then filled with sand, dirt or gravel.

When set up, these barriers are 60 cm thick and can block the bullet from a Taliban insurgent's AK-47 assault rifle.

When three sandbags are placed in a row behind each other, the resulting 1 m 80 cm is more than enough to protect those within the compound from a Rocket-propelled Grenade (RPG). As an additional precaution, state-of-the-art perimeter surveillance and protection also limit the potential for attacks on the base.

These surveillance radars can pick up any human movement up to a distance of 20 miles.

The airfield at Camp Bastion was set up by two RAF personnel in 2006. Within three years, the gravel and dirt track has been transformed into the fifth-busiest UK-operated airport. When the airfield was first built, it was intended to handle no more than three flights per week; it now it deals with 400 flights per day, or 12,000 per month.

This adds up to more take-offs and landings than at Luton, Edinburgh or Birmingham airports, making Bastion busier than Leeds-Bradford and Coventry airports combined.

The largest planes using the 2,350-metre-long runway are the C-130 Hercules and the TriStar passenger transport aircraft.

In addition, double-propeller Chinook helicopters and Apache gunships also operate out of Bastion's helipads.

The huge base also boasts a 50-bed field hospital, employing a total of 170 staff, all specialists in battlefield trauma injuries.

Camp Bastion now has its own mineral water bottling plant, able to produce more than 70,000 litres of water per day.

The water is pumped out of boreholes 120 metres beneath the Afghan desert.

The water-purification factory cost £11 million to build, but it saves the Army about £18 million because it no longer has to transport imported water into the base via convoys, which are open to attack by the Taliban.

Spare a thought for the chefs that have to serve up grub to the war-weary troops; a whopping 4,000 meals are made in the cookhouse three times a day, or 12,000 meals in total.

The Navy, Army and Air Force Institute is the Armed Forces' official store. The biggest seller in the NAAFI is cans of Coke, which give the soldiers a taste of home. Every week, 5,580 cans are sold there.

The soldiers also keep in touch with Britain via letters and parcels from their loved ones. Approximately 300 bags of post are delivered to the base every single day.

By Andy Crick

JUGROOM FORT

WHEN BRITISH TROOPS SET OUT TO ASSAULT THE TALIBAN BASE OF JUGROOM FORT, NEAR GARMSIR, THEY EXPECTED IT TO BE A ROUTINE OPERATION. WHAT FOLLOWED WAS TO BECOME ONE OF THE MOST DARING MISSIONS IN LIVING MEMORY. AFTER AN ASSAULT ON THE ENEMY BASE BY B1 BOMBERS AND 150 MM ARTILLERY, A 200-STRONG FORCE OF BRITISH TROOPS IN AMPHIBIOUS VIKING ARMOURED VEHICLES, CROSSED THE RIVER HELMAND TO ATTACK THE FORT. WITH THE FIREFIGHT RAGING AROUND THEM, ZULU COMPANY MOVED TOWARDS THE COMPOUND'S WALLS, LEAVING THEIR ARMOURED VEHICLES, AND BEGAN A GROUND ASSAULT AS DAWN BROKE.

THE TROOPS WIPE OUT ONE WAVE OF INSURGENTS, BUT ANOTHER TAKES ITS PLACE. IN THE FIERCE FIGHTING MANY MEN ARE WOUNDED. WITH THE BULLETS FLYING, THE ORDER FINALLY COMES THROUGH: 'WITHDRAW!'

WITH SEVERAL COMMANDOS SUFFERING GUNSHOT WOUNDS, THE TROOPS FIGHT THEIR WAY BACK TO THEIR VIKINGS.
HNH-!
WE'RE FALLING BACK TO THE VIKINGS, GUYS.

THE WOUNDED WARRIORS EXTRACT BACK TO BASE, ONLT TOO GLAD TO LEAVE THE FORT.
THAT WAS ONE HELL OF A DUST-UP. SAY WHAT YOU LIKE, THE TALIBAN PUT UP A GOOD FIGHT.

BUT WHEN AT LAST THEY DRAW BREATH AND TAKE STOCK, THE TROOPERS ARE HORRIFIED TO REALISE THAT ONE OF THEIR NUMBER IS MISSING. LANCE CORPORAL MATHEW FORD HAS BEEN LEFT BEHIND. THE PROSPECT OF WHAT MIGHT HAPPEN TO HIM SHOULD HE FALL INTO ENEMY HANDS IS TOO HORRIBLE TO CONTEMPLATE... WHEN AN APACHE IDENTIFIES WHAT LOOKS LIKE A BODY LYING NEAR ONE OF THE COMPOUND WALLS, THE TROOPS KNOW WHAT THEY MUST DO...
WE ALL KNOW WHAT COULD HAPPEN TO HIM. WE CAN'T LEAVE HIM.

I NEED VOLUNTEERS TO GO BACK AND GET HIM.

I'LL GO!
THE COLONEL SELECTS CAPTAIN DAVE RIGG, WOI COLIN HEARN, ZULU COMPANY MARINE CHRIS FRASER-PERRY AND SIGNALLER MARINE GARY ROBINSON FROM THOSE WHO VOLUNTEER.

WITH NO TIME TO WASTE, ONE OF THE APACHE PILOTS QUICKLY EXPLAINS THE PLAN TO THE VOLUNTEERS.
STRAP YOURSELVES ON TO THE GRAB BARS ON THE SIDE AND HOLD ON! WE SHOULD BE IN AND OUT IN A FEW MINUTES, IT'LL BE QUICKER THAN USING THE VIKINGS.

TWO APACHES WILL SUPPRESS THE ENEMY TO THE NORTH AND EAST OF OUR LANDING POSITION WHILE WE LAND. WE'LL HAVE NO MORE THAN TWO MINUTES ON THE GROUND.
THE MEN CLING TO THE MACHINE AS IT BEATS ITS WAY BACK TO THE SCENE OF THE BATTLE.

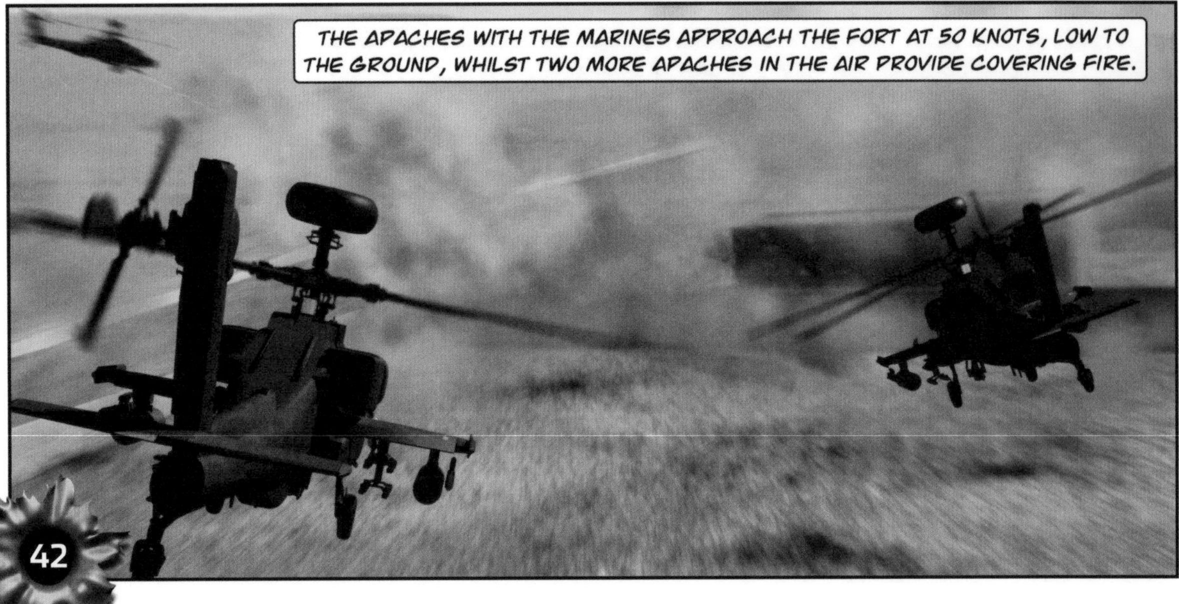
THE APACHES WITH THE MARINES APPROACH THE FORT AT 50 KNOTS, LOW TO THE GROUND, WHILST TWO MORE APACHES IN THE AIR PROVIDE COVERING FIRE.

THE MARINES, FOLLOWED BY SOME OF THE PILOTS, LEAP OFF THE CHOPPERS AMIDST THE SWIRLING DUSTCLOUD THAT THEY'VE CREATED.
GO! GO! GO!

THERE HE IS! MATT!
IS HE STILL ALIVE?

THE APACHES IN THE AIR SMASH ROCKETS AND MACHINE-GUN FIRE INTO TALIBAN POSITIONS AROUND THE FORT WHILST MATHEW FORD IS GRADUALLY LIFTED BACK TO THE CHOPPER ON THE GROUND.
QUICK, LIFT HIM UP! WE'RE GOING TO HAVE TO CARRY HIM BACK TO THE CHOPPER.

£*?@! WE'RE UNDER FIRE! WE NEED TO MOVE FASTER!

THE MEN QUICKLY TIE MATT TO THE APACHE, WHILST TALIBAN BULLETS FLY THROUGH THE AIR AROUND THEM.
COME ON, MATT, HANG IN THERE.

IT TAKES SOME SKILLED FIRING FROM THE OTHER APACHES TO ENSURE THAT THE PILOTS, THE MARINES AND THE CASUALTY ALL MAKE IT BACK ONTO THE GUNSHIPS.

FLYING ONE OF THE SUPPORT APACHES IS CHARLOTTE, A CAPTAIN IN THE ARMY AIR CORPS. SHE IS BRITAIN'S FIRST EVER FEMALE APACHE PILOT, AND ONE OF ITS FIERCEST. OVER THE COURSE OF THE RESCUE SHE UNLEASHES HER ENTIRE SUPPLY OF WEAPONS FROM THE FEARSOME GUNSHIP - 1,200 30 MM CANNON ROUNDS, 76 ROCKETS AND 16 HELLFIRE MISSILES - TO KEEP THE TALIBAN AT BAY.

IN DOING SO CHARLOTTE BECOMES THE FIRST BRITISH APACHE PILOT **EVER** TO RUN OUT OF ROUNDS, ROCKETS AND MISSILES - WHICH IS CODENAMED 'GOING WINCHESTER'. THIS FIREPOWER, WHICH COST CLOSE TO HALF A MILLION POUNDS, IS USED IN JUST SIX MINUTES.

GO! GO! GO!
FINALLY THE GUYS ARE ON BOARD.

AS THE CHOPPER JERKS UPWARDS, TALIBAN GUN-FIRE SMASHES INTO THE FUSELAGE.

...THE APACHES MAKE IT INTO THE AIR WITH THEIR PRECIOUS CARGO.

HANG ON!

I'VE GOT YOU COVERED. JUST GET THOSE GUYS OUT OF HERE!

I HOPE MATHEW'S STILL ON. JUST KEEP IT NICE AND SLOW.

NO ONE'S GONNA AMBUSH US ON THE WAY OUT. TWO MORE HELLFIRES FOR GOOD MEASURE...
BOUM!

WE DON'T HAVE ENOUGH FUEL TO GET HIM TO THE CASEVAC LOCATION. WE'LL HAVE TO DROP HIM AT THE MARINES' FIREBASE AND WAIT FOR A CHINOOK.
ROGER THAT.

USING UP THE LAST OF HER AMMO, CHARLOTTE FIRES ANOTHER ROUND INTO THE FORT...

... AND MAKES BRITISH APACHE HISTORY AS JUGROOM FORT IS LEFT COVERED IN SMOKE AND DUST. THE APACHES HAVE FIRED A TOTAL OF 1,543 ROUNDS OF CANNON FIRE, 15 ROCKETS, 47 FLECHETTES AND 18 HELLFIRES.

ABANDONING WHAT'S LEFT OF JUGROOM FORT, SHE TURNS BACK TO JOIN THE OTHER APACHES...

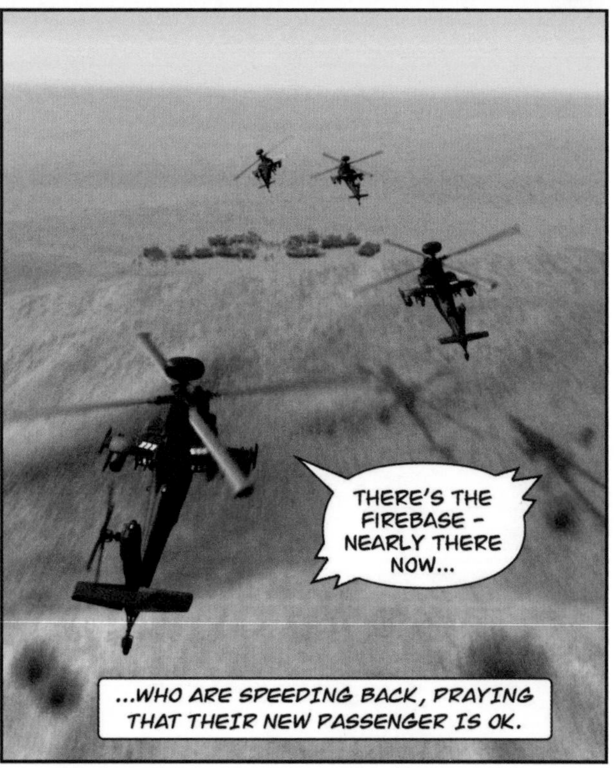
THERE'S THE FIREBASE - NEARLY THERE NOW...
...WHO ARE SPEEDING BACK, PRAYING THAT THEIR NEW PASSENGER IS OK.

IT IS A HEROIC MISSION WITH A TRAGIC OUTCOME: MATHEW FORD, FOR WHOM SO MANY RISKED SO MUCH, IS DEAD.

AND YET DESPITE THIS SAD CONCLUSION, THE DARING RESCUE AT JUGROOM FORT WILL GO DOWN IN HISTORY. THE COURAGE AND DEDICATION OF THE MARINES AND PILOTS WHO WERE PREPARED TO DRAG THEMSELVES BACK INTO THE LINE OF FIRE TO RESCUE A FALLEN COMRADE WOULD BE RECOGNISED IN MULTIPLE AWARDS. MOST IMPORTANLY, FOR FUTURE GENERATIONS OF SOLDIERS, THE DARING RESCUE STANDS AS AN INSPIRING ILLUSTRATION OF THE RULE: **NO ONE GETS LEFT BEHIND.**

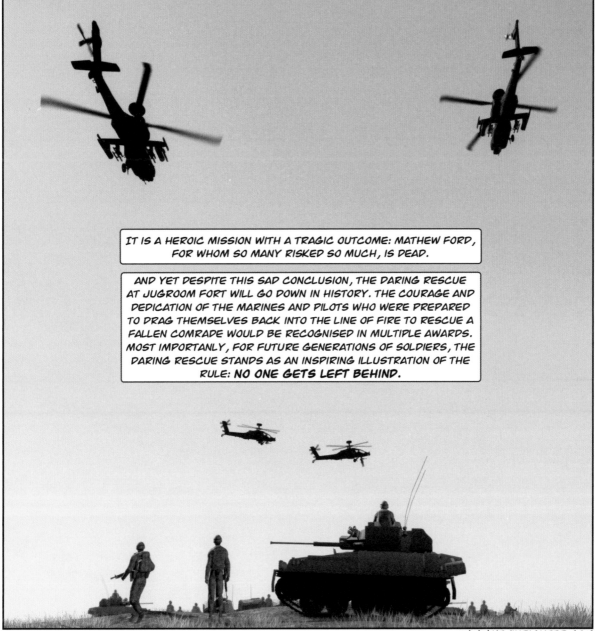

The British Armed Forces consists of the British Army, the Navy and the Royal Air Force. As head of state, the British monarch, Queen Elizabeth II, is nominally the Commander-in-chief of the Armed Forces. In practice, authority for the Forces rests with the prime minister and the Cabinet, although the Queen does retain the right to prevent any unconstitutional use.

The professional head of the Armed Forces is the Chief of the Defence Staff, a position that can be held by an Admiral, an Air Chief Marshal or a General. The three services then have their respective chiefs: the First Sea Lord, currently Admiral Sir Mark Stanhope; the Chief of the General Staff, currently General Sir David Richards; and the Chief of the Air Staff, currently Air Chief Marshal Sir Stephen Dalton.

NAVAL SERVICE

The Naval Service consists of the Royal Navy and the Royal Marines.

The Royal Navy, or 'Senior Service', is the oldest service within the British Armed Forces. It maintains a fleet of over 80 vessels, organised into two flotillas, one based at each of the two naval bases at Portsmouth and Devonport. These ships are supported by the 16 vessels of the civilian Royal Fleet Auxiliary. The Navy also includes the Submarine Service, which maintains 4 strategic missile submarines and 11 attack submarines, and the Fleet Air Arm, the Royal Navy's air force, which numbers about 6,200 people operating about 200 combat aircraft and over 50 support and training aircraft.

With the Royal Navy, personnel are organised according to ratings, unlike in the Army and the RAF, both of which both use ranks. Navy ratings for both non-commissioned and commissioned personnel are as follows, in order of increasing seniority:

Royal Navy NCOs

Leading Rate

Petty Officer

Chief Petty Officer

Warrant Officer 2

Warrant Officer 1

Royal Navy COs

Midshipman

Sub-Lieutenant

Lieutenant

Lieutenant-Commander

Commander

Captain

Commodore

Rear Admiral

Vice-Admiral

Admiral

Admiral of the Fleet

The Royal Marines are the Naval Service's amphibious infantry component. Royal Marine Commandos are specialists in amphibious, Arctic and mountain warfare and are permanently ready to deploy around the world.

STRUCTURE OF THE ARMED FORCES

ROYAL AIR FORCE

The Royal Air Force delivers flexible air power wherever it is needed. The men and women of the RAF are tasked with responding swiftly and effectively to new threats and challenges, preventing escalation in dangerous situations by projecting air power and, if necessary, countering force with superior force and skill. The RAF works increasingly in joint structures with the Royal Navy and the Army.

The RAF is organised into three groups, which are further organised into numerous squadrons. **No. 1 Group** is tasked with generating and developing winning combat air power for use on joint operations, and to support the RAF's support helicopter force. **No. 2 Group** works to generate and develop effective combat support, which consists primarily of air transport and air-to-air refuelling; intelligence surveillance, targeting and reconnaissance; and force protection. And **No. 22 Group** exists to recruit and train RAF personnel and to provide trained specialists to all three of the Armed Forces.

RAF rankings differ from those within the Army, and are structured as follows:

RAF NCOs	RAF COs
	Pilot Officer
Leading Aircraftman	Flying Officer
Senior Aircraftman	Flight Lieutenant
Senior Aicraftman (Technician)	Squadron Leader
Junior Technician	Wing Commander
Corporal	Group Captain
Sergeant	Air Commodore
Chief Technician	Air Vice-Marshal
Flight Sergeant	Air Marshal
Warrant Officer	Air Chief Marshal
	Marshal of the Royal Air Force

THE BRITISH ARMY

The command structure of the British Army is hierarchical, with divisions and brigades responsible for administering groupings of smaller units. It is organised as follows:

Commander-in-Chief, Land Forces

- Commander Field Army
  - 1st Division
  - 3rd Division
  - 6th Division
  - Theatre Troops
  - Land Warfare Centre
- Joint Helicopter Command
  - 16 Air Assault Brigade
- UK Support Command (Germany)
- Commander Regional Forces
  - 2nd Division
  - 4th Division
  - 5th Division
  - London District
  - Army Recruiting & Training Division

BRITISH ARMY DIVISIONS AND BRIGADES

The 1st Division is composed of the **4th Mechanized Brigade**, known as the 'Black Rats'; the **7th Armoured Brigade**, called the 'Desert Rats', and the **20th Armoured Brigade**, known as the 'Iron Fist'.

2nd Division provides properly manned, trained, equipped and motivated operations anywhere in the world, and supports all Army units based within the divisional area (Scotland, Northern Ireland and Northern England). It controls four Regional Brigades: **15 (North East) Brigade**, which trains and administers over 10,500 Regular and Territorial Army (TA) soldiers; **38 (Irish) Brigade**, responsible for administering the TA in Northern Ireland; **42 (North West) Brigade**, which looks after the Army's interests in north-west England and the Isle of Man; and **51 (Scottish) Brigade**, responsible for TA units based in Scotland.

3rd Division is the only division with continual operational readiness within the UK. Under the divisional command are: **1 Mechanized Brigade**, which has served in Egypt, Palestine, Cyprus and most recently Iraq; **11 Light Brigade**, established in November 2007; **12 Mechanized Brigade**, one of the Army's deployable brigades; **19 Light Brigade**, based in Northern Ireland; and **52 Infantry Brigade**, which was recently deployed to Afghanistan, where it successfully reclaimed Taliban strongholds.

4th Division fought with distinction in a number of campaigns, including the Battle of Waterloo, the Crimean War and the First and Second World Wars. The division is responsible for three regional brigades: **2 (South East) Brigade**, which commands and administers about 5,500 soldiers throughout Kent, Surrey, East and West Sussex, as well as Brunei; **145 (South) Brigade**, which is responsible for Hampshire, the Isle of Wight, Berkshire, Buckinghamshire and Oxfordshire; and **43 (Wessex) Brigade**, which covers the counties of Bristol, Cornwall, Devon, Dorset, Gloucestershire, Somerset and Wiltshire.

5th Division is responsible for the training, deployment and administration of troops in Wales, the Midlands and East Anglia, covering almost one-third of Great Britain. It is made up of three brigades: **49 (East) Brigade**, which provides personnel, equipment, barracks accommodation, logistic backup and training facilities, as well as support for training and operations overseas; **143 (West Midlands) Brigade**, which commands Army units throughout the entire West Midlands and also routinely deploys to Iraq and Afghanistan; and **160 (Wales) Brigade**, the hub of the Army in Wales, with an area that includes some of the Army's top training sites.

6th Division was established during the Peninsular War and was active in both the First and Second World Wars. In 2008, it was reformed as a modern, deployable division for service in Afghanistan. The 6th Division is based in York.

KEY ARMY UNITS

Corps: A corps is a formation of two or more divisions, consisting of at least 50,000 personnel.

Divisions: The British Army is made up of six divisions. These divisions each consist of between 10 and 30,000 soldiers, made up of three to four brigades per division and around 20,000 personnel in total. The divisions are commanded by a Major General.

Brigades: A brigade is made up of between three and five battalions and commanded by a Brigadier. Brigades are required to deploy battlegroups.

Battlegroups: A battlegroup is a mixed formation of armour, infantry, artillery, engineers and support units. Its structure is task-specific, and it is formed around a core made up of either an armoured regiment or an infantry battalion. Other units are added or removed as necessary. A battlegroup will typically consist of between 1,000 and 1,200 soldiers under the command of a Lieutenant-Colonel.

Battalions: A battalion consists of between 600 and 700 soldiers organized into five companies. A batallion is also commanded by a Lieutenant-Colonel.

Regiments: A regiment is a military unit made up of a variable number of battalions and commanded by a Colonel.

Companies: A company consists of approximately 100 soldiers divided into three platoons and commanded by a Major.

Platoons: A platoon is made up of around 30 soldiers, and each one is commanded by a Lieutenant, Second Lieutenant or Captain.

A number of elements of the British Armed Forces use alternative terms for battalion, company and platoon. These include the Royal Armoured Corps, Corps of Royal Engineers, Royal Logistics Corps and the Royal Corps of Signals, all of which use regiment (in place of battalion), squadron (in place of company) and troop (in place of platoon).

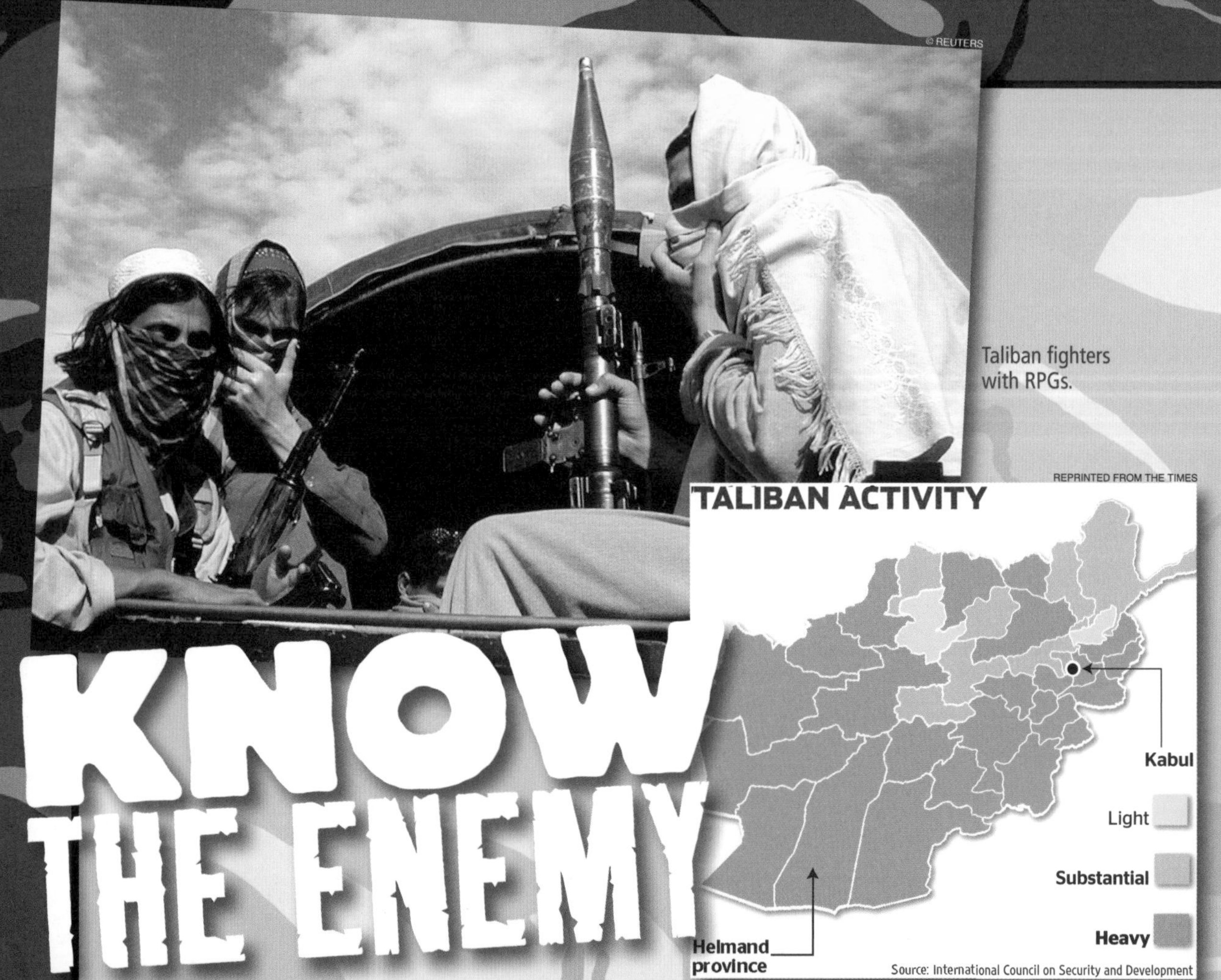

Taliban fighters with RPGs.

KNOW THE ENEMY

The Taliban have changed a great deal since the US-backed Northern Alliance drove them from power in 2001. No longer the rulers of the land, their leadership now live in exile across the border in Pakistan. The insurgent enforcers of strict Islamic codes are now fighting a bitter battle in the mountains, deserts and farmlands.

But there is one thing they have not changed since they swept in from the refugee camps and *madrassas* (religious schools) of Pakistan and Kandahār 15 years ago. They are still masters at exploiting the chaos, division and corruption that have crippled Afghanistan for decades.

For years, the Taliban have been taking advantage of an impoverished population disillusioned with the corruption of its government. According to the gloomiest estimates, the Taliban now have a permanent presence in 80 per cent of Afghanistan.

Insurgent leaders have gloated that the government controls only the cities and that the president hides in his palace, afraid to go out. General Stanley McChrystal, the overall US commander in Afghanistan, said, 'the insurgents control or contest a significant portion of the country, although it is difficult to assess precisely how much'.

Several Taliban leaders have said that the movement continues to attract more recruits. On the ground, the Taliban have perfected their guerrilla warfare, avoiding many of the stand-and-fight battles that they lost so heavily to NATO's superior firepower. Instead, the Taliban now rely heavily on roadside bombs, ambushes and the intimidation of anyone suspected of collaboration, including the use of death threats known as 'night letters'.

TALIBAN BY NUMBERS

Average monthly wage for a Taliban fighter	£250
Average monthly wage for an ANA soldier	£125
Taliban's estimated annual income from heroin	£189 million
Amount spent by Britain on the Afghan military campaign	£5.7 billion
Number of countries contributing personnel	42

The Taliban have studied Western counter-insurgency tactics that emphasize defending the population and winning over their hearts and minds. In the summer of 2009, the Taliban produced a 13-page code of conduct, ordering fighters to avoid civilian casualties. They also ordered their fighters to stop their summary executions, which had lost them popularity in the past.

The Taliban are now also copying the successful 'bombs and charity' approach pioneered by the Middle East hardline groups Hezbollah and Hamas. The Taliban's shadow government – calling itself the 'Islamic Emirate of Afghanistan' – provides a parallel system of courts, clinics and policing to the government's own. They even have an ombudsman's office near Kandahār, where people can complain about any excesses by Taliban commanders.

An insurgent holds his AK-47.

The exact command structure of the new Taliban remains shrouded in mystery. Many believe that overall strategic planning comes from the Quetta Shura, the council of exiled Taliban leaders in Pakistan. But day-to-day attacks are in the hands of local commanders. A former Taliban fighter explained that the Quetta Shura was influenced strategically by al-Qaeda.

Today's Taliban are organised, savvy and ruthless.

General Stanley McChrystal said that while the Taliban made money from heroin trafficking, they were also 'clearly supported by Pakistan'. Al-Qaeda and other extremist movements 'based in Pakistan channel foreign fighters, suicide bombers and technical assistance into Afghanistan, and offer ideological motivation, training, and financial support'.

By James Hilder

IEDs

By Ed Macy

You might have heard the term 'IED' on the news – but what does this mean exactly? An improvised explosive device – or IED – is a home-made bomb, or booby trap. IEDs are highly dangerous and account for numerous deaths and horrific injuries in both Afghanistan and Iraq. The Taliban have grown increasingly skilled at producing IEDs, and their prevalence in Afghanistan has significantly changed the face of modern warfare. At the outset of the war in Afghanistan, British soldiers respected the Taliban fighters' courage, if not their convictions. However, with the increased use of IEDs, this respect has all but disappeared.

A platoon from 2nd Battalion, Royal Anglian Regiment, prepares an IED detection team.

IEDs come in many forms, but all have the potential to cause severe harm. The simplest devices are nothing more than straightforward booby traps. An example of this type of IED is a single piece of wire fed through a grenade pin and attached to a door. When the door opens, the wire stretches tight and pulls the pin from the grenade. This causes the grenade to explode, seriously injuring or killing the person behind the door.

Simple IEDs like this do not need specialist equipment or skill to create. The enemy simply needs to know where troops are going to be, so that the IEDs can be set in the right place. Other IEDs are far more complicated and require a greater level of expertise. In some cases teams of people are involved. For instance, a bomb might begin with a chemist mixing together chemicals into an explosive compound, which is then stored in a special container. An engineer might then build a metal bomb case designed to fracture when the explosives detonate, shooting out red-hot, razor-sharp shards of shrapnel that travel at hundreds of metres per second, causing terrible injuries. Some IEDs are detonated using radio or mobile telephone signals. In these cases, an electronics engineer or technician might be required to build the necessary hardware. Finally, there will be an agent whose job is to get past security in order to place the primed bomb in a concealed location on a military base or other valuable target. Once the bomb is in place, the terrorists can detonate it remotely, from almost anywhere in the world, killing and maiming dozens of service personnel and, often, innocent bystanders.

A soldier inspects a suspected IED by hand, as other troops stay well clear.

There are two main ways in which IEDs are used in combat: one is to take the IED direct to the soldiers; the other is to wait for the soldiers to come to the IED. In Afghanistan and Iraq insurgents employ both techniques to devastating effect.

One way of delivering an IED to soldiers is to use a suicide bomber – someone who is willing to blow himself or herself up in order to maim and kill others. Usually a suicide bomber will wear a concealed vest that holds together plastic explosives (PE). Often, nails, nuts, bolts and pieces of metal will be packed over the PE to act as shrapnel once the bomb detonates, thereby causing maximum damage. A button connected to an AA battery will be wired to a detonator in the PE. The bomber then walks into a crowd, presses the button to detonate the bomb and sets off an explosion, with lethal effect for both themselves and those around them.

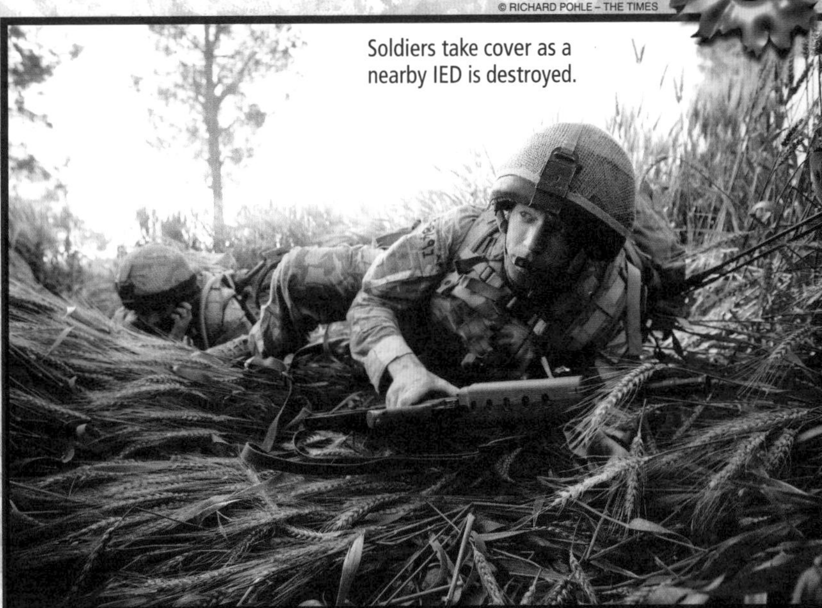

Soldiers take cover as a nearby IED is destroyed.

Insurgents are also known to rig up IEDs to explode when soldiers pass through certain areas. For example, the roads surrounding a terrorist hideout might be packed with IEDs to prevent the attacking force from reaching its target. In some cases insurgents will dig a deep hole in the middle of a dirt track and stack it with three to five anti-tank land-mines, one on top of the other. They then add some PE and a detonator. The wire from the detonator is laid out in a long line away from the IED, running just below the surface of the ground. The hole is filled in and the track is brushed over so that oncoming troops can't see where the explosives have been buried. The insurgents then sit and wait. As soon as a target vehicle drives over the IED, they push the detonator button and blow up the mines under the vehicle, seriously wounding and often killing the troops inside.

All of our troops in Iraq and Afghanistan are trained to look out for IEDs, but they can be impossible to spot before it is too late. They exact a terrible toll on the soldiers who are too often killed or terribly injured in IED attacks.

Ed Macy is the author of *Apache* and *Hellfire*. Find out more at www.edmacy.com.

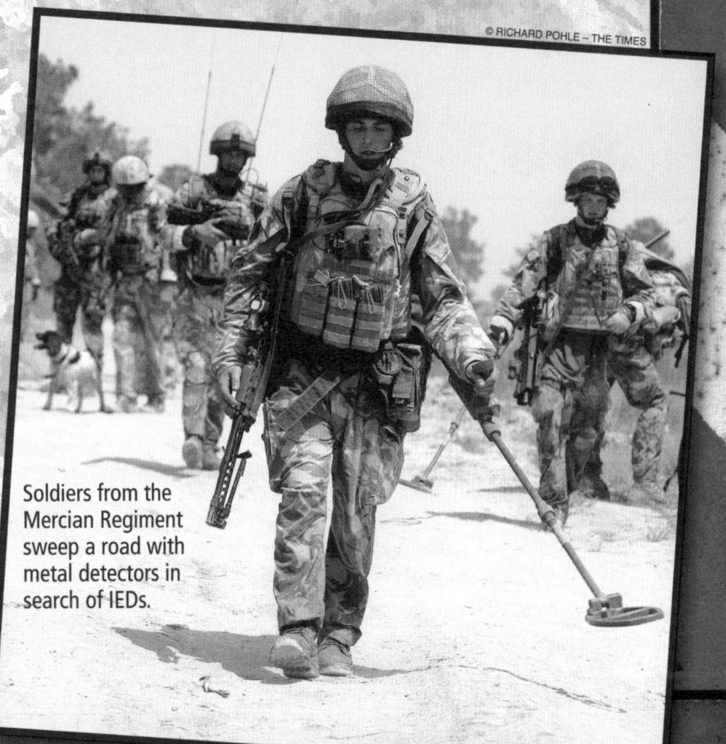

Soldiers from the Mercian Regiment sweep a road with metal detectors in search of IEDs.

MINE AWARENESS

Landmines have been used in warfare for centuries. They are different to improvised explosive devices (IEDs) because they are specifically made to be triggered by a target, whether that is a person (anti-personnel mines) or a vehicle (anti-tank mines). Landmines remain dangerous long after they are set, even beyond a particular conflict, which makes them one of the most controversial weapons on the battlefield. They can kill and injure civilians and leave large areas of land unusable for many years. Even today in the UK landmines are occasionally still detected or set off. Most of these are left over from the First and Second World Wars.

Afghanistan is still the worst-affected country in the world by landmine explosions. About 150,000 Afghans have disabilities resulting from mine blasts and on average 45 to 50 people are killed or maimed each month, according to the United Nations, this despite ambitious efforts to clear them.

It is compulsory for everyone in the British Armed Forces to carry this card about mine awareness and what to do if encountering a mine.

MINE AWARENESS

MINES - WHERE?

- Confrontation lines
- Routes, gravel roads
- Military establishments
- Road blocks /checkpoints
- Strategic areas
- Abandoned equipment
- Abandoned buildings
- Defensive positions
- Field fortifications
- Constricted localities

INDICATORS

- Mine signs
- Blast signatures
- Mine casualties
- Mines debris
- Mine packaging
- Untended fields
- Disturbed ground
- Trip wires and cables
- Mined areas may not be marked

PRECAUTIONS

- Attend mine awareness training
- Obtain mine information
- Use local knowledge
- Stick to approved routes
- Stay on known safe areas
- Stay on tarmac/concrete
- Avoid verges
- Plan routes
- Think mines

ASSISTANCE

- Mine data
- Advise
- Training

} UK MITC

DON'T TOUCH MINES/UXO

034/09(d)

PAMPHLETS COURTESY OF THE MUSEUM OF ARMY FLYING

MINE ENCOUNTER - IMMEDIATE ACTION

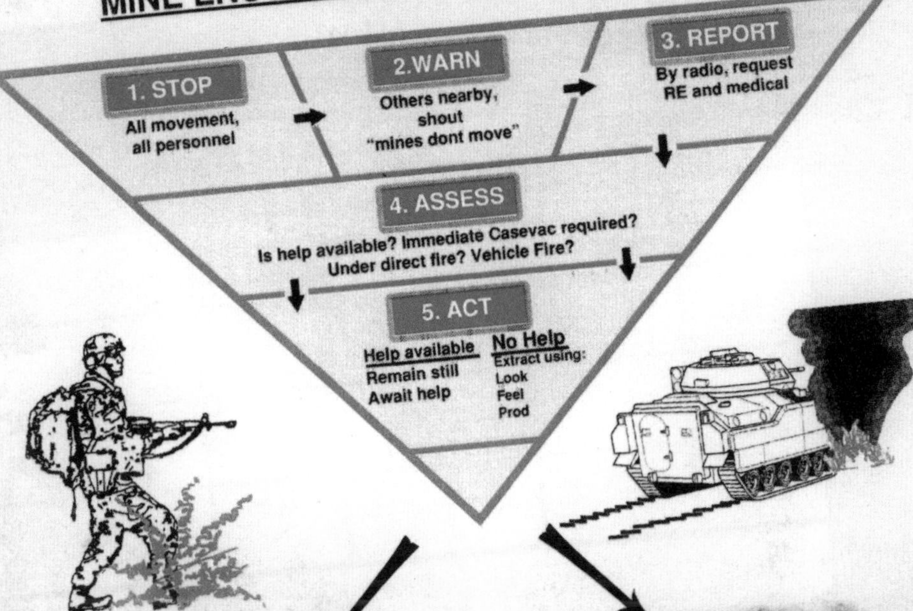

1. STOP
All movement, all personnel
2.WARN
Others nearby, shout "mines dont move"
3. REPORT
By radio, request RE and medical
4. ASSESS
Is help available? Immediate Casevac required? Under direct fire? Vehicle Fire?
5. ACT
Help available
Remain still
Await help
No Help
Extract using:
Look
Feel
Prod

ON FOOT

Stand
- Look, Feel, Prod (LFP)
- Lie prone

Extract
- LFP
- Mark, Avoid, Move (MAM) to closest safe area

IN A VEHICLE

Exit
- rear, not side
- emergency move along tracks?

Extract
- LFP before dismounting
- LFP } to safe area
- MAM }

SAFE AREA

When clear; report to HQ, mark clearly, record on map

CASUALTY EXTRACTION

- Reassure casualty
- LFP to clear upto and around
- Administer first aid
- As appropriate:
  - Extract
  - Wait for help

30°

LOOK, FEEL, PROD

- LOOK for, then
- FEEL for, then
- PROD for mines at 25mm intervals to a depth of 75mm.

PROD

- Firmly, carefully
- Contact side not top
- Thoroughly
- Steadily and patiently

MARK, AVOID, MOVE

- MARK
- AVOID
- MOVE to the closest safe area using LFP

PRODDER

- Issue prodder
- Bayonet
- Trip wire picket
- Any thing suitable

A HERO'S SACRIFICE

ONE OF THE MANY COURAGEOUS ACTS PERFORMED DURING THE CONFLICT OCCURRED NOT IN THE HEAT OF BATTLE, BUT IN THE QUIET OF THE AFGHAN NIGHT, AS A SMALL BAND OF MARINES – FRIENDS, AS WELL AS BROTHERS IN ARMS – PATROLLED THE SEEMINGLY EMPTY LANDSCAPE...

24-YEAR-OLD LANCE CORPORAL MATTHEW CROUCHER, A RESERVIST FROM 40 COMMANDO GROUP'S RECONNAISSANCE FORCE, AND THREE OTHER MEN CREEP SILENTLY THROUGH THE DARKNESS. **THEIR TASK**: TO IDENTIFY IED MAKERS THOUGHT TO BE BASED IN A NEARBY COMPOUND.

OK, LADS, THE COMPOUND'S JUST AHEAD. LET'S KEEP IT NICE AND QUIET AS WE COME IN.
INTEL HAS THE COMPOUND RIGHT ROUND THIS CORNER. ANY SIGN OF IT, MATT?

NOT YET... THOUGH I RECKON WE'RE JUST ABOUT ON TOP OF IT. STAND BY TO GO FIRM WHEN WE SPOT IT.
DON'T WORRY, YOU GOT IT. I'M NOT ANXIOUS TO WAKE THEM UP TILL WE HAVE TO.

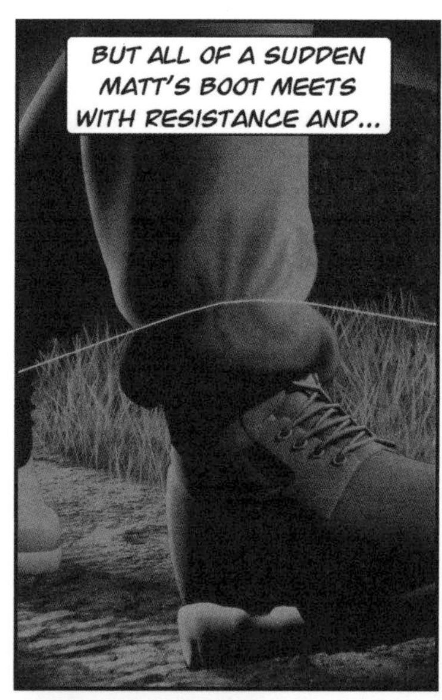
BUT ALL OF A SUDDEN MATT'S BOOT MEETS WITH RESISTANCE AND...

PING!

OH @?$%&*....

GRENADE!
TAKE COVER! TAKE COVER!
QUICK! GET BEHIND THAT WALL!

AS THE MEN RACE FOR COVER, BEFORE THEY REALISE WHAT'S HAPPENING, MATT HAS THROWN HIMSELF ON TOP OF THE GRENADE!
HNK--!

MATT! WHAT THE HELL ARE YOU DOING?! GET OUT OF THERE!
I'M NOT LETTING THEM TAKE ALL OF US OUT! AT LEAST THIS WAY IT'S JUST ME!

IN A FLASH OF BRILLIANT LIGHT, THE GRENADE EXPLODES!
AAAARGH!
BOOM!
QUICK, HELP HIM! IS HE STILL IN ONE PIECE? 
JESUS, MATE, ARE YOU OK?!
MATT? MATT?! CAN YOU HEAR ME?!
UNG-!

I...I...I THINK I'M OK...
LESLEY, CHECK HIM! TOP TO TOE!
THIS CAN'T BE REAL, HE LOOKS OK! THERE'S SHRAPNEL STUCK IN HIS KIT BUT HE LOOKS FINE!
BLOODY HELL, MATE, THAT WAS INSANE...

WHA... WHERE AM I? WHAT...WHAT HAPPENED? WHAT'S THAT RINGING NOISE?
A BLOODY MIRACLE IS WHAT JUST HAPPENED, MATE! YOU ONLY JUST SMOTHERED A GRENADE! LOOK, YOU CAN SEE WHERE IT BLEW UP YOUR BERGEN. AND YOUR BODY ARMOUR DOESN'T LOOK TOO GOOD, EITHER. IT MUST HAVE TAKEN THE BRUNT OF THE EXPLOSION. I'VE NEVER SEEN ANYTHING LIKE IT...

ARE YOU OK TO WALK, MATE? THE ENEMY WILL BE OUT TO CHECK OUT THE EXPLOSION AND I'D RATHER NOT BE HERE WHEN THEY ARRIVE.

YEAH, YEAH, I THINK SO...

MY GOD, MATT, THAT WAS MENTAL! YOUR BERGEN'S STILL SMOKING!

BETTER IT THAN ME, EH LADS! I'VE GOT TO TELL YOU, IT'S GOOD TO HEAR YOUR VOICES.

IT HAS BEEN AN INCREDIBLE DEMONSTRATION OF COURAGE AND SELFLESSNESS – ONE THAT WILL EARN MATT THE GEORGE CROSS, THE HIGHEST MEDAL FOR GALLANTRY NOT IN COMBAT.

AND WHEN THE NOISE OF THE GRENADE THAT SHOULD HAVE KILLED HIM LURES THE TALIBAN OUT TO INVESTIGATE LATER THAT NIGHT, THE COMMANDOS ARE READY... AND TAKE THEM IN AMBUSH.

MATT'S STORY IS JUST ONE AMONG MANY, AS THE MEN AND WOMEN OF THE BRITISH FORCES PIT THEMSELVES DAILY AGAINST DANGER. BUT IT IS ONE THAT WILL GO DOWN IN HISTORY AND THAT HAS FOREVER EARNED HIM THE GRATITUDE OF THE MEN WHOSE LIVES HE SAVED.

SMALL ARMS

SA80 A2 (UK)

The SA80 A2 is the standard-issue service rifle for the British Armed Forces.

Built by the German defence manufacturers Heckler & Koch, the SA80 A2 is one of the most reliable weapons of its type. This top-notch reliability is combined with accuracy, versatility and ergonomic design. It is considered a first-class weapon and the world leader in small arms.

The rifle is part of the SA80 (Small Arms for the 1980s) British family of assault weapons which, when introduced, proved so accurate that the Army marksmanship tests had to be redesigned. Capable of firing both single shot and fully automatic, it has an effective range of over 400 metres when equipped with an optical sight.

The SA80 A2 is a result of a modification to the original SA80, which was prone to jamming in extreme climates, where its plastic components would freeze, melt or break. In operations in Sierra Leone in 2000, members of the Pathfinder Platoon discovered that the safety catches on their SA80s failed in the heat, making their weapons useless.

The SA80 family of weaponry has a forward-mounted pistol grip according to a 'bullpup' layout, in which the action and magazine are located behind the trigger and next to the firer's face. The weapons are fed from a STANAG magazine, a type of detachable firearm magazine, usually with a capacity of 30 rounds. The magazine release button is located above the magazine housing, on the left side of the receiver. The weapon's receiver is made from stamped sheet steel and reinforced with welded and riveted machine-made steel inserts.

The Royal Marines, RAF Regiment, infantry soldiers and other soldiers with a dismounted close combat role use rifles equipped with a SUSAT (Sight Unit Small Arms, Trilux) optical sight with a fixed 4x magnification and an illuminated aiming pointer. A passive night-vision scope can also be used in place of the SUSAT. On some weapons the SUSAT has now been replaced with the Trijicon ACOG (Advanced Combat Optical Gunsight), a series of telescopic reflex sights that provide magnification levels between 1.5– 6x.

The SA80 A2 can also be fitted with a UGL (Underslung Grenade Launcher) system, which consists of a Heckler & Koch AG-36 40 mm grenade launcher and ladder sight. These additional systems are issued to infantry units on a scale of one per fire team.

Calibre: 5.56 mm
Weight: 4.98 kg (when fitted with SUSAT and full magazine)
Length: 785 mm
Barrel length: 518 mm
Muzzle velocity: 940 m/s
Feed: 30-round magazine
Effective range: 400 m
Cyclic rate of fire: over 700 rounds per minute

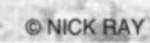

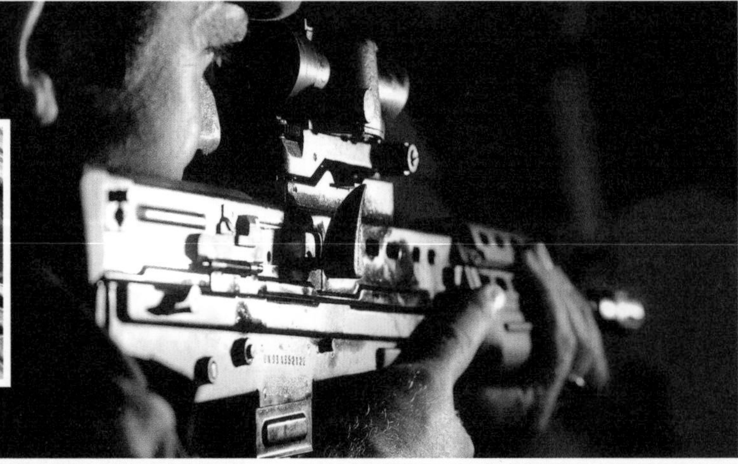

AK-47 KALASHNIKOV/VARIANTS (RUSSIA)

The variants of the Kalashnikov family of weapons are now so numerous that it is not possible to list them all. This illustration shows a Romanian version of the AKM. It should be noted that the distinctive forward pistol grip can be fitted to any standard AK/AKM, so any single component cannot be used as a country identifier without the use of additional data. The most significant difference of the AK-47 series is the solid steel receiver, versus the pressed or stamped metal receiver of the AKM series.

KALASHNIKOV 1974 (AK-74)

The AK-74 is a low-calibre version of the AKM, and it uses the same receiver, hardware and system of operation. The 5.45 mm round is almost the same length as the 7.62 x 39 mm round but of smaller diameter; 7.62 mm x 5.45 mm magazines are not interchangeable. A recognizable feature of this rifle is the laminated plastic and the steel magazine, the design of which has subtly changed since its creation, as stiffening fillets have been added. Another feature is the muzzle brake and compensator, designed to reduce recoil and compensate for the upward jerk always present in automatic weapons. It is highly efficient, reducing the noticeable recoil to a low level and keeping the weapon steady during automatic fire. The AKS-74 version has a folding steel butt that swings to lie along the left side of the receiver. Late-production AK-74s have black, high-impact plastic hardware; this variant is known as the AK-74M.

Cartridge: 5.45 x 39.5 mm
Dimensions: Length: 928 mm; AKS stock-folded: 690 mm
Weight: 3.9 kg
Barrel: 400 mm
Rifling: 4 grooves, rh
Feed system: 30-round detachable plastic box
Rate of fire: 650 rounds/min
Muzzle velocity: 900 m/sec
In production: 1975–
Markings: Model number, factory identifier and serial number on top of receiver
Safety: Standard Kalashnikov combined safety and selector lever on left side of receiver: press all the way up for safety position (obstructs movement of cocking handle and bolt), down one notch for automatic fire, move all the way down for single shots
Unloading: Magazine catch at rear of magazine housing, remove magazine, pull back cocking handle to extract any round in chamber, inspect chamber through ejection port to ensure it is empty, release cocking handle, pull trigger

AK-47

It is estimated that well over 50 million AK-47-pattern rifles have been manufactured worldwide. The original AK-47 was first issued in 1947, and it has since been manufactured or copied in Albania, Bulgaria, China, Egypt, Finland, the former East Germany, Hungary, Iraq, Kazakhstan, North Korea, Poland, Romania and the former Yugoslavia. The original AK-47 had a solid-metal receiver, while the more common AKM uses steel stampings and can be recognized by the small dimple in the receiver, above the magazine well; the AK-47 has a longer dent. The AKM has a folding metal butt stock. Only the markings will indicate the weapon's country of origin, and on some examples only a serial number is provided. Romanian AKMs typically have a forward pistol grip, while other countries have also made small local modifications and dimensional changes. Finishes can vary from poor to excellent, but, in whatever form, the AK-47/AKM is tough and reliable.

Cartridge: 7.62 x 39 mm Soviet M1943
Dimensions: Length, fixed butt: 870 mm
Weight: 4 kg
Barrel: 415 mm
Rifling: 4 grooves, rh
Feed system: 30-round magazine
Rate of fire: 600 rounds/min.
In production: (AK-47) 1947– ; (AKM) 1959–
Markings: Model number, factory identifier and serial number on top of rear end of receiver
Safety: Combined safety catch and fire-selector lever on right rear side of receiver: press all the way up for safety position (obstructs movement of cocking handle and bolt), move down one notch to first mark or letters 'AB' for full-automatic fire and move to bottom position, or letter 'O', for single shots
Unloading: Magazine catch at rear of magazine housing: remove magazine, pull back cocking handle to extract any round which may be in chamber, inspect chamber through ejection port, release cocking handle, pull trigger

© EROS HOAGLAND – THE TIMES

M72 LAW (aka LAW 66)

The M72 LAW (light anti-tank weapon) is a portable, one-shot, 6-mm anti-tank weapon. It was designed in the United States, replacing the bazooka as the US Army's main anti-tank weapon. The M72 LAW consists of a launcher made up of two tubes, one inside the other. Packed inside the launcher is a rocket. The outer tube of the rocket contains the trigger. When fired, the propellant inside the rocket motor combusts.

ROCKET-PROPELLED GRENADE (RPG)

An RPG is an anti-tank weapon. It is launched from the shoulder and consists of two main parts: the launcher and the rocket. The launcher is a tube that rests on the operator's shoulder. A projectile with a small rocket engine is fixed to the front of the tube; a trigger activates the engine to fire the rocket. RPGs have proven themselves to be highly effective against tanks and lightly-armoured vehicles. They are inexpensive and are used by armies across the world, as well as by insurgents and terrorist groups.

Taliban insurgents toting their deadly RPGs.

© WPN

FN MINIMI (BELGIUM)

The Minimi was designed to extract the best performance from the 5.56 mm cartridge and has earned a reputation for reliability. It is gas-operated, using a simple rotating bolt system, but it is unusual in that it is able to fire from an M16-type magazine or a belt without any modifications. A special cover plate closes the belt opening when a magazine is loaded, or closes the magazine opening when a belt is in place, so there is no risk of trying to 'doublefeed'. There is also a lightweight, short-barrelled paratrooper version with a collapsible butt.

Cartridge: 5.56 x 45 mm NATO
Dimensions: Length o/a: 1,040 mm
Weight: 6.9 kg
Barrel: 466 mm
Rifling: 6 grooves, rh
Feed system: 30-round magazine, or 200-round belt
Rate of fire: 700–1,000 rounds/min
In production: 1982–
Markings: 'FN MINIMI 5.56' on left side of receiver
Safety: Push-through safety catch on left side of receiver: push from right to left to fire, from left to right for safety position
Unloading: Press in two spring catches at top rear of receiver and lift cover: remove belt or magazine, pull back cocking handle, examine chamber and feedway, release cocking handle, press trigger

A camouflaged sniper takes aim

SNIPER RIFLE

Unveiled earlier this year the L115A3 sniper rifle is a larger calibre weapon which provides state-of-the-art telescopic day and night all-weather sights. The first batch was deployed to Afghanistan with members of 16 Air Assault Brigade in May 2008. Designed to be accurate to 600 metres, with a maximum range of 1,100 metres, the L115A3 long-range rifle fires an 8.59 mm bullet.

LIVING IN A BATTLEFIELD

By Christina Lamb

When Abdul Hadi heard the British were coming to Helmand province, he was surprised. 'Every Afghan grows up with the stories of how the British came here three times and were always set back, and we have a saying, "A clever man does not get bitten by a snake from the same hole twice."'

Locals like this elderly man often don't know what to make of the soldiers in their midst.

The elders in his home town of Nowzad met to discuss the development. Some thought they should take up arms against these latest 'invaders'. Others thought the foreign forces would end the long decades of war. One said he hoped the British would help them to take back the border areas of Pakistan that they considered to be part of Afghanistan.

Abdul Hadi thought he would wait and see. As a man in his thirties (like many Afghans, he doesn't know his exact age), he had only ever known war and then the Taliban. His eldest daughter Farida was eight when the Taliban came and closed the schools to girls. After the Taliban fell, the school reopened, but there had recently been threats against those who sent their daughters to school and some schools in other districts had been burnt down. Abdul didn't like the way that some Taliban had started reappearing on

Clash of cultures: an Afghan boy rides his donkey past Paras on patrol in Kajakī.

motorbikes, wearing their big black turbans.

As a child, his family used to grow pomegranate trees, and he fondly remembers the trees' red flowers, splitting the fruits to see the pips shining like rubies and sucking the delicious seeds. However, there was no local market for the fruit and no cold storage, so the pomegranates would rot. Soon he, like almost everyone else in the district, switched to growing poppy for the drug opium.

Even so, with six children to feed, Abdul was very poor and when the big helicopters came, bringing in British troops, he hoped the foreigners might bring water and electricity. But heavy fighting broke out in Nowzad between the Taliban and British troops, who had moved into the district centre. As fighting intensified, the British called in air strikes, and in early 2007 Abdul fled, along with most of Nowzad's ten thousand residents.

Today Abdul lives in a tent not far from the state capital of Lashkar Gāh. His family have had to move four times in less than two years. 'First we moved to Garmsir,' he said. 'Then last summer the conflict broke out in Garmsir and we sought shelter in Marja. The war followed us into Marja and we moved to Bodam desert, and from there we came to Lashkar Gāh.'

The pomegranate trees he played in when he was a boy seem like a dream. 'We don't want the Taliban to come back, but we don't like this fighting with the British,' he said. 'We have lost everything. We don't have food, medicine, shelter, water, clothes or even matches to light a candle, and none of my children go to school.'

'OPIUM BRIDE' © ALIXANDRA FAZZINA

THE OPIUM BRIDE By Christina Lamb

Twenty-year-old Nadia loves music and dreams of becoming a singer. She wears jeans and a red-checked shirt, just like any English girl her age. But she jumps whenever there is a sound at the door and her home is a secret women's shelter in Herāt, Afghanistan's second-largest city.

Nadia was only thirteen when she was sold by her brothers into marriage with a fifty-year-old man. 'I had been promised to him when I was a child,' she explained. 'He had married someone else and had a family in Iran, then, when I reached puberty, he came back to my village near Shindand to get me. I didn't want to, so I ran away. But my brothers are opium addicts so they wanted to sell me to have money and they handed me over.'

Nadia was sold for 3,500 Afghanis (£40). After the marriage, Nadia was made to work as the man's slave, doing everything that he ordered. If the house wasn't clean enough or the food not cooked well, he would beat her. One day when her husband was out tending his goats, she cut her hair like a boy's, dressed in boys' clothes and secretly made her way to Kabul on a bus, travelling for two days and nights.

She had planned to try to get work as a singer, but she was prevented. 'When I got to Kabul, the hostel owner realized I was a girl and took me to the police,' she said. 'They put me in a shelter for six months, then a women's organization transferred me here to Herāt to be nearer my home.'

Nadia is now trying to get a divorce, even though life for divorced women is very difficult in Afghanistan. 'In our culture it's very easy for a man to get a divorce and almost impossible for a woman,' she said. She first appealed to the elders of her village, who held a *jirga*, a traditional tribal meeting, to discuss the case, but they ruled that she should return to her husband. 'Now I have gone to the courts, but the place where all the documents are kept burnt down,' she shrugged. 'But I won't give up. I don't want to spend the rest of my life just singing to goats.'

Christina Lamb is a bestselling author and award-winning foreign correspondent. Find out more at www.christinalamb.net

PIXEL HEROES

When it came to depicting battle scenes, early video games leaned towards science-fiction combat. There's a very good reason for this. There are countless people who will tell you that the Challenger 2 battle tank, represented in your game by a few chunky pixels, doesn't look right or move right. However, there isn't anyone alive who is more qualified to talk about your futuristic hovering cyber-tank than you are.

Video games have evolved an extraordinary amount in a very short time. The blocky graphics used in the 1992 alternative history game set during the Second World War, *Wolfenstein 3D*, have become almost photorealistic in the game's 2009 recreation. That is, if you can call murderous Nazi zombies realistic.

One of the major turning points in the world of first-person shooters was the publication of user-editing tools, which enabled gamers to roll their own maps, weapons and sometimes entire games, based on commercial releases. In 1999 two students created their own spin-off from the massively popular sci-fi shooter *Half Life*. This was a contemporary warfare scenario called *Counter-Strike*.

Counter-Strike changed everything. One of the most popular first-person shooters ever, it marked the beginning of a move away from plasma pistols and wave-motion cannons towards the kinds of weapon that we see in war movies and read about in Tom Clancy thrillers.

Call of Duty 5

And Tom Clancy was quick to spot the potential for his brand of technically detailed action in the new world of video games. *Rainbow 6*, a tactical shooter based on characters in his novels, was released shortly before the all-conquering *Counter-Strike*. Featuring a more realistic style of play than standard 'run and gun' games, the *Rainbow 6* series dovetails with Clancy's *Ghost Recon* and *Splinter Cell* to evoke a whole spectrum of modern combat.

But modern combat is not the whole story. That same year, 1999, also saw the release of the first *Medal of Honor* game, putting the player in the

boots of US Army Lieutenant Jimmy Paterson as he creates havoc behind Nazi lines.

Call of Duty 4

Medal of Honor was followed by the even more ambitious *Call of Duty* series. This gave an even greater insight into the achievements of the 'Greatest Generation' by covering two of the major war zones of the Second World War.

For the first time, gamers could not only parachute into Normandy with US forces on D-day, they could also engage in a sniper duel on the harsh, unforgiving Russian Front and sabotage a dam as part of an SAS strike force. The SAS team provided the first glimpse of Captain Price, a bluff, fearless leader who has brought his distinctive mutton-chop whiskers to almost every version of the *Call of Duty* series so far – including the wildly popular *Call of Duty: Modern Warfare* – despite the sixty-year gap between the time periods of the games.

Call of Duty: Modern Warfare 2

The *Call of Duty* series is renowned for its authenticity, but if you *really* want to get a sense of realistic military tactics, you need to go to the professionals. *America's Army* was developed by the US military as a tool to reach out to potential recruits and, not incidentally, to provide an absorbing gaming experience for those of us who aren't eligible to join the US Army but are still excited about a team-based tactical shooter with realistic weaponry.

The military professionals use gaming technology to train, too: *VBS 1*, an incredibly detailed immersive 3D environment, lets infantrymen rehearse situations such as convoy ambushes and house-to-house fighting, in the same way that pilots have been using flight simulators for years.

Call of Duty 4

Already, fighter pilots are outnumbered by unmanned aerial vehicle (UAV) pilots controlling drone aircraft over Afghanistan and Iraq. Perhaps a decade from now, ground wars will be fought by robots, controlled by operators stationed a safe distance from the war zone using telepresence to identify potential targets.

Do you want to be ready for that brave new world? Better get gaming.

'SOMETHING OUR PARENTS WILL UNDERSTAND'

IN THE SUMMER OF 2009, THE MEN AND WOMEN OF 16 AIR ASSAULT BRIGADE WERE SET THEIR TOUGHEST CHALLENGE YET. **THE MISSION**: TRANSPORTING A HUGE HYDRO-ELECTRIC TURBINE 160 KM TO KAJAKĪ DAM, A NOTORIOUS HOTSPOT AND FAVOURITE TALIBAN TARGET. **THE ODDS**: NOT GOOD. BURDENED WITH DELICATE PARTS WEIGHING UP TO 29 TONNES, THE 200-VEHICLE CONVOY TRANSPORTING THE TURBINE WILL HAVE A TOP SPEED OF JUST OVER 3 KM/H. MEANING THE JOURNEY ALONG DIRT TRACKS WILL TAKE A GRUELLING FIVE DAYS. IF THEY GET THERE AT ALL...

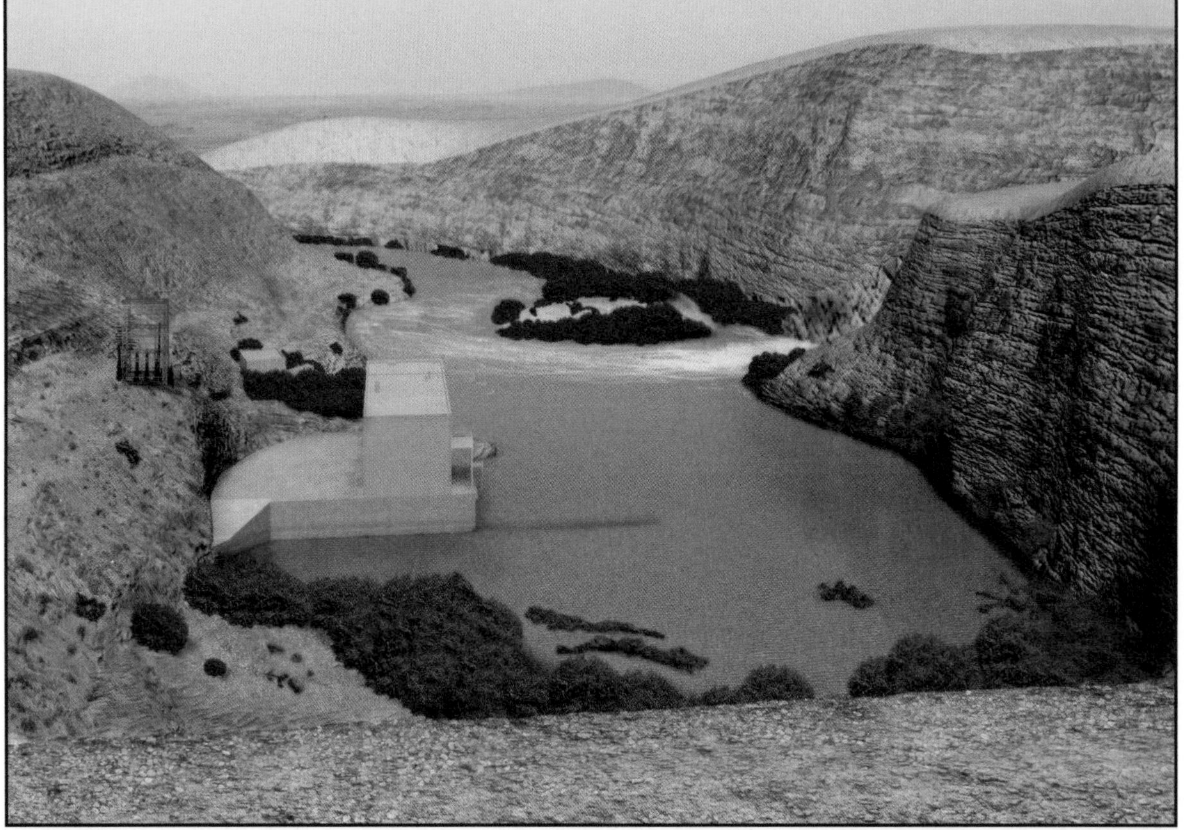

AND HELMAND'S ROUGH ROADS AREN'T THE ONLY DANGER. THE TURBINE IS TOO HEAVY TO TRANSPORT BY AIR, AND THE ONLY LAND ROUTE TO KAJAKĪ, ROUTE 611, LIES THROUGH TALIBAN-INFESTED COUNTRYSIDE. THE SLOW-MOVING CONVOY WILL MAKE AN EASY TARGET FOR IEDS AND AMBUSHES. THE GUYS ON THE GROUND WILL NEED TO USE SUBTERFUGE, AS WELL AS FIREPOWER, TO MAKE IT THROUGH...

BEFORE THE MISSION BEGINS, THE PARAS STRIKE OUT TO FORCE THE INSURGENTS ONTO THE DEFENSIVE.
GRENADES IN! OK LADS, MOVE IN!

RIGHT BEHIND YOU, BOSS!

TALIBAN COMPOUNDS PEPPER THE AREA AROUND KAJAKI, EACH ONE A POTENTIAL DEATH TRAP. THEY NEED TO BE CLEARED BEFORE THE CONVOY CAN SET OUT. A PLATOON OF PARAS BEGINS THE DANGEROUS TASK...
BOOM!
GO, GO, GO!

WE'RE IN! FOLLOW ME!
TONROE AND PETERS, TAKE THE PERIMETER! WE NEED EYES ON THE ENEMY!

WE HAVE EYES ON, DAWESY! ENEMY SIGHTED IN BUSH. RANGE 200. RAPID FIRE!

$%&*@! CONTACT! THEY'RE NOT LETTING UP! WE NEED FIRE SUPPORT – CALL IN THE MORTARS!
I'M ON IT, SIR. DAVEY, I NEED COMMS!
ON IT!

AT THE FIRE SUPPORT GROUP OUTSIDE THE COMPOUND, A MORTAR TEAM SETS UP AND...
FIRE!

IT'S A DIRECT HIT! GOOD WORK, LADS.
WHUMPH!

MEANWHILE, ON THE OPPOSITE END OF THE COMPOUND, ROYAL ENGINEERS SET A BAR-MINE AGAINST ONE OF THE THICK WALLS, PREPARING TO BLAST AN ENTRY HOLE.
EASY DOES IT, MATE – DON'T DROP IT.
YOU'RE ALL RIGHT, I'VE GOT IT. IT'S THE BLOODY HEAT – MAKES MY HANDS SWEAT.

BAROOUM!
OK, THE WALL'S DOWN – GET INTO THE COMPOUND! MOVE!

BACK AT KANDAHĀR AIRFIELD, THE CONVOY STEELS ITSELF FOR OP 'OQAB TSUKA'*. AS NIGHT SETTLES OVER THE BASE, THE MASSED FORCES ASSEMBLE FOR THEIR HERCULEAN EFFORT. TWO HUNDRED VEHICLES, INCLUDING HETS**, ARMOURED WMIKS, VIKINGS AND MASCOTS, LINE UP IN THE DARKNESS, WHILE HUNDREDS OF TROOPS AWAIT THE ORDER TO DEPLOY. THE MEN ARE USED TO LONG HOURS WITHOUT SLEEP IN THE CRIPPLING HEAT OF THE DESERT, BUT THIS PROMISES TO BE THE MOST PHYSICALLY DEMANDING OP OF ALL. ONCE IT STARTS, THE CONVOY WON'T STOP UNTIL IT REACHES ITS DESTINATION FIVE DAYS LATER – UNLESS FORCED TO HALT BY ENEMY ACTION.

SIR, WE'RE READY.
ALL RIGHT, CAPTAIN. TELL THE MEN TO STAND BY FOR DEPLOYMENT AT 0100 HOURS.

* 'EAGLE'S SUMMIT' ** HEAVY EQUIPMENT TRANSPORTERS

THE PRECIOUS TURBINE COMPONENTS ARE CONCEALED WITHIN CONTAINERS COVERED IN POSTERS DISPLAYING VERSES FROM THE KORAN. THEY MAY LOOK LIKE REGULAR CARGO CRATES BUT, INVISIBLE TO AN OUTSIDE EYE, THE DELICATE TURBINE PARTS ARE ENCASED IN CAREFULLY WELDED STEEL BOXES. STILL, A LUCKY ROUND FROM AN AK-47 OR AN RPG COULD WRECK THE ENTIRE PROJECT.

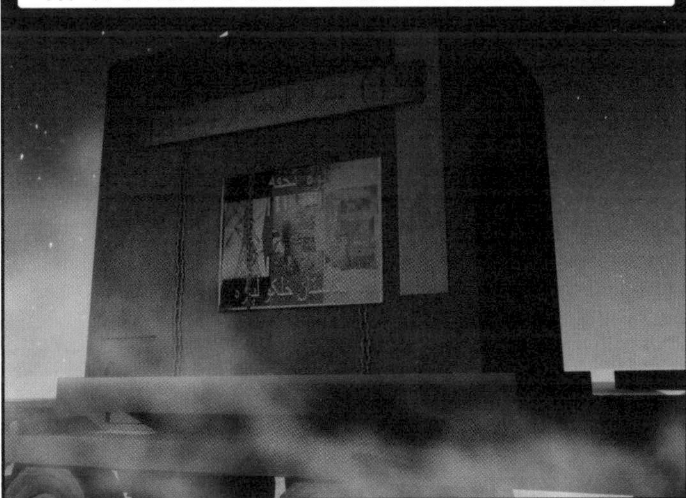

THE CANADIANS AND THE AMERICANS LEAD THE CONVOY SLOWLY OUT OF KANDAHĀR AIRFIELD...

SO THIS IS IT...

...AND INTO THE VAST, STILL EXPANSE OF THE AFGHAN NIGHT.

HOW LONG TILL THE FIRST CONTACT, I WONDER?

DAWN BREAKS OVER THE DUSTY PLAINS OF HELMAND...
WELL, THAT'S ONE NIGHT WITH NO TROUBLE, THANK GOD.
YEAH, MATE, BUT DON'T SPEAK TOO SOON. THEY'RE GOING TO HIT US AS SOON AS IT'S LIGHT ENOUGH TO SEE, AREN'T THEY? THAT'S MY BET.

AN APACHE GUNSHIP HOVERS PROTECTIVELY OVERHEAD. AS THE POUNDING HEAT OF THE DAY BEGINS TO BUILD, PHASE II OF THE OP COMES INTO EFFECT. THE CONVOY SPLITS – THE HETS CARRYING THE TURBINE VEER OFF ROUTE 611 AND ON TO WHAT LOOKS LIKE A DIRT TRACK.
WORKING IN SECRET TO FOIL TALIBAN SPIES, THE ELITE PATHFINDERS FORCE HAVE UNCOVERED A DESERT TRACK – CODENAMED ROUTE HARRIET – LEADING THROUGH THE MOUNTAINS TO KAJAKI. AS THE BULK OF THE CONVOY TURNS ON TO ROUTE HARRIET, SEVERAL VEHICLES CONTINUE DOWN ROUTE 611 TO ACT AS DECOYS.

SO FAR SO GOOD, EH MATE?
AYE, BUT THERE'S A LONG WAY STILL TO GO. JUST KEEP YOUR EYES AND EARS OPEN, EH?

THE HEAVILY LADEN TRUCKS GROAN THEIR WAY UP THE NARROW ROUTE.
EASY DOES IT, LADS! WE DON'T WANT THE TRUCKS ROLLING OR WE'RE STUFFED.

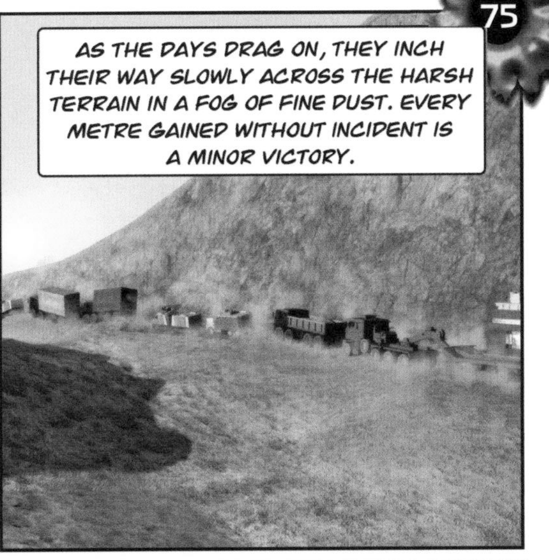
AS THE DAYS DRAG ON, THEY INCH THEIR WAY SLOWLY ACROSS THE HARSH TERRAIN IN A FOG OF FINE DUST. EVERY METRE GAINED WITHOUT INCIDENT IS A MINOR VICTORY.

ALERT TO THE THREAT OF IEDS, ROYAL ENGINEERS SWEEP EVERY INCH OF THE ROAD AHEAD OF THE CONVOY.
HANG ON, I THINK....THAT LOOKS...YES... STOP! MINES! BOSS, I'VE GOT ONE!
THIS IS 3 PLATOON. WE HAVE A MINE SIGHTING. GO FIRM, REPEAT GO FIRM.
ROGER THAT!
WOAH, WATCH IT, LADS, IT'S A REALLY NASTY ONE - WE'RE GOING TO HAVE TO BLOW IT.

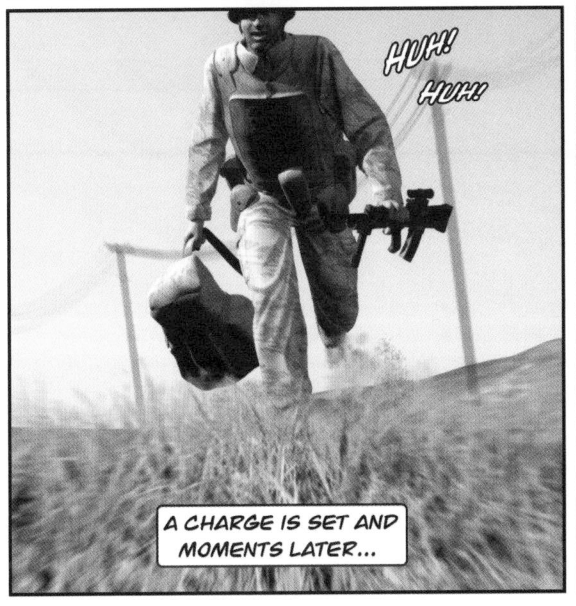
HUH!
HUH!
A CHARGE IS SET AND MOMENTS LATER...

£*?@"% THAT WAS CLOSE. TOO CLOSE! EVERYONE OK?
BOOUM!

THE DANGER DEALT WITH, THE CONVOY CREEPS ON. UNTIL SUDDENLY...

ALL VEHICLES GO FIRM! REPEAT, GO FIRM! WE HAVE A PROBLEM.

NOW WHAT?!

ALL RIGHT, LADS, YOU KNOW WHAT TO DO. EYES WELL AND TRULY PEELED TILL WE FIGURE OUT WHAT THE HOLD UP IS.
THAT MEANS YOU, PRIVATE! LOOK ALIVE. THIS IS THE PERFECT SPOT FOR AN AMBUSH.

HOW LONG TILL YOUR ENGINEERS CAN FILL THIS IN, SERGEANT? I DON'T NEED TO REMIND YOU THAT TIME IS OF THE ESSENCE. WE'RE SITTING DUCKS HERE.
IT'S THE WEIGHT OF THE LORRIES, SIR, THEY'VE CAVED IN THE ROAD - IT'S JUST NOT BUILT TO TAKE THIS KIND OF WEIGHT. GIVE US HALF AN HOUR, THOUGH, AND WE'LL BE ON THE MOVE AGAIN.

WHAT'S THE HOLD UP? I'M BEING ROASTED ALIVE IN HERE ... 55 DEGREES! IT'S INHUMAN.

THE ENGINEERS WORK QUICKLY, AND THE TRUCKS SOON ROLL OUT ONCE MORE. BUT THE SLOW RATE OF PROGRESS HAS LEFT TIME FOR WORD OF THE NEW ROUTE TO LEAK OUT TO THE INSURGENTS.
THIS DUST! I CAN HARDLY SEE...IT MUST BE A FOOT THICK.

ALL AT ONCE... CONTACT!
DAMN IT, THEY'VE GOT RPGS! I CAN SEE FOUR OF THEM. THEY'RE JUST OUT OF RANGE AND... %£*?$, THEY'RE FIRING AGAIN! GET ME AIR SUPPORT! NOW!

AN APACHE, NEVER FAR AWAY, SPEEDS INTO THE ACTION AND UNLEASHES A MIGHTY BARRAGE. THERE IS THE SHRIEK OF THE FEARSOME AIRCRAFT'S FLECHETTE ROCKETS BEING FIRED, THE THUD OF IMPACT, THEN SILENCE.
THIS IS UGLY 51. TARGET IDENTIFIED AND ELIMINATED. YOU ARE CLEAR TO CONTINUE.
AFFIRMATIVE. NICE WORK, UGLY 51. CONVOY, ROLL OUT.

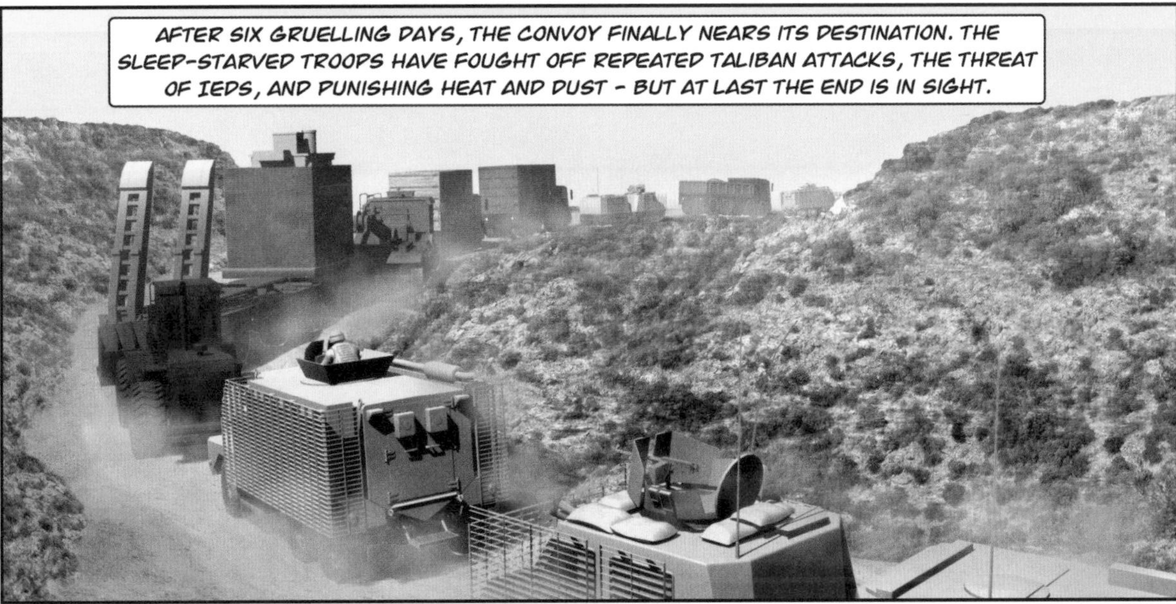
AFTER SIX GRUELLING DAYS, THE CONVOY FINALLY NEARS ITS DESTINATION. THE SLEEP-STARVED TROOPS HAVE FOUGHT OFF REPEATED TALIBAN ATTACKS, THE THREAT OF IEDS, AND PUNISHING HEAT AND DUST - BUT AT LAST THE END IS IN SIGHT.

THAT'S IT, LADS, WE'RE HERE! WE MADE IT. MISSION ACCOMPLISHED.
NOT QUITE YET, WRIGHTY – WE'VE STILL GOT TO UNLOAD THE THING. COME ON, YOU LOT, LET'S GET IT DONE FAST. I FANCY A SWIM BEFORE WE HAVE TO HEAD BACK. SOMETHING TO FRESHEN US UP BEFORE WE TACKLE THAT LOT AGAIN.

THE TURBINE COMPONENTS ARE CAREFULLY WINCHED OFF THE DUSTY HETS.
EASY THERE, SERGEANT! DON'T WANT TO BASH THE THING TO PIECES AFTER LUGGING IT ALL THIS WAY.

THERE SHE IS, LADS – SOMETHING TO FEEL GOOD AND PROUD OF.
SHE'S A BEAUT, BOSS.

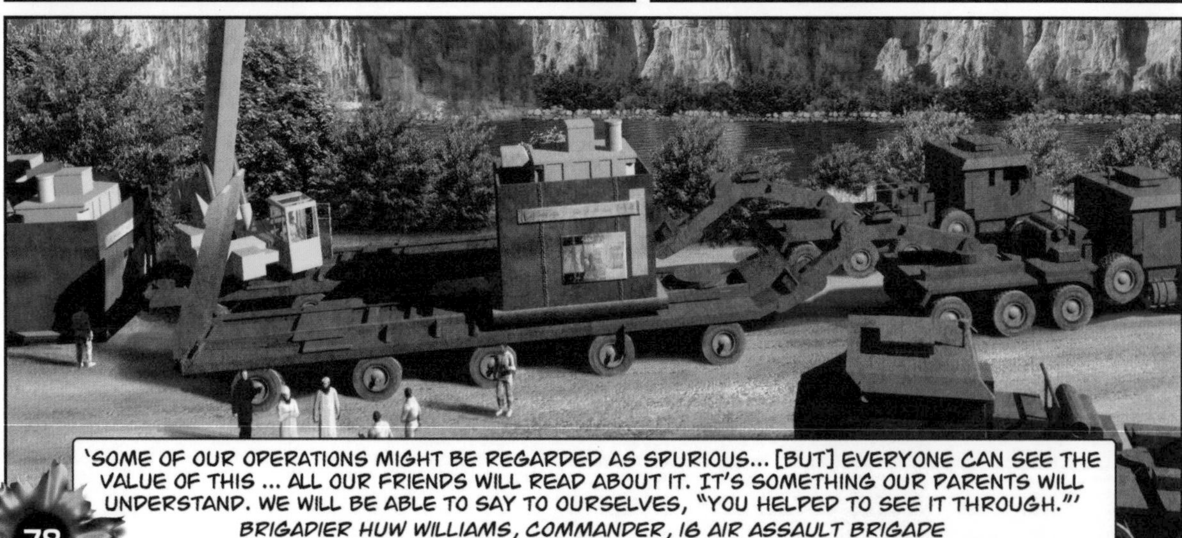
'SOME OF OUR OPERATIONS MIGHT BE REGARDED AS SPURIOUS... [BUT] EVERYONE CAN SEE THE VALUE OF THIS ... ALL OUR FRIENDS WILL READ ABOUT IT. IT'S SOMETHING OUR PARENTS WILL UNDERSTAND. WE WILL BE ABLE TO SAY TO OURSELVES, "YOU HELPED TO SEE IT THROUGH."'
BRIGADIER HUW WILLIAMS, COMMANDER, 16 AIR ASSAULT BRIGADE

16 AIR ASSAULT BRIGADE HAD ACCOMPLISHED WHAT THEY SET OUT TO DO – AND WHAT MANY THOUGHT WOULD PROVE IMPOSSIBLE. THEY COULD LEAVE AFGHANISTAN FEELING PROUD OF THE REAL CONTRIBUTION THEY MADE TO THE LIVES OF ORDINARY PEOPLE.

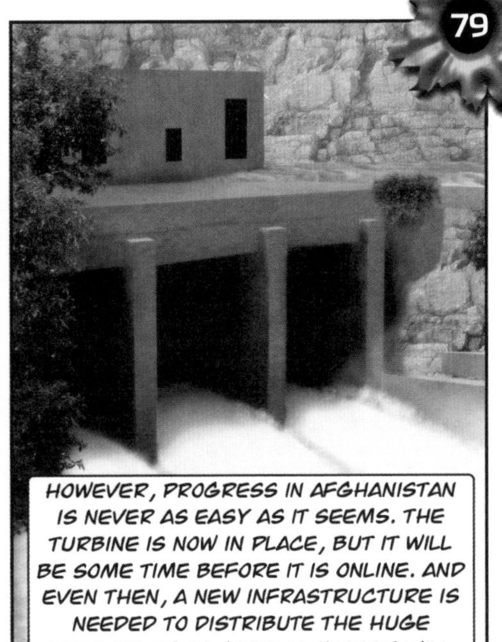

HOWEVER, PROGRESS IN AFGHANISTAN IS NEVER AS EASY AS IT SEEMS. THE TURBINE IS NOW IN PLACE, BUT IT WILL BE SOME TIME BEFORE IT IS ONLINE. AND EVEN THEN, A NEW INFRASTRUCTURE IS NEEDED TO DISTRIBUTE THE HUGE AMOUNTS OF POWER THE SYSTEM WILL GENERATE.

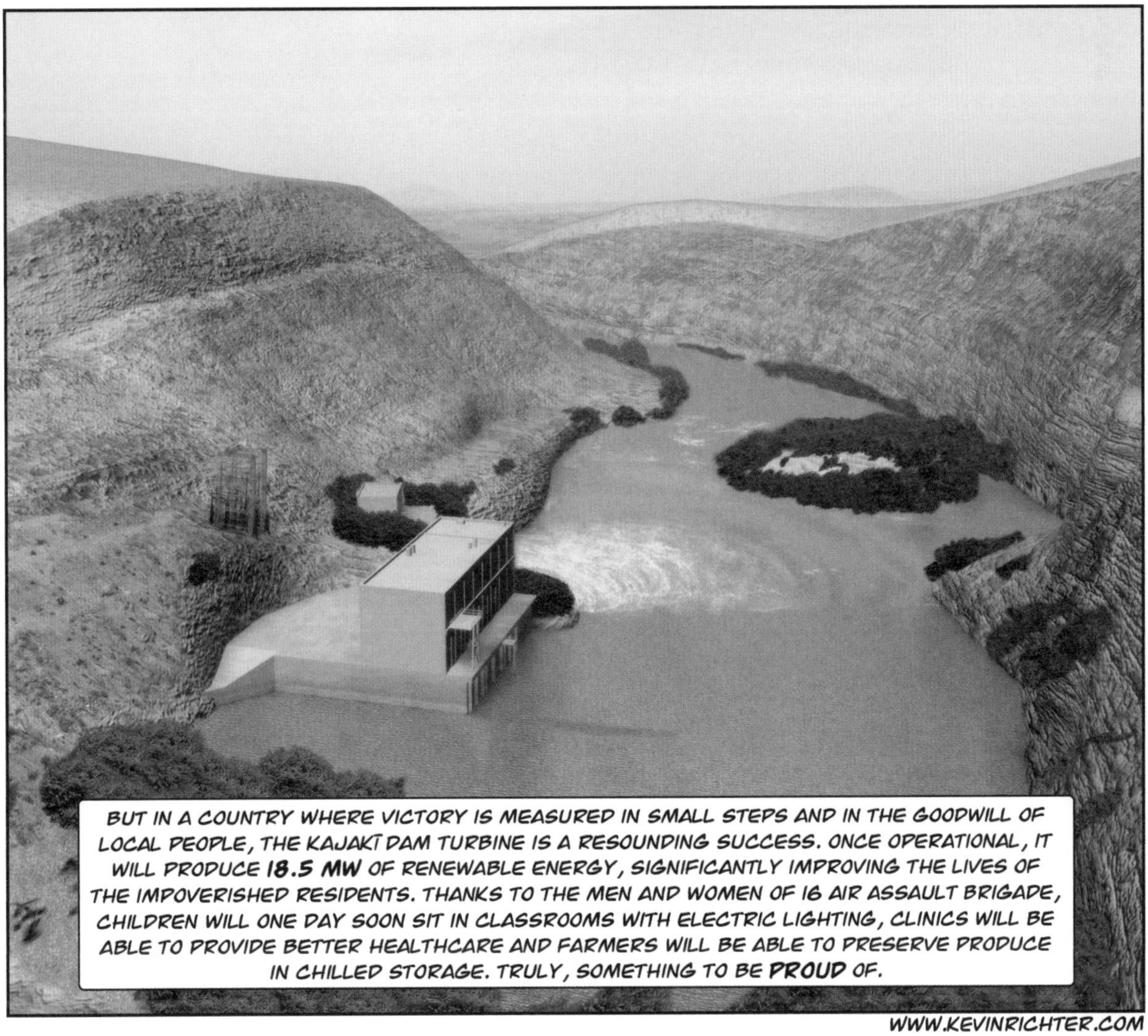

BUT IN A COUNTRY WHERE VICTORY IS MEASURED IN SMALL STEPS AND IN THE GOODWILL OF LOCAL PEOPLE, THE KAJAKI DAM TURBINE IS A RESOUNDING SUCCESS. ONCE OPERATIONAL, IT WILL PRODUCE **18.5 MW** OF RENEWABLE ENERGY, SIGNIFICANTLY IMPROVING THE LIVES OF THE IMPOVERISHED RESIDENTS. THANKS TO THE MEN AND WOMEN OF 16 AIR ASSAULT BRIGADE, CHILDREN WILL ONE DAY SOON SIT IN CLASSROOMS WITH ELECTRIC LIGHTING, CLINICS WILL BE ABLE TO PROVIDE BETTER HEALTHCARE AND FARMERS WILL BE ABLE TO PRESERVE PRODUCE IN CHILLED STORAGE. TRULY, SOMETHING TO BE **PROUD** OF.

THE AFGHAN CONFLICT: YESTERDAY & TODAY

By James Holland

A British soldier who had been serving in the First Anglo-Afghan War in the late 1830s, or in the Second Anglo-Afghan War between 1878 and 1880, or again in the third war in 1919, and who then found himself miraculously transported to the twenty-first century, would find a landscape hardly changed and much that was very familiar. Admittedly, in the towns there are now vehicles and a few proper roads, but the hubbub of the market, the number of wooden carts and animals, and the dress of the Afghans is much the same. In the rural areas, there has been even less progress.

COLOURED LITHOGRAPH BY JAMES BATTRAY, 1842 © PUBLISHED BY HARING AND REMINGTON, LONDON, 1847

Afghan foot soldiers in 1842.

In fact, much has barely changed for not just hundreds, but thousands of years. Crossing the desert, it is possible to find small farming communities nestling beneath harsh, jagged mountains. The people live in rectangular compounds, in the corner of which will be a flat-roofed house. Both the house and the farmstead walls are made of mud and straw. There is no electricity, and water is drawn from a well or a nearby river. The children wear no shoes and have no modern facilities whatsoever. Alexander the Great passed through Helmand Province in 329 BC – he would recognize parts of it today without any difficulty at all.

Today, in Helmand, British troops can be dropped into remote spots by helicopter and can call upon Apache gunships and supersonic jets to help them if things get really bad. The skies were empty of all but the birds in the nineteenth century, but in many ways, the experiences of the

TINTED LITHOGRAPH FROM 'SKETCHES OF AFGHANISTAN', 1838–1842, BY LOUIS AND CHARLES HAGHE AFTER JAMES ATKINSON, PUBLISHED BY HENRY GRAVES AND CO. AND J.W. ALLEN AND CO., 1 JULY 1842

Afghanistan in the 1830s: the entrance to the Bolan Pass.

THE FIRST ANGLO–AFGHAN WAR

© LITHOGRAPH BY W. TAYLOR AFTER LT T WINGATE, 1839

'The Storming of Ghuznee', 1839. Note the British soldiers' distinctive red tunics.

The First Anglo–Afghan War, 1839–42, began during a time of massive conflict between the empires of the day. This period, known as the 'Great Game', centred on the rivalry between the British and Russian empires for supremacy in Central Asia. The Anglo–Afghan War marked one of the worst setbacks of British power in the region.

Crucially, India, Afghanistan's neighbour, was still a British colony, with strong British military control. Britain feared a Russian invasion of India through Afghanistan, and sought to protect its empire. General Sir John Keane led the British–Indian Army in claiming large areas of Afghanistan and installed Shah Shuja as emir, exiling the previous leader, Dost Mohammed Khan. The Afghan people resented Britain's occupation. This increasingly violent tension between the Afghans and the British–Indian force, paired with the country's fierce climate, eventually wore down the British–Indian garrison.

In January 1842, the garrison's five thousand troops and their twelve thousand followers were guaranteed safe passage to leave their fortification outside Kabul. But as these men and women made their way along treacherous, snow-bound passages, they were ambushed. Dr William Brydon is the only Briton known to have escaped alive. The rest were massacred.

Ultimately, British troops in the rest of Afghanistan succeeded in pulling out of the country, but not before pillaging the countryside as an act of revenge for their defeat.

PHOTOGRAPH BY JOHN BURKE © FROM AN ALBUM BY BOURNE AND SHEPHERD, 1878–1880 (ASSOCIATED WITH MAJ GEN FREDERICK SLEIGH ROBERTS, 2ND AFGHAN WAR)

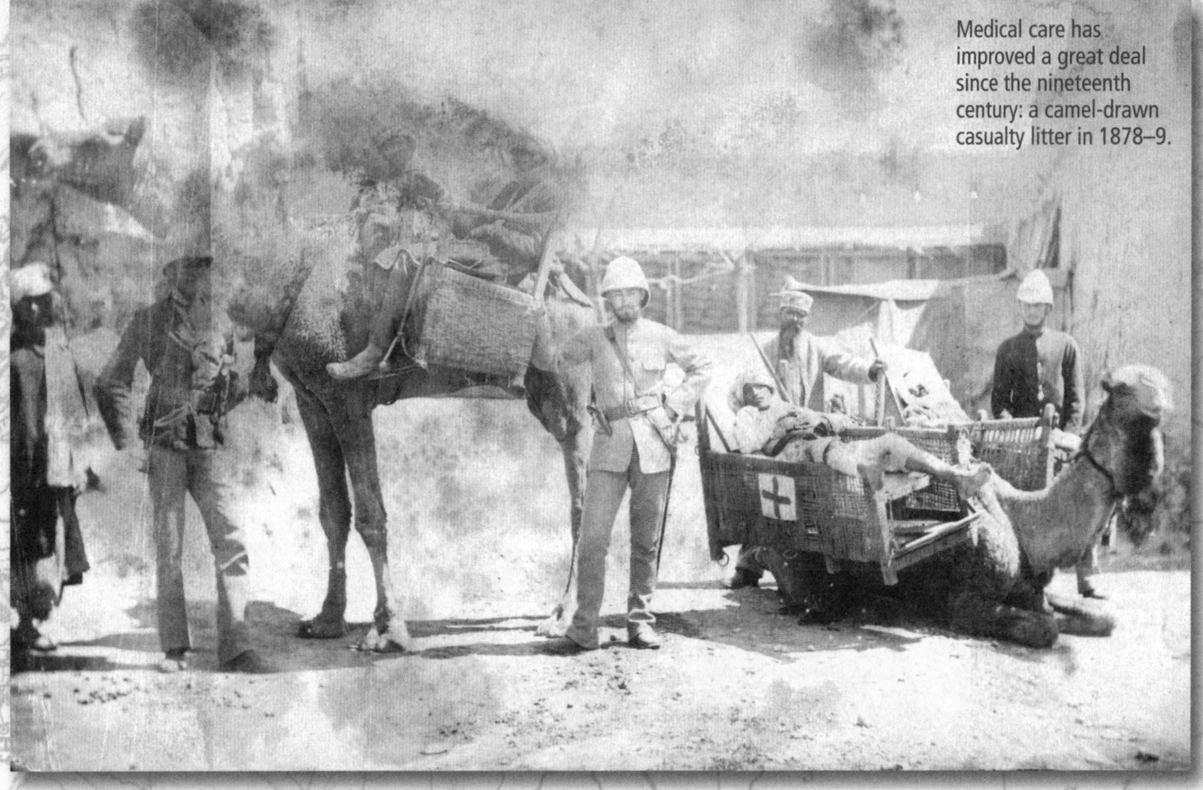

Medical care has improved a great deal since the nineteenth century: a camel-drawn casualty litter in 1878–9.

THE SECOND ANGLO–AFGHAN WAR

Thirty years after the first Anglo–Afghan War, tensions in Europe were still simmering. Russia was dissatisfied with a clampdown on its European expansion and, as a result, returned its attention to Central Asia.

In the summer of 1878, Russia sent an uninvited diplomatic mission to Kabul. In response, the British insisted that reigning Emir Sher Ali Khan accept a British mission. The Emir refused, but a British mission was sent regardless. When the mission reached the Khyber Pass, it was turned back, as the Emir had threatened, triggering the Second Anglo–Afghan War. In response, 40,000 British troops invaded Afghanistan. Sher Ali hoped for Russian support, but died before assistance arrived.

British forces soon occupied most of the country. Sher Ali's son and successor, Mohammed Yaqub Khan, took power and signed the Treaty of Gandamak in May 1879, to prevent Britain invading the rest of Afghanistan. Yaqub handed over control of foreign affairs to the British, in return for British subsidy and protection, British representatives were set up around Afghanistan.

Soon after, an Afghan uprising led to the assassination of a British diplomat and his staff, sparking unrest. General Frederick Roberts commanded a British force to defeat the Afghan Army, before moving on to occupy Kabul. Yaqub was forced to step down. As his successor, the British chose his cousin, Abdur Rahman Khan. With the treaty signed and foreign policy now in British hands, Britain withdrew from Afghanistan.

Pathan tribesmen, c. 1879.

FROM A PHOTOGRAPH ALBUM BY MAJ. GEN. SIR ALEXANDER ROBERT BADOCK

THE THIRD ANGLO–AFGHAN WAR

The end of the Second Anglo–Afghan War ushered in forty years of friendly relations. However, Abdur Rahman's death in 1901 set the ball rolling for what would become the Third Anglo–Afghan War. His successor, Amir Habibullah, was fickle, alternating sides between Britain and Russia. In 1915, Habibullah accepted a German– Turkish mission to Kabul, where Turkish officers stirred up anti-British unrest. By the time the mission left in 1916, they had convinced Habibullah to pursue full independence. Three years later, however, Habibullah was assassinated.

A power struggle between his two sons followed, and the fiery Amanulla seized the reins of government. However as the third son, his claim to rule was weak – he needed a diversion. Sensing the exhaustion of post-war Britain, Amanulla attacked the British in India on 3 May 1919. The British were taken by surprise and, initially, the Afghans triumphed. But soon Britain's greater forces, more sophisticated weaponry and, crucially, airpower gained ground. However, following the First World War, British and Indian fighting power was low. Many experienced officers had died, and those left had little will to fight, resulting in widespread desertions. War was short-lived. By 3 June, an armistice was signed, followed by the Peace Treaty of Rawalpindi on 8 August.

The war's outcome was not clear. The British repelled the Afghan invasion, but the British–Indian Army suffered twice as many casualties. As a result of the treaty, Britain withdrew its subsidy, the controversial Afghan–Indian border was reaffirmed and Afghanistan regained control of its foreign affairs as a fully independent state.

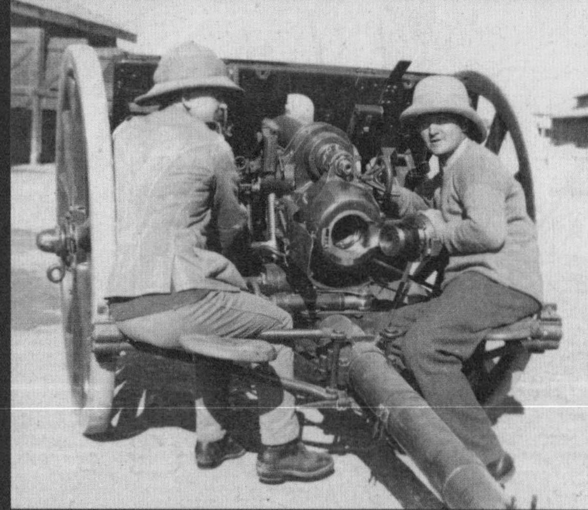

Field guns have long played a vital role in Afghanistan: the open breech of an 18-pounder field in 1919.

FROM A PHOTOGRAPH ALBUM RELATING TO THE 101ST BTY ROYAL FIELD ARTILLERY IN INDIA 1917–19

troops have not greatly changed. For much of the time, today's British servicemen are on their own, operating from Forward Operating Bases (FOBs) or Patrol Bases (PBs). FOBs are very basic encampments, with a protective wall around them and a camp inside. The troops sleep in camp beds – if they have beds at all – often under canvas, just as troops did in Victorian times, and they survive off basic rations.

In some ways, a serviceman's kit is very different today. Now, troops have radios, satellite telephones and computers with Internet access that can be set up in some of the most remote places, keeping a link with the main bases and camps. Their weapons are far more sophisticated, as are their uniforms, helmets and body armour.

FROM AN ALBUM, 1912–1919, COMPILED BY W.K. FRASER-TYTLER

Motor transportation, like these motorcycle combinations and cars, proved extremely valuable during the Third Anglo–Afghan War.

However, in other ways, there are many similarities. For most of the Victorian era, British troops wore scarlet and coloured tunics, but by 1919 they wore cotton khaki drill, not so very different from today's basic jacket and trousers. Soldiers today carry their kit in rucksacks, pockets and pouches just as they did in 1839, 1879 and 1919. The weight of the kit would also have been much the same. Today's SA80 rifle weighs about 3.8 kilos – about the same as the Short Magazine Lee Enfield that the troops would

PHOTOGRAPH FROM AN ALBUM BY RICHARD BEZZANT HOLMES, 1919–1920

The Afghans have always taken pride in their fierce warriors.

Afghan tribesmen mount an ambush during the Second Anglo–Afghan War.

ENGRAVING BY V. HAMILTON

have had in 1919 and the Martini-Henri rifle used in the Second Anglo-Afghan War of the late 1870s. In the past, British troops would have travelled into a campaign with a long column carrying their equipment and would have been resupplied in much the same way. Today, troops might be dropped by air into a specific place, but an FOB or urban base is still resupplied by a long column in what is called a Combat Logistic Patrol. Large trucks are used rather than carts and wagons, but from a distance the long dusty line crawling through the desert looks much the same.

The First, Second and Third Anglo-Afghan Wars were even more violent than the kind of fighting British troops are experiencing today. In 1841, the British Army suffered one of its worst defeats when the garrison of Kabul decided to retreat into India. Four thousand troops and some twelve thousand non-combatants set out, but only one solitary person reached the border. The rest were massacred. Even during the brief Third Anglo-Afghan War in 1919, the British suffered around two thousand casualties in two months. After that war, British troops stayed out of Afghanistan, but they continued to have considerable problems with tribesmen along the North-West Frontier between India and Afghanistan. Throughout the 1920s and 1930s, British and Indian troops fought a series of campaigns against troublesome tribesmen in these mountainous regions. The fighting then was much the same as it is now in Helmand – they could even call upon air support, although biplanes were not nearly so fast or effective as helicopters, let alone jets. Casualties during these campaigns were also comparable with today's.

British troops in Helmand are also commanded by a brigadier, just as they were on the North-West Frontier in the 1930s. Brigadiers Auchinleck and Alexander, for example, led successful campaigns there and later went on to become celebrated generals during the Second World War.

If the level of communications and the sophistication of the modern weaponry are

Royal Marines at Kajakī.

THE SOVIET WAR IN AFGHANISTAN

In April 1978, Afghanistan's communist party, the People's Democratic Party, seized power, renaming the country the Democratic Republic of Afghanistan (DRA). Immediately, Islamic and conservative uprisings began. The beleaguered new government signed a friendship pact with the USSR, increasing Soviet military and financial support in existence since the 1950s.

After a bloody reorganization of government, Hafizullah Amin emerged as DRA leader, and more Soviet troops were sent to fight the growing *mujahideen* (meaning 'struggler') rebellion. By late December 1979, the *mujahideen* were in revolt and Amin's loyalty to the Soviet Union had come under suspicion. The Soviet government decided to invade. After heavy fighting, Amin was killed, to be replaced by Soviet-backed Babrak Kamal.

Mujahideen in Kunar province, Afghanistan, 1987.

Soviet troops pull out of Afghanistan, 1988.

Over the next two years, resistance grew. Under the umbrella of the Cold War, the US, Saudi Arabia and Pakistan supplied money and arms to the Afghan mujahideen, increasing their strength against Soviet and DRA forces. In 1982, the United Nations General Assembly called for Soviet withdrawal. By the time five million Afghans were displaced, in 1985, Soviet leader Mikhail Gorbachev was ready to end the war. However, an increase in Soviet troops aimed at a quick victory resulted in the war's highest bloodshed.

In 1988, with one million Afghans and thirteen thousand Soviet soldiers dead, all parties were eager for the war to end. Peace accords were signed by the DRA, USSR, US and Pakistan. On 15 February 1989, the USSR announced the departure of the last Soviet troops from Afghanistan.

two major differences between today's and yesterday's troops, the other big change is in the standard of medical care.

CASEVAC – casualty evacuation – takes precedence over nearly all other flying requirements, and helicopter crews are superb at flying in and retrieving wounded soldiers as soon as they possibly can. The wounded are then rushed to the hospital at Camp Bastion in the centre of Helmand Province. This hospital is more sophisticated and better equipped than just about any NHS hospital in Britain. Camp Bastion's surgeons reckon that if a wounded serviceman or woman is still alive when he or she gets there, the chances are that he or she will survive. In the nineteenth century medicine was still undeveloped. Even minor wounds could easily turn septic, while the biggest killer was not a Pashtun spear, but disease. Things had improved somewhat by 1919, but it is only in recent times that medicine has advanced such an enormous degree. Fatalities in Afghanistan would be far, far higher were it not for the brilliance of the British medical teams in Helmand today.

James Holland is a bestselling writer and historian. Find out more at www.secondworldwarforum.com.

VEHICLES

© CHRISTOPHER PLEDGER / EYEVINE

WMIK

One of the vehicles with the most impact on the ground is a type of protected Land Rover equipped with a special weapons mounted installation kit (WMIK). Tough, manoeuvrable and armed with huge amounts of fire power – from the rapid-fire grenade machine gun and .50-calibre heavy machine gun to new night-vision sights and Javelin missiles – WMIKS have been dubbed 'porcupines' by local Taliban because of the spiky appearance of their mounted weapons. They are used to advance ahead of patrolling infantry in order to help hold back the enemy. The Land Rover can also be modified for use as an ambulance. The Land Rover battlefield ambulance can either carry up to six soldiers seated or four stretcher casualties, and it provides a high standard of medical equipment on board.

PANTHER

The Panther command and liaison vehicle is one of the British Army's newest additions. It weighs around 7 tonnes and can be transported by air, suspended beneath a Chinook helicopter. The Panther is armed with a 7.62 mm general-purpose machine gun (GPMG) and its weapon system is fired by remote-control. This enables the gunner to operate the GPMG from within the relative safety of the vehicle, using a joystick and camera. It also has a sighting system for both day and night.

© CROWN COPYRIGHT

JACKAL

The Jackal is a 'high-mobility weapons platform'. This means that it can be used for a range of tasks, including rapid assault, convoy protection, fire support and reconnaissance. Weighing 6.65 tonnes, the Jackal is one of the most agile vehicles on operations. It is extremely mobile off-road, where it can reach speeds of up to 80 km/h (its top speed on paved roads is 130 km/h). This versatility allows troops to avoid well-trodden routes, giving them a degree of unpredictability which is an essential tactical asset. The design of the vehicle's hull incorporates advanced armour protection features.

JACKAL 2

The enhanced Jackal 2 features improved manoeuvrability and reliability, and can carry four crew members, including the driver – one more than its predecessor. The position of the top-mounted .50-calibre machine gun has been moved forward, allowing a greater range of movement. The chassis has also been upgraded, enabling the vehicle to carry a heavier load and giving it greater strength – vital if a vehicle is to survive the blast from a roadside bomb. The armoured door now locks back into the open position, allowing troops a wider field of fire. And the rear of the Jackal 2 has also been redesigned so that fuel or water containers can be carried on the outside of the vehicle, along with troops' Bergen backpacks, extra ammunition or other equipment.

© ANDREW LINNETT/MOD CROWN COPYRIGHT/PA WIRE

COYOTE

The Coyote was bought by former Secretary for Defence, John Hutton, in October 2008 as part of a £700-million package of protected patrol vehicles. A 6x6 lightly armoured tactical support vehicle, the Coyote supports the high-mobility Jackals across difficult terrain and provides enhanced protection for British troops.

© PETER TARRY

SPRINGER

The Springer is an all-terrain vehicle, specifically designed for desert conditions. It carries a crew of two and is capable of hauling a combat load of 1 tonne. Its primary role is to transport combat equipment from helicopter landing sites to forward operating bases (FOBs), enabling front-line troops to receive the supplies that they need.

SCIMITAR

The Scimitar armoured reconnaissance vehicle entered active service in 1971, and is occasionally classed as a light tank. Its small size and low ground pressure make it particularly useful in difficult terrain. It carries a crew of three. Its main armament is a 30-mm L21 Rarden cannon, and it also boasts a co-axial 7.62 mm general-purpose machine gun and smoke grenades. On operations, it carries 160 rounds of 30 mm and 3,000 rounds of 7.62 mm ammunition. Relatively slow on the ground, its maximum speed is 80 km/h. Currently used in Afghanistan, the Scimitar was also used by British forces on UN and NATO peacekeeping duties in former Yugoslavia and Iraq.

SPARTAN

The Spartan is a very small armoured personnel carrier. It is manned by a crew of three and is capable of carrying up to four additional soldiers. Rather than simply a general personnel carrier for infantry, the Spartan is used to transport specialized groups, including reconnaissance teams, mortar fire controllers and ambush parties, Royal Engineer technicians and anti-aircraft missile teams, across the battlefield. It is armed with one 7.62 mm general-purpose machine gun, and can travel at up to 96 km/h.

VIKING

The Viking is an amphibious vehicle, with a body made from armoured steel. It weighs approximately 12 tonnes and can be lifted by a Chinook helicopter in order to move it between locations. Its turbo diesel engine enables it to produce speeds of up to 65 km/h. The Viking can operate in temperatures ranging from -46°C to 49°C, and it has been credited with saving many British lives in Afghanistan due to its capability in the intense heat found there. It is armed with a 7.62 mm GPMG, a 0.5 mm heavy machine gun (HMG) and two smoke-grenade dischargers.

QUAD BIKE

The quad bike is an all-terrain vehicle that allows troops to move quickly through harsh terrain. Its main role is to deliver crucial combat supplies to troops on the ground. It is capable of reaching troops in areas that are particularly difficult to access, in order to provide them with food, water and ammunition. As well as providing logistical support, the quad bike also assists with the quick evacuation of casualties from the battlefield.

WARRIOR

The Warrior infantry fighting vehicle can carry three crewmembers – commander, gunner and driver – and seven additional soldiers. The driver sits in the front hull, while the commander and gunner sit in the rear hull. The embarked infantry section sits in the rear hull. The Warrior entered active service in 1988, and it continues to provide excellent mobility, lethal fire power and protection for troops. It weighs an impressive 25.4 tonnes.

MASTIFF

The Mastiff is a heavily armoured 6x6 patrol vehicle, which protects troops against mines, small arms and IEDs (improvised explosive devices). The first Mastiffs were deployed in 2006, to protect British troops in Iraq. In June 2009 the Mastiff 2 was introduced. This has been improved to include greater crew capacity (from six to eight), bigger axles, a tougher suspension and increased electrical power. The Mastiff 2 can travel at a maximum of 90 km/h and is armed with the latest weapons systems, including a 7.62 mm GPMG, 12.7 mm HMG or a 40 mm automatic grenade launcher. These wheeled patrol vehicles have a less intimidating profile than tracked vehicles, such as tanks, and give commanders on the ground in Afghanistan more options to deal with the threats they are facing.

RIDGEBACK

The Ridgeback is a mine-resistant, multi-role vehicle that is available in both a 6x6 and a 4x4 model. The 6x6 layout can transport up to nine soldiers. Both Ridgeback models can be operated on a wide range of terrains. The Ridgeback is used to transport weapons, as a recovery vehicle and even as an ambulance in emergencies. Its surface is covered by large plates that act as armour to ensure that crews are protected from explosions.

As well as the range of vehicles used by the British Armed Forces for protection, patrol and transportation during operations, there are any number of support vehicles vital to the construction of bases like Camp Bastion, as well as for engineering and logistical purposes. Combat engineers depend on top-end equipment to clear routes, repair airfields and harbours and bridge rivers – all at high speed and often under fire. They also need to be able to build structures to protect troops on the ground. Vehicles such as the heavy equipment transporters (HETs) that can carry 70-tonne tanks, the family of Support Vehicles that can transport up to 15 tonnes of weaponry, ammunition or other cargo, and the tankers used to transport fuel and water are all of vital significance to the progress of the British Army in Afghanistan.

© ASSOCIATED PRESS

Special forces play a crucial role behind the scenes in Afghanistan.

While soldiers from front-line units take the fight direct to the Taliban, elite servicemen and women are constantly carrying out covert surveillance work to hunt out the enemy.

At any one time there are between sixty and seventy of these highly trained and incredibly skilled troops in the badlands.

During the early years of the Afghan conflict, the Special Boat Service (SBS) was based there. But more recently, following the end of combat operations in Iraq, soldiers from the world-famous Special Air Service (SAS) have taken over.

Men from the 'Who Dares Wins' Regiment currently on the ground play a vital role supporting the war.

A top SAS source said: 'The main job of special forces is information gathering. What they do is target members of the enemy [forces]; they secretly watch and wait for the target to come. They don't always kill them. Quite often, they just record what they are up to, who they are speaking with, where they go. They are long-term observation posts (OPs); they can last as long as two or three weeks, sometimes. So, as you can imagine, being discreet, patient and highly observant is essential.'

SPECIAL

By Andy Crick

In Afghanistan it is vitally important to know who the major players are in the Taliban. It is a highly organized and well-structured organization, so it is important that the British Armed Forces are aware of the enemy chiefs.

The SAS source added: 'It is all about identifying who is who, what they do and the role they play. The Taliban works as a cell system, so you have different tribes working together. But you have guys who, for example, are responsible for bringing in weapons for the insurgents. Then you have other guys who deal with the finance and funding their fight against us. By identifying and targeting the Taliban chiefs, you hit right at the heart of them.'

Operation Panther's Claw is a UK-led military operation, involving thousands of troops, that is ongoing in Helmand Province. Its aim is to secure river and canal crossings in order to establish a permanent security presence in the area. British Special Forces were especially useful in the operation.

An additional but no less important aim of the massive operation involved clearing a dangerous Taliban heartland near Babaji of insurgents ahead of the Afghan presidential elections in August 2009, allowing locals to vote.

'During the operation, SAS were brought in to take out strategic targets, Taliban personnel and equipment. But they also did all the preparation work and they would be on the ground long before the infantry came in.'

© GETTY

FORCES

A huge focus for the elite soldiers in recent months has been combating the threat of improvised explosive devices (IEDs). Also known as roadside bombs, they are the biggest killer of British soldiers.

IEDs are cheap and easy to build, and they are well hidden by insurgents, making them the Taliban's deadliest weapon.

© EPA

Special Forces have been tasked with tracking down the bomb-makers to ensure that fewer bombs are set, resulting in fewer deaths and injuries.

In July 2009 a Taliban bombing team killed five young soldiers from 2nd Battalion, the Rifles – three of them just eighteen years old.

One month later, SAS troops tracked down the killers. A twelve-person SAS team was dropped by helicopter near their Taliban hideout in Sangin.

The SAS source explained: 'When the five British soldiers were killed in a cynical double bomb blast, the SAS were tasked with finding the bombers who made the bombs and killing them – which they did. If you can take out the key people that make and lay the IEDs, it lessens the problem.'

The SAS team used unmanned drones to track down the Taliban hideout. These drones are pilotless aircraft that are crucial for tracking enemy targets from the air.

'The drones are vitally important, they are up in the skies all the time. The Taliban are aware of them, but there is nothing they can do about them,' the SAS source added.

Although British Special Forces carry out high-risk tasks in Afghanistan, they are certainly not taken for granted.

'The lads cost £3 million each to train, so they are not put at risk unless the risk is worth it,' the SAS source concluded.

DRONES

Drones are unmanned vehicles. They can be autonomous, able to carry out a specific task without outside assistance, or teleoperated, which means that they are remotely operated. Drones have found widespread usage in military operations, as a drone can perform a high-risk task in place of a soldier, thereby protecting the soldier from unnecessary harm. Drones are used in the air, on the ground and underwater. With their top-of-the-line cameras and radar systems, drones can be used for reconnaissance – detecting and relaying information, such as the location of enemy troops or missing soldiers – or for attack purposes, as such vehicles can often move undetected behind enemy lines. The technology behind drones has accelerated rapidly, and their use in Afghanistan has been very effective in the fight against the Taliban.

A gunner launches the new 'Desert Hawk 3' UAV (Unmanned Aerial Vehicle) spy plane.
© SOUTH WEST NEWS SERVICE

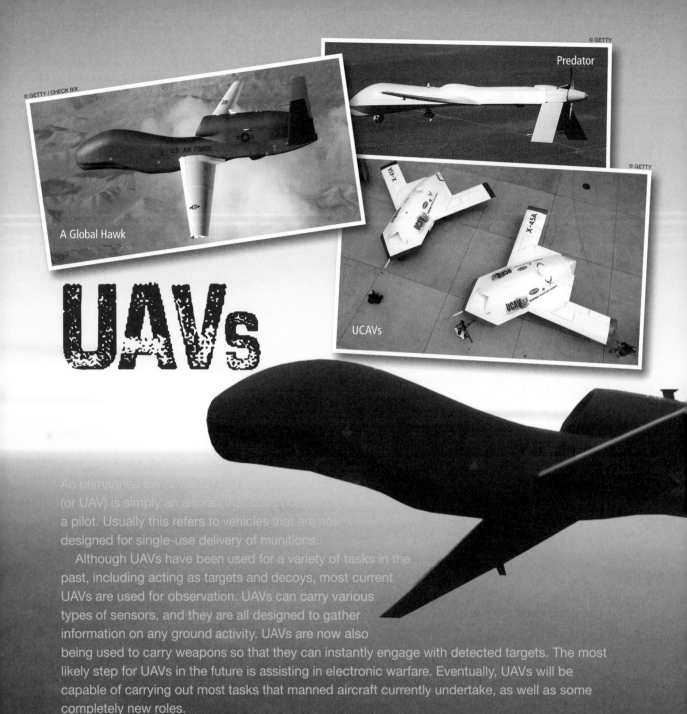

© GETTY / CHECK SIX

A Global Hawk

© GETTY

Predator

© GETTY

UCAVs

UAVs

An unmanned aerial vehicle (or UAV) is simply an aircraft that does not carry a pilot. Usually this refers to vehicles that are not designed for single-use delivery of munitions.

Although UAVs have been used for a variety of tasks in the past, including acting as targets and decoys, most current UAVs are used for observation. UAVs can carry various types of sensors, and they are all designed to gather information on any ground activity. UAVs are now also being used to carry weapons so that they can instantly engage with detected targets. The most likely step for UAVs in the future is assisting in electronic warfare. Eventually, UAVs will be capable of carrying out most tasks that manned aircraft currently undertake, as well as some completely new roles.

UAVs can be controlled in several ways. With remote piloting or remote operation, the vehicle is flown by a pilot on the ground, with signals transmitted by radio. The pilot operates a set of instruments that relay the UAV's altitude, airspeed and other important measurements. This system has been in use for many years with a variety of drones.

Another means of controlling a UAV is through autonomous operation. This type of UAV either follows a pre-set flight path that is loaded before take-off, or can be directed – but not directly piloted – from the ground. This often involves pre-setting waypoints or pre-setting the area to be observed. The UAV's computers can then take care of the altitude, power and airspeed.

While remote piloting is technically the simplest and most flexible way of controlling UAVs, it means that qualified pilots are still required to fly them. This increases the cost of using UAVs, particularly for long-endurance flights, where shifts of pilots are needed.

ADVANTAGES OF UAVs

There are a number of reasons why interest has recently increased in UAVs and UCAVs. This is partly due to advances in technology, which have enabled UAVs to operate autonomously, improving their capability and usefulness.

However, the main reason that UAVs and UCAVs are of such interest to the Armed Forces is their ability to lower the number of deaths and casualties during operations. Although many modern UAVs are expensive, they involve no risk of losing personnel from enemy action. UAVs can therefore perform tasks in situations that are too risky to allow the use of a manned aircraft. Additionally, UAVs have longer endurance than manned vehicles as they are limited only by fuel, rather than by pilot fatigue. This enables the vehicle to hover for long periods, either for intelligence gathering, or to act as a continuous threat, thereby providing cover to troops on the ground.

A US soldier prepares a Mini UAV in Kunar province, Afghanistan.

MODERN UAV TYPES

HALE – High Altitude, Long Endurance. These UAVs tend to be large vehicles that require standard runways and that are flown from bases some distance from the areas being observed. These machines are often used for reconnaissance and surveillance. An example of a HALE UAV is the Global Hawk, which can fly for 36 hours at an altitude of 20,000 m and a maximum speed of 650 km/h (400 mph).

MALE – Medium Altitude, Long Endurance. Smaller than HALE UAVs, these machines also require prepared runways. An example of a MALE is the Predator, which can fly for an impressive 40 hours at 25,000 m at a cruise speed of 129 km/h (80 mph). It is used for surveillance, but it also has a tactical role in inspecting the battlefield.

Tactical UAVs tend to operate over a smaller area and shorter timescale than MALE and HALE UAVs. Many tactical UAVs can be launched and recovered from unprepared sites, using vertical take-off and landing (VTOL), ramp systems, rockets and other methods. This enables the UAVs to be operated closer to the frontline and to support commanders in the field directly. An example of a tactical UAV is the Phoenix. This smaller UAV can be launched within one hour of reaching a launch site. It has a wingspan of 5.5 m and a maximum launch weight of 175 kg. Flights can last more than four hours and its maximum altitude is 2,700 m.

Micro/Mini UAVs. This definition covers a huge range of UAVs with differing roles and capabilities, most of which are still experimental. An example is the tiny Pointer UAV, which weighs only 4 kg and can fly missions for up to 90 minutes. The Pointer uses a day camera or a thermal-imaging camera for night or low-visibility conditions. The images captured can be viewed in real-time at a ground-control station, giving fighters an aerial picture of their surroundings.

UCAV – Unmanned Combat Air Vehicles. These are armed UAVs. Most current projects that involve these vehicles are aimed at ground attack rather than air-to-air combat. The only UCAV to have been used operationally is the Predator B, armed with Hellfire anti-tank missiles, which has been used by the US.

FOOTBALL IS A GAME OF HEROES

© SWINDON TOWN

From World Cup winner Sir Geoff Hurst to Liverpool's Steven Gerrard, every fan has their idol.

But now football fans are uniting to give Britain's heroes from the Armed Forces the credit they deserve, thanks to a new partnership between Help for Heroes and The Football League.

Help for Heroes is the official charity partner of the Football League for the 2009–10 season, and football is working hard to say 'thank you' to the country's military heroes.

Brave British troops enjoyed a lap of honour at all of the 2008 and 2009 play-off finals at Wembley Stadium as tens of thousands of fans showed their gratitude. The troops were then treated to a special VIP behind-the-scenes experience at Wembley.

The public will get their chance to say thank you again at the 2010 play-off finals.

Clubs from across the Coca-Cola Championship, Coca-Cola League 1 and Coca-Cola League 2 have been raising money for Help for Heroes; Swindon Town even had their match ball delivered by a Scimitar tank! Fans at the club donated a massive £1,864 for three military charities, including Help for Heroes.

Nottingham Forest, Reading, Colchester United and Leyton Orient are just a few examples of Football League clubs pulling out all the stops to raise as much money as possible for the courageous men and women fighting for their country.

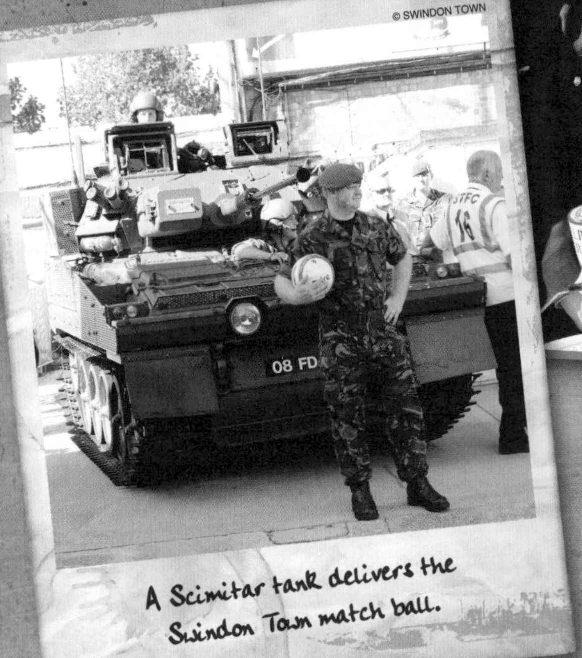

A Scimitar tank delivers the Swindon Town match ball.

A HERO'S WELCOME

© PA IMAGES

Private Carl Clowes, a Leeds United fan injured in Afghanistan, recently spoke about his experience as one of 200 members of the Armed Forces honoured before all three of the 2008 play-off finals at Wembley.

Carl followed Leeds on their famous rise to the 2001 Champions League semi-finals. Seven years later, Carl was waiting for a prosthetic leg from Headley Court Defence Medical Rehabilitation Centre, after suffering appalling injuries when a mine exploded while he was on tour.

'I was top-covering an armoured Land Rover, and the back tyre hit a mine,' said Carl. 'It severely damaged both legs and I had to have an amputation on the left leg. I broke my jaw, my cheekbone, both knees, both ankles, both feet and got a burn on my back. The Army contacted Leeds when I was injured. Leeds came back with a signed flag. That was brilliant. I'm Leeds through and through. Leeds then invited me to their Thorp Arch training ground, where the players were brilliant. Paul Huntington, the central defender, said to me, "We have to make decisions as players, but it's nothing compared to the decisions you guys have to make."

'Nothing will make up for what happened to me, but it is a consolation. It shows people recognize what we do out in Afghanistan and Iraq.'

© PA IMAGES

ON YOUR BIKE

Former Lincoln City striker Simon Yeo is gearing up to raise money for Help for Heroes with a charity bike ride from Blackpool to Lincoln.

Currently leading the line at Conference North side Droylsden FC, Simon is planning to pedal the 240-km trip before the Imps' home tie against Morecambe in April 2010. This is just the latest in a series of fund-raising events by the ex-serviceman who saw action in Bosnia and Northern Ireland during his stint in the 22nd Cheshire Regiment.

'I was in Bosnia in 1992–3 and I saw a lot of stuff that still affects me today,' admitted Simon. 'The guys and girls that come back from Afghanistan and Iraq are going to need help. Some of them are missing limbs and they have to live the rest of their lives with that and they deserve to be helped. I was fortunate enough to come back having not been injured, but others weren't so lucky and I want to raise money for them. I am still in contact with people in the Army – I still have mates out in Afghanistan and Iraq. Someone from my old regiment was killed the other day and it really hits home.'

Boot camp for Ipswich players

Ipswich Town Chief Executive Simon Clegg has pledged his support to the new partnership between The Football League and Help for Heroes. Clegg spent a decade in the Armed Forces, travelling across the globe while serving under the 7th Parachute Regiment, Royal Horse Artillery. He still actively maintains his Army links, as Roy Keane and his squad discovered during a tough two-day pre-season boot camp at Colchester Garrison.

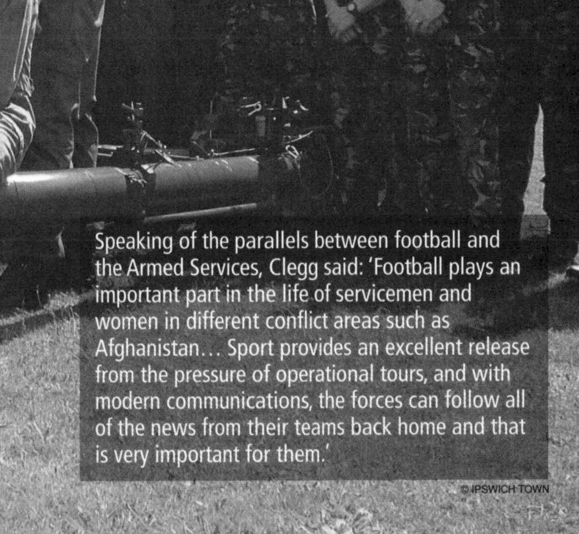

Speaking of the parallels between football and the Armed Services, Clegg said: 'Football plays an important part in the life of servicemen and women in different conflict areas such as Afghanistan… Sport provides an excellent release from the pressure of operational tours, and with modern communications, the forces can follow all of the news from their teams back home and that is very important for them.'

© IPSWICH TOWN

MISSING IN ACTION

By Ed Macy

A lone soldier is particularly vulnerable to attack and capture.

'Missing in action', or 'MIA', is the term used to describe a soldier who has become separated from his unit during combat. As soon as a soldier goes MIA, a search operation will be launched to try to ensure his safe recovery.

British Armed Forces are prepared to accept injury and even death in the line of duty. In Afghanistan, a soldier's worst nightmare is to be captured by insurgents. The Taliban, al-Qaeda and HIG (*Hezb-I Islami Gulbuddin*) are not interested in kidnapping. These groups have a history of torturing and killing lone soldiers and of posting videos of these appalling acts on the Internet. If a soldier is caught by these groups, there is little chance of survival.

All of our Armed Forces are taught what to do if they become separated from their unit. Here is a concise guide on how to escape capture and survive.

Being separated from your unit during combat is terrifying: you're all alone in an unfamiliar terrain and you are aware of the potential consequences of capture.

Your best chance of survival is to link up with your unit as quickly as possible. The longer this takes, the lower your chances of success. However, always be mindful that the enemy may not know that you are MIA. If they don't know that you're missing, then they won't be looking for you. In this case, it can be best to lie low.

If your unit appears to have moved on from your location, do not think they that have left you behind. They will know that you are missing and they may have simply changed location to fool the enemy. Meanwhile, your position will be being observed or, if they haven't yet found you, they will be searching.

Whatever happens, you must be prepared to be decisive and keep in mind your two survival options: link up or escape. Your willpower will be crucial during this time.

Follow the flow diagram on the opposite page to determine what you should do if you are separated from your unit during combat.

Ed Macy, MC, is an Apache helicopter pilot and bestselling author of *Apache* and *Hellfire*. Find out more at www.edmacy.com.

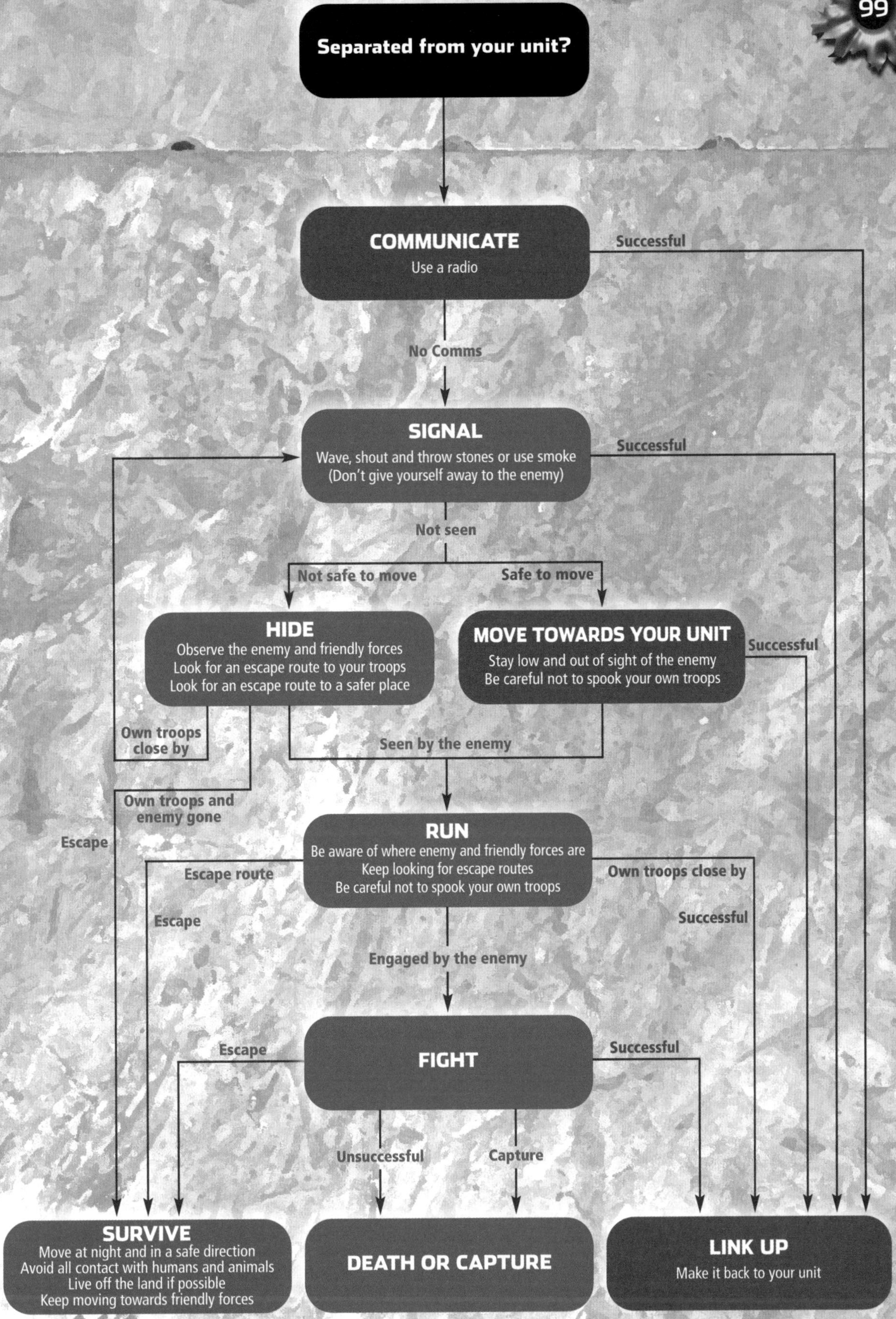

Separated from your unit?

↓

COMMUNICATE
Use a radio

- Successful → LINK UP
- No Comms → SIGNAL

SIGNAL
Wave, shout and throw stones or use smoke
(Don't give yourself away to the enemy)

- Successful → LINK UP
- Not seen → Not safe to move → HIDE
- Not seen → Safe to move → MOVE TOWARDS YOUR UNIT

HIDE
Observe the enemy and friendly forces
Look for an escape route to your troops
Look for an escape route to a safer place

- Own troops close by → SIGNAL
- Own troops and enemy gone → Escape → SURVIVE
- Seen by the enemy → RUN

MOVE TOWARDS YOUR UNIT
Stay low and out of sight of the enemy
Be careful not to spook your own troops

- Successful → LINK UP
- Seen by the enemy → RUN

RUN
Be aware of where enemy and friendly forces are
Keep looking for escape routes
Be careful not to spook your own troops

- Escape route → Escape → SURVIVE
- Own troops close by → Successful → LINK UP
- Engaged by the enemy → FIGHT

FIGHT

- Escape → SURVIVE
- Successful → LINK UP
- Unsuccessful → DEATH OR CAPTURE
- Capture → DEATH OR CAPTURE

SURVIVE
Move at night and in a safe direction
Avoid all contact with humans and animals
Live off the land if possible
Keep moving towards friendly forces

DEATH OR CAPTURE

LINK UP
Make it back to your unit

THE SIEGE OF ROSHAN TOWER

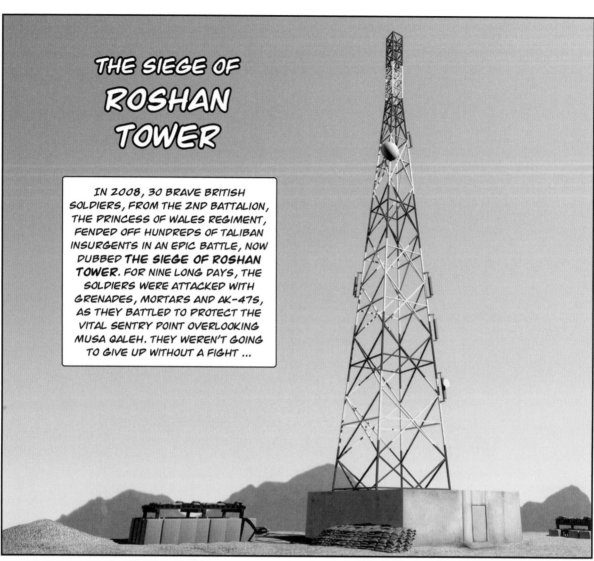

IN 2008, 30 BRAVE BRITISH SOLDIERS, FROM THE 2ND BATTALION, THE PRINCESS OF WALES REGIMENT, FENDED OFF HUNDREDS OF TALIBAN INSURGENTS IN AN EPIC BATTLE, NOW DUBBED **THE SIEGE OF ROSHAN TOWER**. FOR NINE LONG DAYS, THE SOLDIERS WERE ATTACKED WITH GRENADES, MORTARS AND AK-47S, AS THEY BATTLED TO PROTECT THE VITAL SENTRY POINT OVERLOOKING MUSA QALEH. THEY WEREN'T GOING TO GIVE UP WITHOUT A FIGHT ...

BELOW THE SENTRY POSITION, ALL APPROACHES TO THE OBSERVATION POST ARE OBSCURED BY ENDLESS CORNFIELDS.

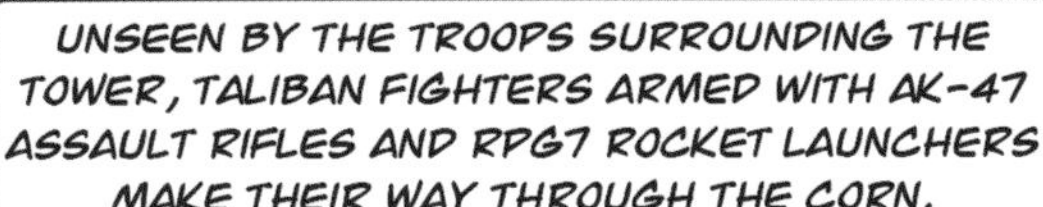

UNSEEN BY THE TROOPS SURROUNDING THE TOWER, TALIBAN FIGHTERS ARMED WITH AK-47 ASSAULT RIFLES AND RPG7 ROCKET LAUNCHERS MAKE THEIR WAY THROUGH THE CORN.

AS THE SCORCHING 'WINDS OF 120 DAYS' RUSTLE THE TALL CROPS, THE TALIBAN ADVANCE AS SILENTLY AS POSSIBLE.

THEY LEVEL THEIR ROCKET LAUNCHERS, TAKING AIM AT THE BRITISH OUTPOST...

ONE OF THE SENTRIES, SCANNING WITH HIS BINOCULARS, SPOTS THE TALIBAN JUST IN TIME.
*%$#! ENEMY FRONT! THEY'RE IN THE CORNFIELD!

THE TROOPS LEAP INTO ACTION AS THE ENEMY OPEN FIRE.
SWING RIGHT. ON TARGET!
GOT 'EM! PASS ME ANOTHER BELT OF AMMO - QUICK!
CHH! CHH! CHH! CHH!

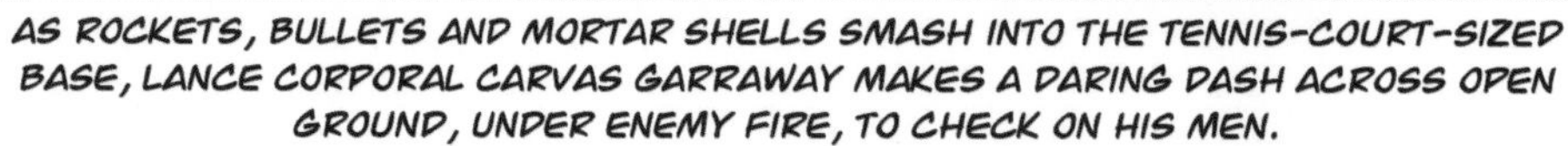
AS ROCKETS, BULLETS AND MORTAR SHELLS SMASH INTO THE TENNIS-COURT-SIZED BASE, LANCE CORPORAL CARVAS GARRAWAY MAKES A DARING DASH ACROSS OPEN GROUND, UNDER ENEMY FIRE, TO CHECK ON HIS MEN.

HQ, THIS IS ROSHAN TOWER. THEY'RE POUNDING US TO HELL! WE NEED BACKUP - NOW!

JESUS, GARRAWAY, BE CAREFUL!
NEGATIVE, ROSHAN TOWER, WE CAN'T GET TO YOU - THE FIRE'S TOO HEAVY! YOU'RE GOING TO HAVE TO HOLD OUT ALONE!

GARRAWAY TAKES COVER, BUT WITH ROCKETS FLYING IN IT SEEMS LIKE ONLY A MATTER OF TIME BEFORE THE BESIEGED TROOPS SUFFER A DIRECT HIT.
IS EVERYONE OK?

THE FIRING CONTINUES ALL DAY AND ALL NIGHT, AS THE TALIBAN THROW THEMSELVES INTO BATTLE IN A FRENZIED ATTEMPT TO STORM THE POSITION.
ANOTHER RPG HIT! I'M NOT SURE HOW MUCH MORE WE CAN TAKE!

AS THE DAYS DRAG ON, THE EXHAUSTED TROOPS HUDDLE IN WHAT LITTLE SHELTER THEY HAVE...
TRY TO GET SOME REST, MATE, BEFORE IT'S YOUR TURN ON THE GUN...

I WISH I COULD! I DON'T KNOW HOW HE CAN SLEEP WITH ALL THAT NOISE.
I RECKON HE'S PRETTY BLOODY KNACKERED. I KNOW I AM.

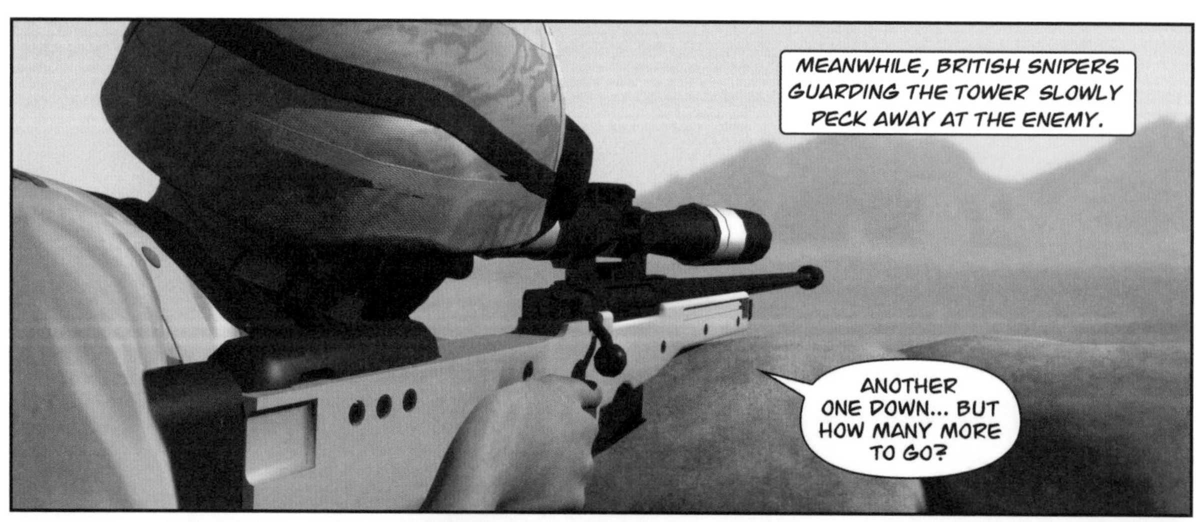

MEANWHILE, BRITISH SNIPERS GUARDING THE TOWER SLOWLY PECK AWAY AT THE ENEMY.
ANOTHER ONE DOWN... BUT HOW MANY MORE TO GO?

THE TALIBAN FIRE VOLLEY AFTER VOLLEY OF RPG MISSILES, THEIR DEADLY SHRAPNEL BURSTING IN THE AIR ABOVE THE TROOPS.

AARGH!

LOOK OUT! ENEMY ATTACKING FROM THE SOUTH!

ONE FRENZIED FIGHTER ATTACKS FROM ONLY A FEW HUNDRED YARDS AWAY...

...AND IS CUT DOWN.

HNH-!

THAT'S THE LAST ROCKET YOU FIRE, MATE!

THE BATTLE DRAGS ON, AS THE BONE-WEARY TROOPS MUSTER THEIR LAST RESERVES OF STRENGTH...
BLOODY HELL, THAT WAS CLOSE!
WAY TOO CLOSE – MY EYES ARE WATERING.

FSG, I'VE GOT MULTIPLE ENEMY ATTACKING MY POSITION...
THE BELEAGUERED TROOPS USE EVERYTHING THEY'VE GOT TO KEEP THE RELENTLESS ENEMY AT BAY.

STANDBY FOR COORDINATES – THEN HIT THEM AS HARD AS YOU CAN!

AT THE BASE OF THE TOWER, MORTAR TEAMS POUND THE TALIBAN FIGHTERS AS, AGAIN AND AGAIN, THEY TRY TO STORM THE TROOPS' POSITIONS.
RELOAD! FASTER, DAMMIT, THEY'RE NOT STOPPING!

SALVO AFTER SALVO OF DEADLY 81 MM HIGH EXPLOSIVE SHELLS, WITH THEIR JAGGED SHARDS OF SHRAPNEL, FLY AT THE TALIBAN BY DAY...
RELOAD! AGAIN!

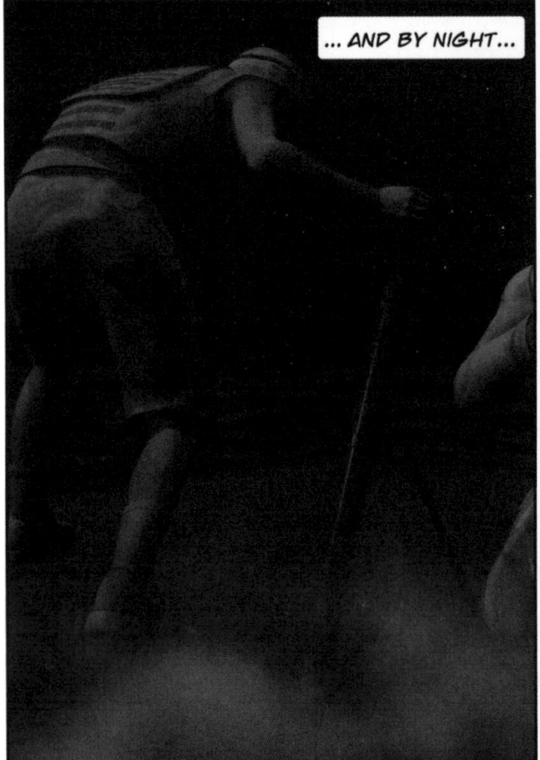

... AND BY NIGHT...

RE–
I KNOW! RELOAD!

...THEIR DESPERATE EFFORTS ECHOING ACROSS THE EMPTY AFGHAN SKY.

THE VASTNESS OF THE STARRY NIGHT DWARFS THE SMALL BAND OF SOLDIERS WHOSE EPIC EFFORTS ARE ALL THAT STAND BETWEEN THE TALIBAN AND THEIR MATES ON THE GROUND BELOW.

BOOM!

AT LAST, EXHAUSTED, THE ENEMY RETREAT, AND APACHES RACE IN TO MAKE SURE THEY STAY AWAY.
ROSHAN TOWER, THIS IS UGLY 63. GLAD WE CAN FINALLY JOIN YOU!

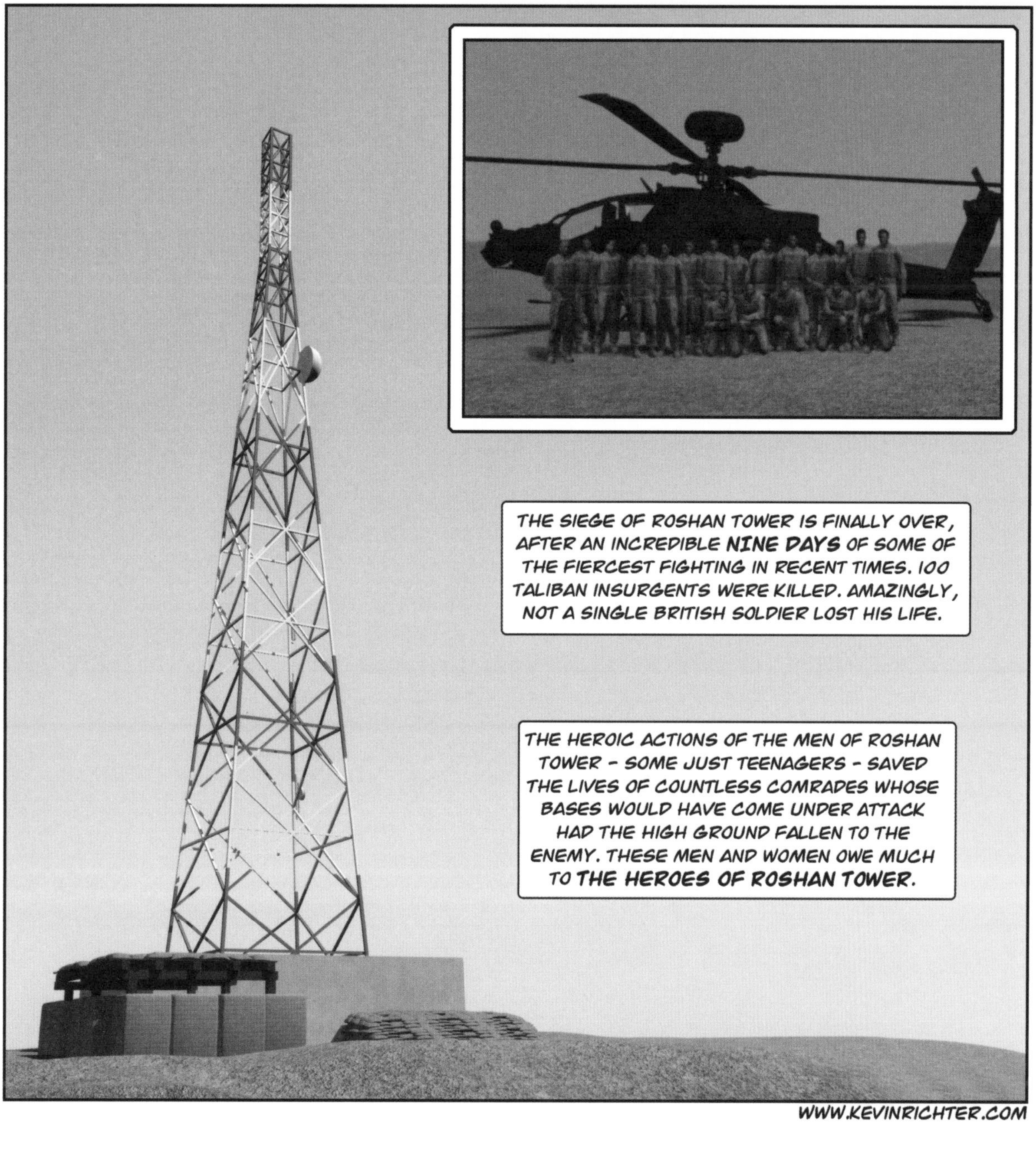

THE SIEGE OF ROSHAN TOWER IS FINALLY OVER, AFTER AN INCREDIBLE **NINE DAYS** OF SOME OF THE FIERCEST FIGHTING IN RECENT TIMES. 100 TALIBAN INSURGENTS WERE KILLED. AMAZINGLY, NOT A SINGLE BRITISH SOLDIER LOST HIS LIFE.

THE HEROIC ACTIONS OF THE MEN OF ROSHAN TOWER – SOME JUST TEENAGERS – SAVED THE LIVES OF COUNTLESS COMRADES WHOSE BASES WOULD HAVE COME UNDER ATTACK HAD THE HIGH GROUND FALLEN TO THE ENEMY. THESE MEN AND WOMEN OWE MUCH TO **THE HEROES OF ROSHAN TOWER**.

HELP FOR HEROES

Help for Heroes (H4H) was founded in 2007 by Bryn and Emma Parry out of a desire to help wounded members of the Armed Forces coming back from Afghanistan and Iraq. Help for Heroes believes that anyone who volunteers to serve during wartime, knowing that they may risk all, is a hero. These are extraordinary people doing extraordinary things, and some of them continue to live with the consequences of their service for the rest of their lives.

The current focus of the charity is raising money to build a series of regional Army Recovery Centres (ARCs) across the UK. These will serve as the last stage of rehabilitation before a serviceman or woman returns to their unit or moves back into civilian life.

Soldiers who are wounded in the service of their country receive excellent medical care. However, once the soldier has stopped being an 'in patient', problems can arise.

Most wounded soldiers are able to return to their homes, but not all families can provide the level of support, supervision and care required to help someone with a serious injury.

And although it is hoped that all soldiers wounded in the service of their country will be able to return to duty, there will be many who leave the services. It is important that these individuals receive assistance and guidance in this step, allowing them to make a smooth transition to a skilled and supported civilian life.

ARCs will help soldiers to make the swiftest possible return to duty or a smooth transition to civilian life. Soldiers live in comfortable individual rooms within the centre, which is attached to a garrison so that wounded soldiers can stay within a military environment and close to friends and family. In addition to medical support, ARCs will also provide wounded soldiers with individually tailored programmes, including career management and counselling, as well as assistance with resettlement. The first ARC was opened in Edinburgh on 17 August 2009, and Help for Heroes hopes that more will soon follow.

HELP FOR HEROES IN NUMBERS

£30 million raised to date – in just two years
On average, over £40,000 received per day – or 46p per second
£1,521,659.93 collected in a single day on 20 October 2008
Over 10,500 fundraising events so far
Over 1.4 million people wearing H4H wristbands
Over £23.5 million allocated to projects that support the wounded
98p of every £1 donated to the charity contributed directly to grants

'When we started, we had no idea just how much generosity and support we would encounter from the public, all desperate to do their bit to help the wounded. The money raised is going to help some extraordinary young men and women wounded in the service of our country. We may not be able to stop them being wounded, but together we have shown that we are not helpless, we can help them to get better.' BRYN PARRY, CHIEF EXECUTIVE OF HELP FOR HEROES

www.helpforheroes.org.uk

The X-Factor charity single for Help for Heroes was the fastest selling single of 2008.

MEET THE PARAS

Q&A WITH THE MEN OF THE PARACHUTE REGIMENT

PRIVATE AARON THOMAS

Who are you? I'm 19 years old and a Private in the Parachute Regiment. I'm from a town called Redruth in Cornwall. I have been in the Army for just over three years and was in Afghanistan in 2008 on Op Herrick 8.

What does your job involve? My job involves keeping fit and being a good shot. We do lots of physical training and have to go on the ranges to use our weapons regularly.

What does your average day consist of? In Colchester, my day consists of fitness training in the morning and then briefs or lessons throughout the day. In Afghanistan it's a lot different: you wake up and check you have enough water to last through the day, check you have all the kit that you may need, clean your weapon and prepare for the first patrol. It's all about the patrols, so you have to stay focused on being ready all the time. It's hard work but we train hard, so it comes naturally.

Best bit of army kit? I would say the bomb (the sleeping bag).

CORPORAL PETE 'PREECY' PREECE

Who are you? I'm 27 years old and am currently a Corporal in 3 Para's Mortar Platoon. I've been in the Army for 11 years and have completed three tours of Northern Ireland, a tour of Iraq in 2003 and two tours of Afghanistan.

What does your job involve? I'm a Mortar Fire Controller so when I'm on operations with the battalion, my job requires me to direct mortar fire. I work closely with the rifle companies at the front of any battle, and make sure the mortars are hitting the right target at the right time.

What does your average day consist of? Whilst back in camp, we focus hard on training but my passion is boxing so I'm currently involved in preparing the battalion's boxing team for the next season's Army Competition. We're training three times a day at the moment. The pressure is on because we've been pretty successful as a boxing team over the years and we don't want to lose!

Best bit of army kit? My favourite piece of military equipment is the 81 mm mortar!

LANCE CORPORAL JAMES ALLEN

Who are you? I'm from Northern Ireland. I'm currently in the Patrols Platoon of 3 Para; we're the reconnaissance specialists for the battalion. I've been in the Army for about four years. Since joining, I've been to Afghanistan twice; once as a signaller and last year as a recce soldier.

What does your job involve? On my first tour of Afghanistan I was employed as a signaller with a rifle company. It was an eye-opening experience because we were the first infantry battalion to go into Helmand and were there on our own, so

things were a bit intense at times. Last year, I served as a heavy machine gun operator with the Patrols Platoon. We were responsible for various tasks, including route clearance and setting up overwatch[1] positions. My job specifically included providing overwatch with my gun when on the vehicles and operating the general purpose machine gun when on foot as part of a six-man patrol.

What does your average day consist of? When you have to look after vehicles, there is always a lot to do. Even when we were not deployed on the ground last year, we were preparing vehicles and ensuring our kit was always good to go. When we deploy, we tend to work independently of the battalion, which is great because it means you have yourself to rely on and you have to be good at what you do. We have a lot of responsibility, gathering information for the rifle companies and clearing routes for them.

Best bit of army kit? The best piece of military equipment has to be 'the bomb' which is what we call our big sleeping bags. There's nothing better than crawling into one when you're wet and cold!

CAPTAIN ANDY MALLET

Who are you? I'm 30 and from Jersey, Channel Islands. I've been in the Armed Forces for four and a half years. Previous tours include Op Herrick 4 (in 2006) and Op Herrick 8 (2008).

What does your job involve? I'm the Officer Commanding for Patrols Platoon, 3 Para battlegroup reconnaissance platoon of 32 men. I'm responsible for gathering information on the enemy, on the ground and on the situation for the Commanding Officer (CO) of the battlegroup. I also lead the patrol element of the battlegroup.

What does your average day consist of? A typical 24 hours involves battle preparation – including planning, issuing orders, making sure kit is prepared, weapons are cleaned and vehicles are prepared – and patrol deployment, which involves patrolling up to 100 kilometres, independently, in front of the battlegroup, to conduct reconnaissance and gather information on the enemy. I also conduct ground studies and prove routes so that I can provide 'ground truth' to the CO. I measure atmospherics and conduct *shuras*[2] with local tribesmen and elders to gather information. Then I report back and provide up-to-date SITREPs (situation reports) to battlegroup HQ.

Best bit of army kit? LLP (Low Level Parachute).

1. 'Overwatch' means covering the movement of your colleagues with your weapon system.
2. Meetings

Battling Back from the Battlefield

By Antony Lloyd

A casevac is rushed to a waiting ambulance.

There is one shout common to almost every fire fight or bomb strike in which British soldiers are wounded in Afghanistan: 'Medic!'

As soon as that cry goes out, this specially trained soldier – formally known as a combat medical technician – must move forward to reach the casualty, regardless of the level of incoming fire. Carrying a trauma kit containing tourniquets, dressings, blood coagulants (to thicken the blood and stop bleeding), morphine, fluids and chest seals, as well as a rifle, their job is to keep critically wounded soldiers alive for long enough that they can be evacuated from the scene of battle for more sophisticated treatment, a period of time traditionally known as 'the golden hour'.

In past conflicts it was common to have one medic attached to each company of infantry troops. Now, however, due to the intensity of fighting and level of casualties, many infantry units in Helmand have one medic accompanying each platoon.

But though they carry weapons, the medics seldom use them.

'Medics usually get pushed to one side in a contact,' explained Serjeant Graham Wright, 37, the senior medical non-commissioned officer (NCO) in Sangin. 'The blokes don't want to see the medic fight. They want them with the platoon serjeant in a known location, ready to treat the casualties.'

As the medic moves forward to treat the wounded, step one in the seven-stage treatment pathway experienced by soldiers injured in Afghanistan, a simultaneous request will be relayed by radio to Camp Bastion for a Medical Emergency Response Team (MERT) to evacuate the casualties. Comprising an anaesthetist, A&E specialist, further medics and force-protection troops, the MERT is flown to the incident site aboard a CH47 Chinook, accompanied by two Apache attack helicopters providing top cover.

Meanwhile, regardless of the extent of the wounds and unless it is blatantly obvious that the casualty is dead, the medic on the ground will continue exhaustive attempts to keep

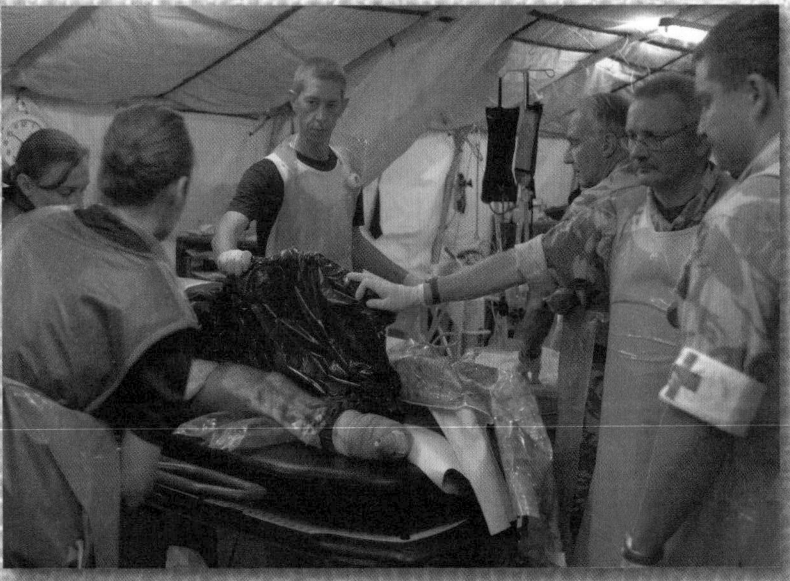

In the operating theatre top medical teams leap into action.

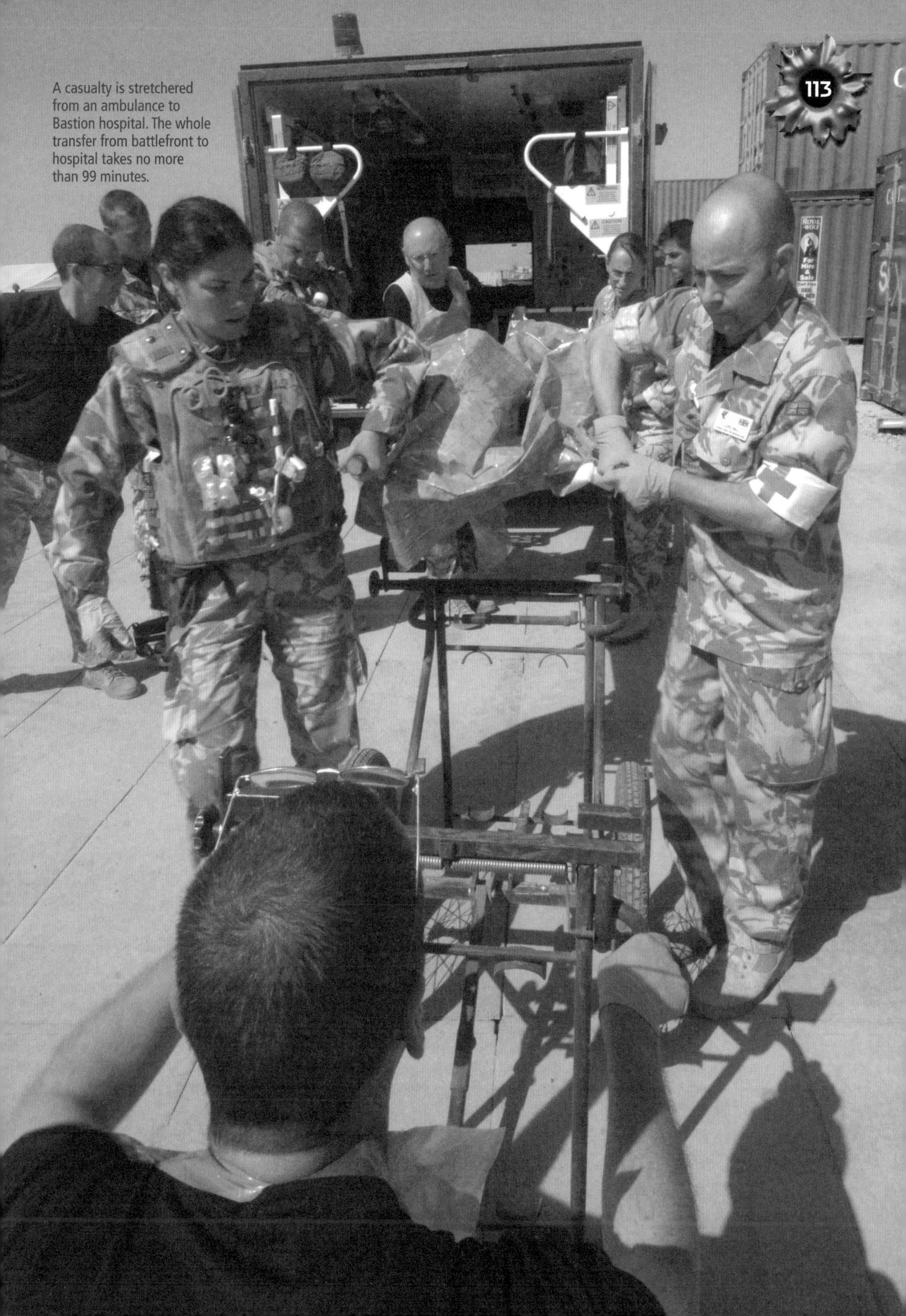

A casualty is stretchered from an ambulance to Bastion hospital. The whole transfer from battlefront to hospital takes no more than 99 minutes.

wounded troops alive. This summer a medic attached to 2 Rifles in Sangin was attempting to revive a severely injured soldier who had lost both legs before she herself was blown up and wounded. In another incident in the same area, a medic kept alive a wounded soldier who had suffered a triple bomb blast amputation.

The casualties are rushed aboard the Chinook the moment that it lands. Neither the MERT's Chinook nor its US equivalent, the Black Hawk 'Pedro' (also used to evacuate British soldiers), spend a second longer than necessary on the ground before lifting off again on the return journey to Camp Bastion.

In many instances these helicopters will themselves come under fire from the moment they first approach the scene of the incident. In July this year, a Pedro carrying wounded soldiers was brought down by Taliban fire. A second Black Hawk managed to land and cross-load the wounded. Yet there was no room aboard for the crew of the first damaged aircraft. They had to clip themselves to the skids of a third helicopter, a tiny OH-58 Kiowa, and escape the scene hanging beneath the aircraft while still under fire.

At Camp Bastion the wounded are stretchered straight from the landing site into the state-of-the-art field hospital there, where a combined emergency team of British, American and Danish surgeons and nurses take up the task of treatment. This year the average time soldiers spent between being seriously wounded and arriving in Bastion hospital was just 99 minutes.

'The speed and aggressiveness with which we resuscitate,' said Colonel Tim Hodgetts, director of the hospital, 'the tools we use, it's way beyond what most hospitals are capable of... Get them to our hospital alive. That gives us an opportunity to do what we can do, which is a paradigm so far beyond my NHS experience, it is hard to explain.'

British-run, but staffed by a tri-nation group of about 170 predominantly Danish medical personnel, the hospital has a limited number of beds, making it essential for the more serious casualties to be flown back to the UK as soon as possible aboard a specialist Aeromed C17 plane.

Once in the UK, in the fifth stage of treatment, severely wounded soldiers are cared for at Birmingham's Selly Oak Hospital.

Seriously wounded soldiers are evacuated back to the UK aboard giant C17s.

The rehabilitation facilities at Headley Court are among the best in the world. The top-end prosthetic limbs they supply can cost as much as £20,000.

Some will have been unconscious since the moment they were first wounded and the process of waking them up in Selly Oak's intensive care ward must be carefully managed. On first regaining consciousness, many believe they are still under fire and immediately ask for their rifle.

As the sixth step, those requiring further treatment for orthopaedic and neurological injuries are moved next to Headley Court, which hosts the famed limb-fitting and amputee centre that enables soldiers who have lost legs to learn to walk again.

Finally, in the seventh step of treatment, wounded troops leave hospital. Those unable to continue in the Armed Forces are given continuation treatment as civilians. But whenever possible, injured soldiers return to duty. In April 2008 Corporal Stuart Hale, 3 Para, became the first of several amputees to return to Helmand on an operational tour, less than two years after losing his right leg to a land mine in Kajakī.

Programmes like Battle Back work with wounded service men and women to recover their levels of fitness and take on new challenges. Lance Corporal Terry 'Tel' Byrne lost his leg in August 2008. He began training in May 2009 and on 20 October 2009 achieved a time of 1 minute 13 seconds in the 1 km time trial at the British Track Championships – a time that would have gained him 6th place at the Beijing Paralympic Games.

An Army medic, Dr Captain Sivan Sivaloganathan, in Malgir, near Lashkar Gāh.

'IT IS ALL ABOUT KEEPING THEM ALIVE'

Camp Bastion hospital

by Andy Crick

British soldiers who survive serious battle wounds in Afghanistan owe a huge debt of gratitude to everyone working at Camp Bastion's main field hospital.

Currently, the staff of one hundred and seventy medical staff, including nurses, doctors, consultants, surgeons and radiographers, deal with an average of twelve emergency patients per day, seven days a week. They serve Afghan civilians, members of the Afghan National Army and coalition troops, but the majority of their patients are members of the British Armed Forces.

In addition to its location in the middle of a desert, the fifty-bed hospital is unlike any you would visit in Britain.

Its primary function is to deal with trauma injuries sustained on the battlefield.

Surgeon Rear-Admiral Lionel Jarvis, Assistant Chief of the Defence Staff (Health), believes that amazing things occur at Camp Bastion on a daily basis. And it all started back in the spring of 2006, when it was built in just over a week.

'Building a hospital in the middle of a remote, austere, desert environment presents some challenges. It's not a matter of putting up tents, although enough for twenty-five beds could be put up in a day. You are building something that can cope with patients that are in intensive care so there are obvious issues with ensuring everything is kept sterile. But you've also got to have electricity, running water and everything that is needed to run a hospital.'

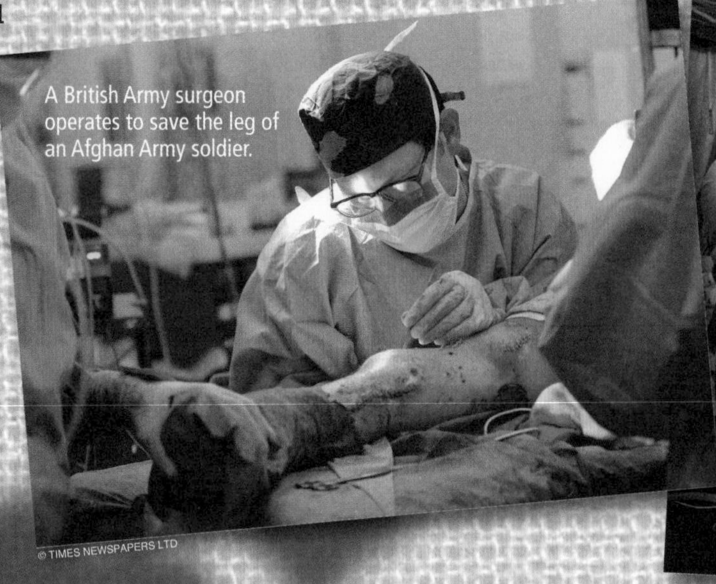
A British Army surgeon operates to save the leg of an Afghan Army soldier.

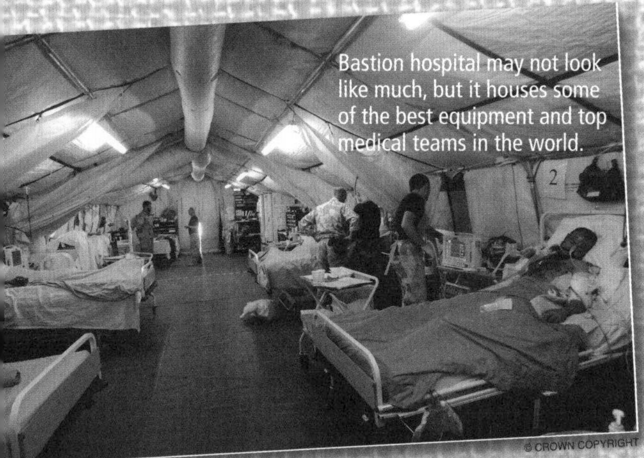
Bastion hospital may not look like much, but it houses some of the best equipment and top medical teams in the world.

© CROWN COPYRIGHT

Because of its remote location north-west of Lashkar Gāh, the capital of Helmand Province, generators are needed to power the hospital's life-saving equipment.

Rear-Admiral Jarvis said: 'It's a fifty-bed hospital and it is dedicated almost entirely to trauma. Unlike a civilian hospital, where you have got a children's ward and a general medicine ward, etc., this is primarily for battle trauma.'

But he was keen to point out that before the Camp Bastion teams can begin saving lives on the operating table, they rely on the professionalism and bravery of the medics out in the field. 'It is a team effort; it starts on the front line with the team medics and the helicopter evacuation teams. Imagine trying to save someone's life. Then add being under enemy fire, but also with the heat and dust and dirt of battle against you. These guys are doing the most heroic things.'

But despite Bastion's location, new equipment and medical advances are constantly evolving. If there is anything that can be done to help save the lives of the troops, these methods and techniques are drafted in. For example, if a soldier needs a blood transfusion, the medical teams rely on the blood donations flown over from Britain. The blood has to be kept at a constant temperature of between 20 and 24 degrees Celsius during the entire 6,000-km journey. Once the blood donation is five days old it can no longer be used, so a constant supply into Afghanistan is required.

Bastion's medical bosses are also awaiting the delivery of a second CT scanner. The vital piece of equipment will double the doctors' effectiveness in detecting injuries and ailments.

Rear-Admiral Jarvis said: 'We are using all the advances we can to give the soldiers the best chance of survival. We are really making a difference.'

Since 2003, a staggering seventy-five soldiers classified as 'unexpected survivors' have defied their prognosis by surviving life-threatening injuries. Lionel added: 'Some of these guys suffered multiple amputations and severe brain injuries. But they are walking around and more physically fit than you could ever imagine now.'

Summing up the work of Camp Bastion's doctors and nurses, Rear-Admiral Jarvis concluded: 'It is high pressure, involves incredible teamwork, often with casualties coming in at short notice. The doctors at Bastion,' he said, 'are all highly specialized and highly skilled, trained specifically in battle trauma. The pressure is to respond to saving the lives of young men, and occasionally young women, and get them back to the UK.

'It is all about keeping them alive.'

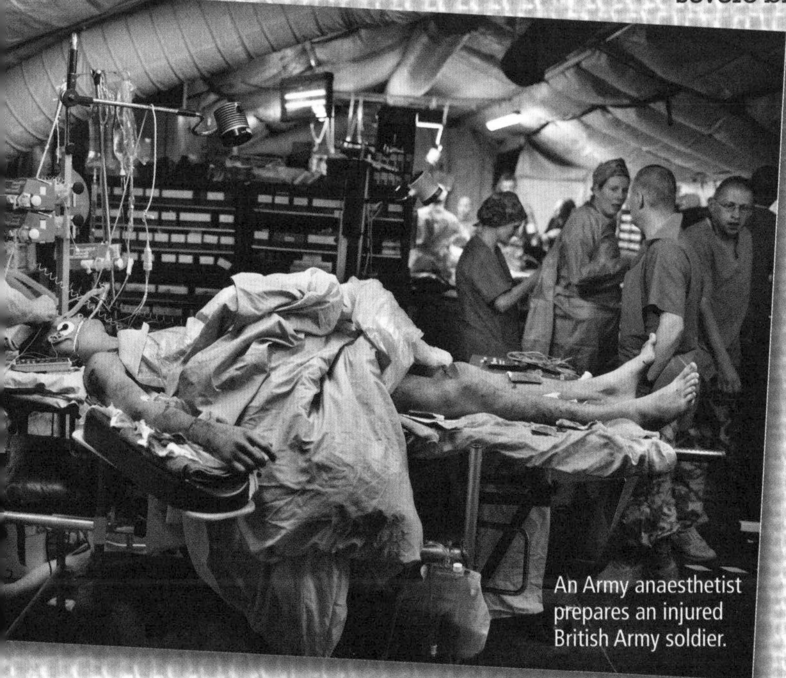
An Army anaesthetist prepares an injured British Army soldier.

© GETTY

SURVIVING THE DESERT ENVIRONMENT

Afghanistan has a continental dry climate with large differences between daytime and night-time temperatures, as well as quick seasonal changes. Summer temperatures in the plains can reach almost 50 degrees Celsius, while in the higher plateaus winter temperatures can fall to -25 degrees Celsius. The 'Winds of 120 Days', which occur between June and September, can have velocities of up to 180 km/h (108 mph). The rainy season lasts from October to April, although rainfall is very irregular.

Large areas of Afghanistan, including the Dasht-e-Margo or 'Desert of Death' that surrounds Camp Bastion, are near-desert conditions. The scorching temperatures on these hot, dusty, inhospitable plains make daily life exhausting for the heavily kitted, padded, helmeted and booted soldiers. Survival in this brutal environment is no easy matter. The survivor must learn to make the most of any available shade, to create protection from the sun and to reduce moisture loss.

WATER

Water needs are essential, and finding water is vital. If you have it, you must ration it immediately. If you are stranded due to mechanical failure during a planned desert crossing, you will have plotted your route with an awareness of available oases, wells and water holes. Wells can be very deep and the water level can require that a container be lowered on a line to reach it. Small water holes in the bottoms of wadis are often seasonal. These are usually covered with a stone or brushwood.

Away from known water holes, try digging at the lowest point on the outside bend of a dry stream bed or at the lowest point between dunes. Do not dig in the heat of the day, as the exertion will use up too much fluid and you may not find any to replace it. You

must always balance fluid loss against any possible gain. Take advantage of cacti and roots as water sources and, in deserts where the temperature range between daytime and night-time is great, use this to produce water by condensation.

LIFE EXPECTANCY

Life expectancy depends on available water, as well as your ability to protect your body from exposure to the sun to minimize perspiration. Allow a slight negative balance. Drink 1.5 litres for every 2 litres lost and then drink at the rate that the body is sweating. Efficiency is then little impaired and no water is wasted. Less fluid will not result in decreased sweating. Sweating is a cooling mechanism, not a way of losing moisture. If more fluid is drunk than is actually needed, it will be expelled from the body.

Without water, you will last about two and a half days at 48 degrees Celsius if you spend the whole time resting in the shade. However, you could last as long as twelve days if the temperature stays below 21 degrees Celsius.

If you are forced to walk to safety, the distance you are able to travel will directly relate to the water available. With none, at a temperature of 48 degrees Celsius, walking only at night and resting all day, you could cover 40 km (25 miles). Attempting to walk by day, you would be lucky to complete 8 km (5 miles) before you collapse. At the same temperature, with about 2 litres of water, you might cover a distance of 56 km (35 miles) and last for three days. Your chances are not significantly increased until available water reaches about 4.5 litres per person, although training and a determination to survive could contradict these predictions.

SHELTER AND FIRE

Make a shelter from the sun and rest in its shade. You'll also need protection from strong winds and low night-time temperatures. Do not stay in a metal vehicle or aeroplane, as it may quickly become overheated. Instead, use it to support a shelter, or make use of the shadow created by an aircraft's wing. Also utilize rock outcrops and the shadow provided by the sides of a wadi. Where temperatures are very high and shelters directly exposed to the sun, make roofs in two layers with an air space in between to aid cooling. Much of the heat will dissipate on striking the upper layer, and the air passing between the two layers lowers the temperature of the covering beneath. The distance between layers should be 20–30 cm.

DEHYDRATION

Water makes up 75 per cent of a person's body weight – about 50 litres for the average man. Survival is unlikely if more than one-fifth of this is lost. As more body fluid is lost, dehydration becomes increasingly noticeable. The following is a list of what happens to a person with increasing dehydration.

Fluid loss 1–5 per cent: Thirst, vague discomfort, lack of appetite, flushed skin, impatience, sleepiness, nausea

Fluid loss 6–10 per cent: Dizziness, headache, difficulty breathing, no salivation, indistinct speech, unable to walk

Fluid loss 11–20 per cent: Delirium, swollen tongue, unable to swallow, dim vision, numb and shrivelled skin

In the latter stages: Severe muscular weakness and impaired mental capacity. You must make any escape or survival plans when you can think clearly – and then stick to them.

FORAGING FOR FOOD

Almost any animal can provide food, and anyone lost in the desert must get used to eating unusual ones such as worms and insects.

Insects are likely to be the survivor's most reliable source of animal food. Although usually very small, they can be found almost everywhere and are often so plentiful that enough for a meal can soon be gathered.

Weight for weight, insects give more food value than vegetables. Rich in fat, protein and carbohydrates, they are life-savers, especially their larvae – those succulent grubs.

Many insects are inactive during the heat of the day, although most will emerge to collect moisture if it rains. Look for them in the tissue and seed pods of plants, as well as in any moist and shady spots. Ants' and termites' nests are often immediately recognizable mounds.

Collect only living specimens. Avoid any that look sickly or dead, have a bad smell or produce skin irritation or a rash when handled. Take care when foraging for insects. Their hiding places may also harbour unwelcome creatures, such as scorpions and spiders or, in larger crannies, snakes.

Do not gather insects feeding on refuse, carrion or dung – they are likely to carry infection. Remember that brightly coloured insects – including their caterpillars – are usually poisonous. Their bright colours are a warning sign to predators.

Most insects are edible raw and usually more nutritious that way, but they are more palatable cooked. Boiling them is safest, as it destroys harmful bacteria and parasites, but roasting them is easier if adequate containers and plentiful water are not to hand. Just place your meal on hot stones or in the embers of a fire.

Remove the legs and wings from larger insects, as hairs on insects' legs can irritate or even block the digestive tract and the fine hairs on some caterpillars can cause rashes. If you must eat a hairy caterpillar, squeeze it to extract the innards – don't eat the skin. Remove the armour-like casing from beetles.

Smaller insects such as ants and termites can be mashed into a paste and then either cooked or dried to a powder. Use this powder to thicken other food or for later eating – it will keep for some time.

Remove the wings from large termites before eating them. They can be boiled, fried or roasted, but are also more nutritious when eaten raw. Their eggs have good food value, too. A chunk of termites' nest put on the coals of a fire will produce fragrant smoke that will keep away mosquitoes and similar insects. It will smoulder all night and help to keep the fire going.

Ants quickly gather round the smallest scrap of food, where they can be collected, or you can break into a nest. Take care. Most ants have a stinging bite – go for small ones.

Many desert creatures spend the day beneath the surface, where the daytime temperature is much lower and the nights are much warmer. Sand will not permit tunneling, so you will have to make a support structure before attempting this.

Having provided yourself with immediate shade, build your shelter in the cool of the evening in order to conserve energy and fluids. Pile up rocks to make a windbreak and make use of wadi walls (except when rain and consequent flash floods seem likely).

If using fabric for your shelter walls, leave the bottom edges lifted and loose during the day to increase air circulation. At night, weigh these edges down with rocks. Avoid lying directly on the hot ground. If you make a raised bed, air is able to circulate beneath you.

You will need fire for warmth at night, as well as for boiling water. Smoke will be very noticeable: useful for signalling, but dangerous if enemy eyes are about. Desert scrub is dry and burns easily. If the land has no material for burning, vehicle fuel and oil mixed with sand in a container will burn well, otherwise use a string wick. Camel, donkey and other animal droppings also burn well.

KEEP COVERED

Do not strip off your clothes. Apart from the risk of severe sunburn, an uncovered body will lose more sweat through evaporation, which then requires even more fluid to cool it. But keep your clothes as loose as possible so that there is a layer of insulating air. Sweating will then cool you more efficiently.

FOOD

Heat usually produces a loss of appetite – so do not force yourself to eat. Foods high in protein increase both metabolic heat and water loss, and liquids are also needed for digestion. If water is scarce, keep eating to a minimum and then try to eat only moisture-containing foods, such as fruits and vegetables.

HEALTH

In the desert even the most trivial wound is likely to become infected if it is not dealt with immediately. Thorns are easily picked up and these should be pulled out as soon as possible. Where the skin is broken, a large and painful sore may develop which, if on the feet, could prevent walking. Bandage all cuts with clean dressings and use whatever medical aids are available.

Most desert illnesses are caused by excessive exposure to sun and heat. These can mostly be avoided by keeping the head and body covered and remaining in the shade until sundown. The following symptoms may appear:

Constipation and pain during urination are common, and salt-deficiency can lead to cramping.

Continued heavy sweating on the body, combined with the rubbing of clothing, can produce blockages in the sweat glands and an uncomfortable skin irritation known as prickly heat.

Heat cramps, leading to heat exhaustion, heatstroke and serious sunburn, are dangerous. A gradual increase in activity and daily exposure to the sun will build up a defence – as long as plenty of drinking water is available.

Various microorganisms attack the moist areas of the body – the crevices of the armpits, groin and between the toes. The best methods of prevention and treatment are to keep these areas clean and dry.

AIRCRAFT

UAV

A UAV, or unmanned aerial vehicle, is an aircraft that operates without a pilot or crew on board. A UAV can carry cameras, sensors, communications equipment or other payloads, including weaponry. Unlike missiles, which can only be fired once, UAVs are reusable. They're also capable of sustained flight, powered either by a jet or reciprocating engine. They come in a range of shapes and sizes and can either be remote-controlled by a pilot on the ground or flown according to pre-programmed flight plans.

C-17 GLOBEMASTER

The C-17 is a large military transport aircraft. It is used to airlift troops and cargo to main and forward operating bases across the globe and is able to deploy combat units to potential battle areas and sustain them with supplies. The C-17 was developed for the United States Air Force and is now also used by the United Kingdom, Australia, Canada, Qatar and NATO forces.

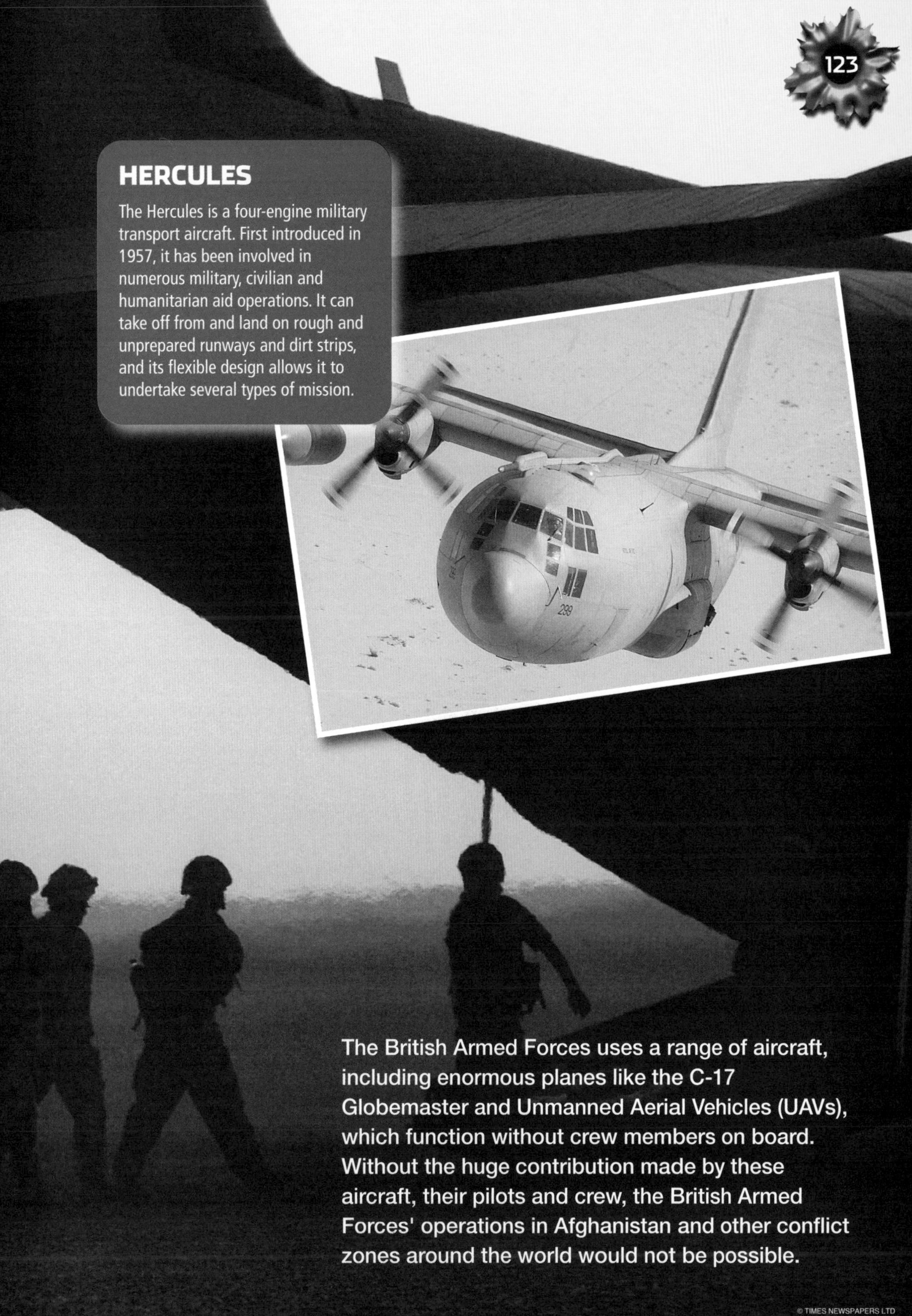

HERCULES

The Hercules is a four-engine military transport aircraft. First introduced in 1957, it has been involved in numerous military, civilian and humanitarian aid operations. It can take off from and land on rough and unprepared runways and dirt strips, and its flexible design allows it to undertake several types of mission.

The British Armed Forces uses a range of aircraft, including enormous planes like the C-17 Globemaster and Unmanned Aerial Vehicles (UAVs), which function without crew members on board. Without the huge contribution made by these aircraft, their pilots and crew, the British Armed Forces' operations in Afghanistan and other conflict zones around the world would not be possible.

HARRIER GR9

The Harrier is a British-designed military strike aircraft. It is capable of vertical and/or short take-off and landing (V/STOL), using a system of power known as thrust vectoring. This involves directing the thrust from the jet's main engines in directions other than parallel to the ground. The jet's thrust – which measures between 21,800 and 24,750 lbf – can therefore be directed towards the ground to allow the jet to 'jump' straight up into the air. The thrust can also be manipulated to allow various manoeuvres during combat situations. The Harrier can take off and land using airfields and even smaller aircraft carriers at sea. It combines the best aspects of a helicopter with those of a fighter jet and can fly at a blistering 1,177 km/h (730 mph).

TORNADO GR4

The Harrier jet is being replaced in Afghanistan by the Tornado GR4. This is a two-seater, day or night, all-weather attack aircraft, capable of delivering a wide variety of weapons. Powered by two engines, the GR4 is equipped with a laser ranger and a marked target-seeker system that provides accurate information on ground targets. It also carries a range of bombs and missiles as well as a Mauser cannon that can fire up to 1,700 rounds per minute.

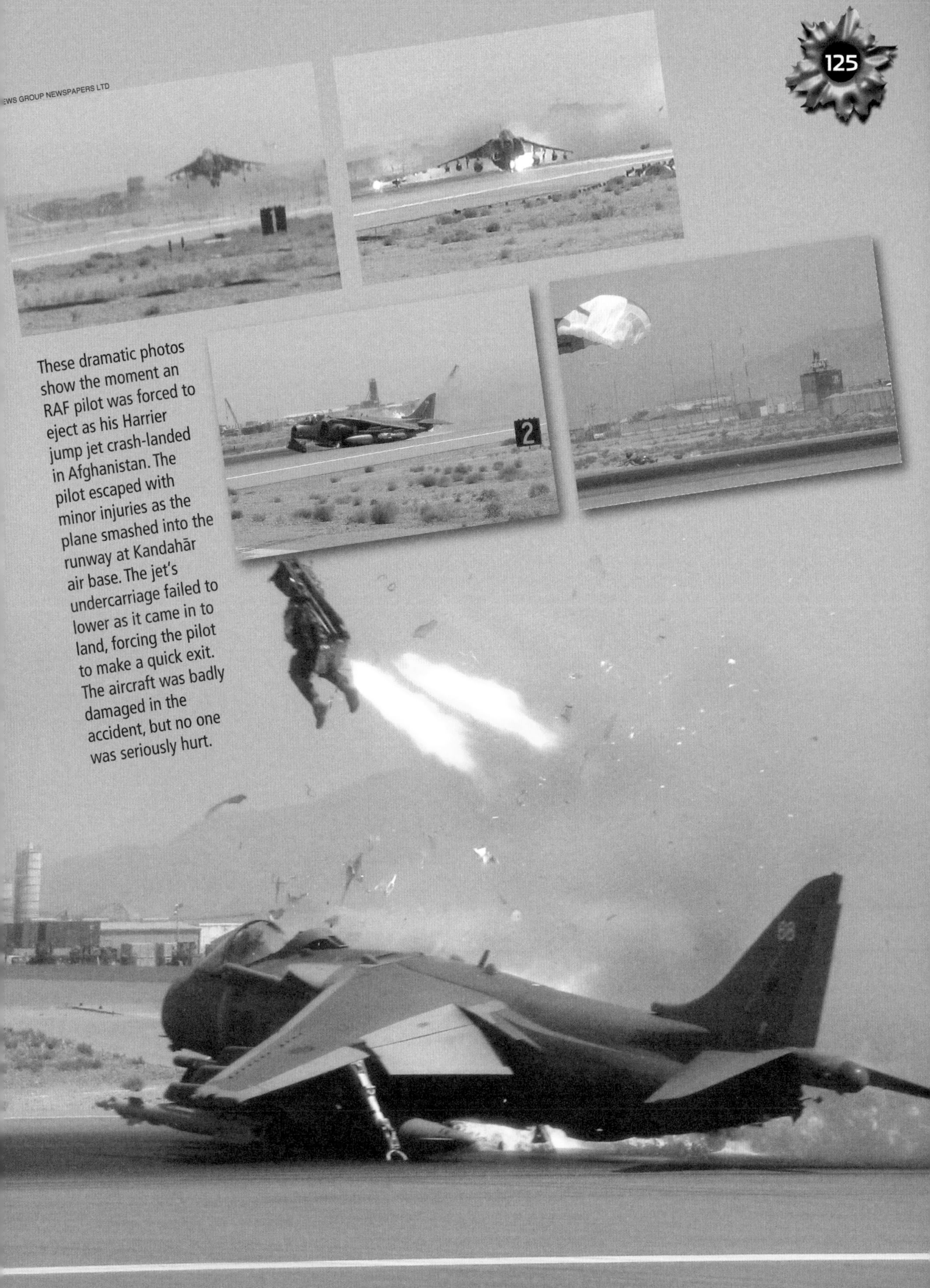

These dramatic photos show the moment an RAF pilot was forced to eject as his Harrier jump jet crash-landed in Afghanistan. The pilot escaped with minor injuries as the plane smashed into the runway at Kandahār air base. The jet's undercarriage failed to lower as it came in to land, forcing the pilot to make a quick exit. The aircraft was badly damaged in the accident, but no one was seriously hurt.

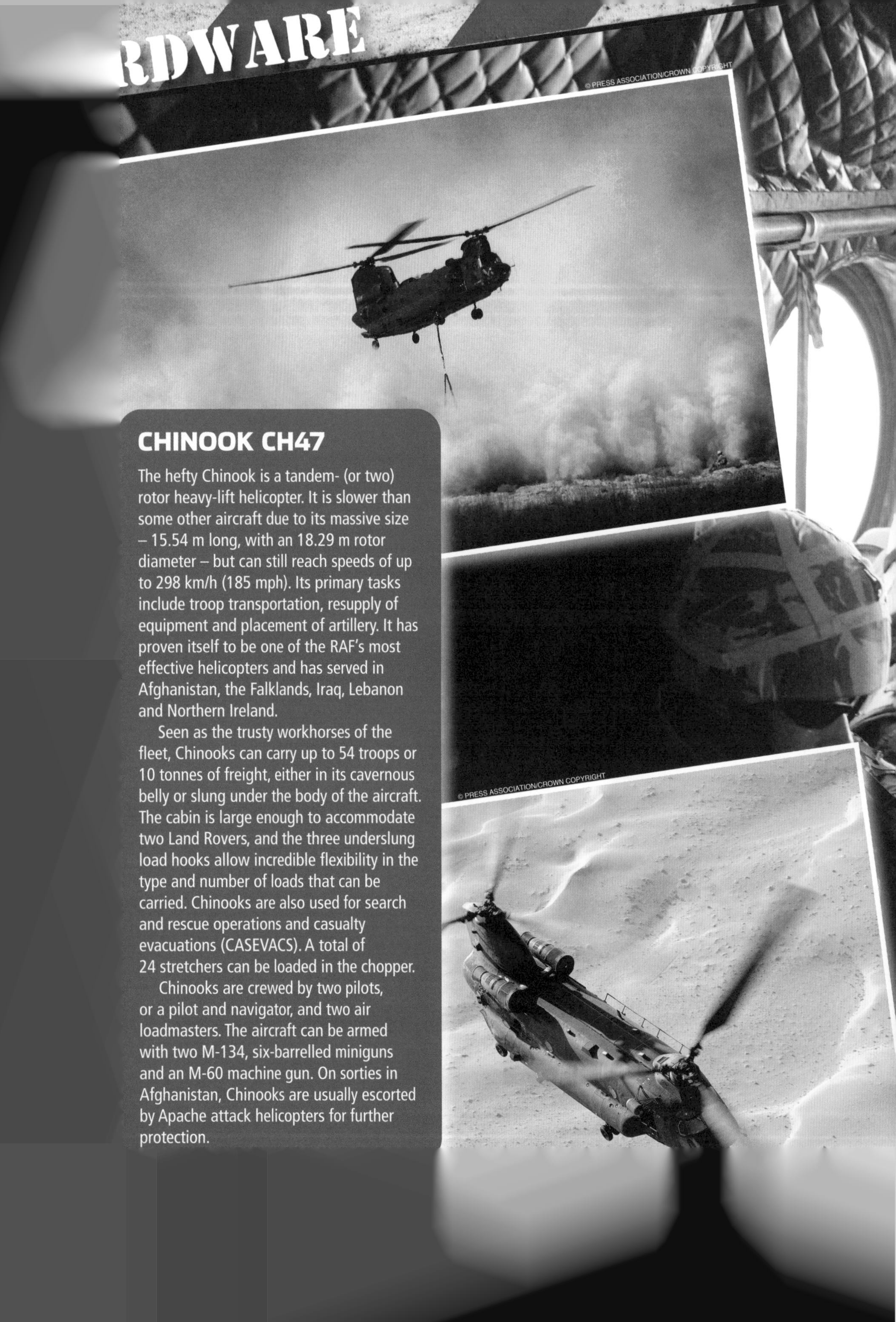

CHINOOK CH47

The hefty Chinook is a tandem- (or two) rotor heavy-lift helicopter. It is slower than some other aircraft due to its massive size – 15.54 m long, with an 18.29 m rotor diameter – but can still reach speeds of up to 298 km/h (185 mph). Its primary tasks include troop transportation, resupply of equipment and placement of artillery. It has proven itself to be one of the RAF's most effective helicopters and has served in Afghanistan, the Falklands, Iraq, Lebanon and Northern Ireland.

Seen as the trusty workhorses of the fleet, Chinooks can carry up to 54 troops or 10 tonnes of freight, either in its cavernous belly or slung under the body of the aircraft. The cabin is large enough to accommodate two Land Rovers, and the three underslung load hooks allow incredible flexibility in the type and number of loads that can be carried. Chinooks are also used for search and rescue operations and casualty evacuations (CASEVACS). A total of 24 stretchers can be loaded in the chopper.

Chinooks are crewed by two pilots, or a pilot and navigator, and two air loadmasters. The aircraft can be armed with two M-134, six-barrelled miniguns and an M-60 machine gun. On sorties in Afghanistan, Chinooks are usually escorted by Apache attack helicopters for further protection.

MERLIN

The Merlin is the first of a new generation of advanced, medium support helicopters used by the RAF. It is an all-weather, day and night, multi-role aircraft with one of the most comprehensive defensive aid suites fitted to any helicopter in the world. This suite includes a radar and laser warning receiver, missile approach warners and directional infrared countermeasures equipment. To increase its range, the Merlin is equipped with extended-range fuel tanks and is capable of air-to-air refuelling. The Merlin is able to carry a range of bulky cargo – either internally or slung beneath the body of the aircraft – including everything from artillery to Land Rovers or light-strike vehicles, and over 5 tonnes of freight. The spacious cabin can also accommodate up to 24 fully equipped combat troops and, when required, will convert to carry 16 stretchers for CASEVACS. The Merlin will be in use in Afghanistan by the end of 2009.

© ED MACY

'You do not need to ask them about their contribution, you need to ask those on the ground who depended on them, day after day, to provide the crucial military edge over the enemy. They will leave you in no doubt about what the Apache achieved, and the praise of the praiseworthy is beyond measure.' AIR CHIEF MARSHAL SIR JOCK STIRRUP, CHIEF OF DEFENCE STAFF

APACHE

Crew: 2
Cruise speed: At 500 m, 272 km/h (169 mph)
Armament: Carries 16 x Hellfire II missiles (range of 6,000 m approx.)
76 x 2.75 rockets
1,200 x 30 mm cannon rounds
4 x air-to-air missiles
Engines: 2 x Rolls Royce RTM-332
The Apache attack helicopter is one of the most fearsome fighting machines in existence. A twin-engine, four-blade attack helicopter, it is the world's most technically advanced helicopter and one of the most difficult to fly. The Apache can operate in all weather, day or night. It proved pivotal in Afghanistan in the 2007 rescue mission known as Operation Jugroom Fort.

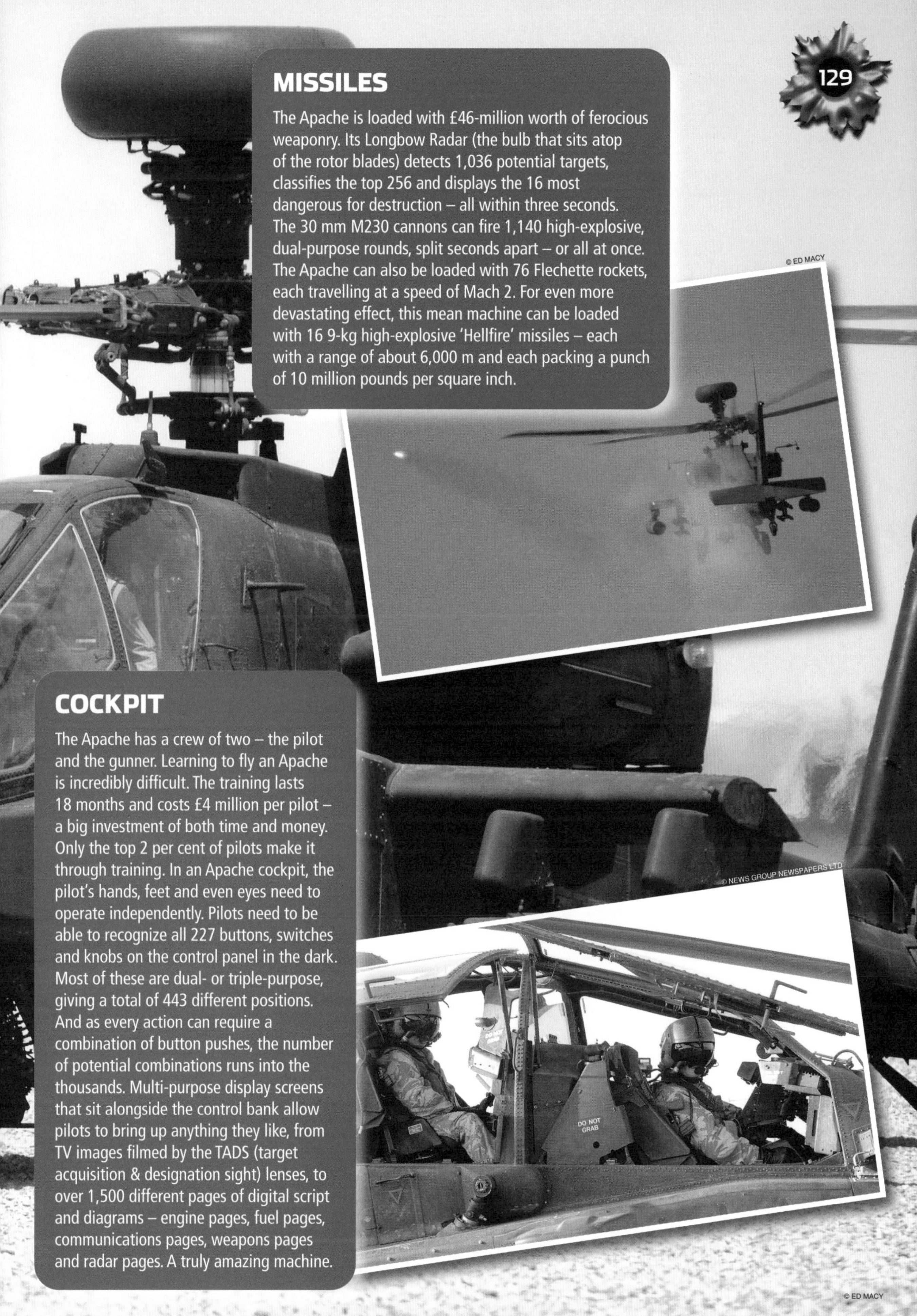

MISSILES

The Apache is loaded with £46-million worth of ferocious weaponry. Its Longbow Radar (the bulb that sits atop of the rotor blades) detects 1,036 potential targets, classifies the top 256 and displays the 16 most dangerous for destruction – all within three seconds. The 30 mm M230 cannons can fire 1,140 high-explosive, dual-purpose rounds, split seconds apart – or all at once. The Apache can also be loaded with 76 Flechette rockets, each travelling at a speed of Mach 2. For even more devastating effect, this mean machine can be loaded with 16 9-kg high-explosive 'Hellfire' missiles – each with a range of about 6,000 m and each packing a punch of 10 million pounds per square inch.

COCKPIT

The Apache has a crew of two – the pilot and the gunner. Learning to fly an Apache is incredibly difficult. The training lasts 18 months and costs £4 million per pilot – a big investment of both time and money. Only the top 2 per cent of pilots make it through training. In an Apache cockpit, the pilot's hands, feet and even eyes need to operate independently. Pilots need to be able to recognize all 227 buttons, switches and knobs on the control panel in the dark. Most of these are dual- or triple-purpose, giving a total of 443 different positions. And as every action can require a combination of button pushes, the number of potential combinations runs into the thousands. Multi-purpose display screens that sit alongside the control bank allow pilots to bring up anything they like, from TV images filmed by the TADS (target acquisition & designation sight) lenses, to over 1,500 different pages of digital script and diagrams – engine pages, fuel pages, communications pages, weapons pages and radar pages. A truly amazing machine.

RED DAGGER

IN DECEMBER 2008, THE BRITISH-LED TASK FORCE HELMAND LAUNCHED A MASSIVE OPERATION TO CLEAR AND SECURE A LARGE AREA OF CENTRAL HELMAND THAT HAD BEEN UNDER TALIBAN CONTROL, WEST OF THE MAJOR HELMAND TOWN OF LASHKAR GĀH. FIGHTING IN RAIN AND MUD, THE OFFENSIVE INVOLVED 1,500 BRITISH, ESTONIAN AND DANISH TROOPS. THE OPERATION WAS CODE-NAMED **RED DAGGER**, AFTER THE COMMANDO PATCH WORN BY MEMBERS OF 3 COMMANDO BRIGADE ROYAL MARINES. THE TROOPS CAME UNDER CONTINUOUS ATTACKS AS THEY FOUGHT HEAD ON WITH THE ENEMY IN QUAGMIRE TERRAIN SUPPORTED IN THE AIR BY ATTACK HELICOPTERS AND ON THE GROUND BY LEOPARD TANKS. IT CERTAINLY WASN'T A WALK IN THE PARK...

UNDER COVER OF DARKNESS THE TROOPS ADVANCE TOWARDS ENEMY POSITIONS.
FSG, WE'RE GOING TO NEED MORTARS AHEAD OF US.

ROGER THAT, BOSS! THIS SHOULD KEEP THEIR HEADS DOWN. FIRE!

ALL TROOPS ADVANCE! STAY WELL BEHIND THE LEOPARDS - WE DON'T KNOW HOW MANY OF THEM ARE WAITING FOR US...
HANG BACK, PRIVATE! LET'S GIVE THEM A BIT OF A POUNDING BEFORE WE RUSH IN!
YES, SIR!
THE TANK TAKES AIM...

...AND FIRES!
BOOM!
IT'S A DIRECT HIT! OK LADS, GO, GO!

THE CHARGING LEOPARD TEARS ACROSS THE MOONLIT LANDSCAPE WITH AN ANGRY ROAR.

THE TALIBAN, SHOCKED AT THE SPEED WITH WHICH THE DANISH TANKS RACE TOWARDS THEM, DESPERATELY FIRE THEIR AK-47S. THE BULLETS PING HARMLESSLY OFF THE HEAVY ARMOUR.
AARGH!

A FIGHTER TAKES AIM WITH AN RPG...

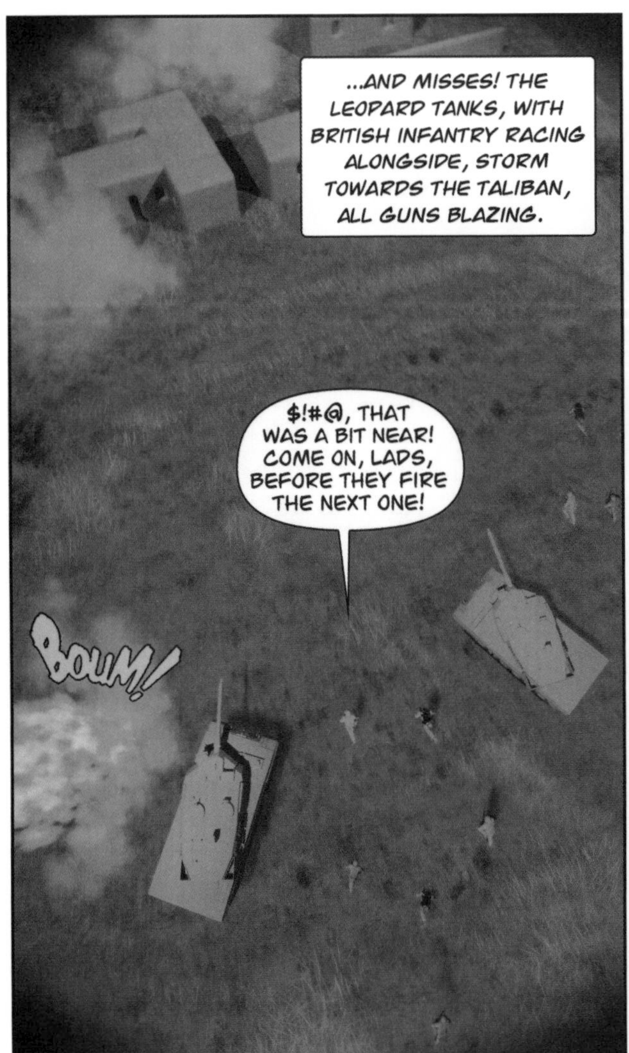
...AND MISSES! THE LEOPARD TANKS, WITH BRITISH INFANTRY RACING ALONGSIDE, STORM TOWARDS THE TALIBAN, ALL GUNS BLAZING.
$!#@, THAT WAS A BIT NEAR! COME ON, LADS, BEFORE THEY FIRE THE NEXT ONE!
BOUM!

DESPERATE TO BREAK UP THE ASSAULT, A TALIBAN FIGHTER SETS UP A CHINESE-MADE 107 MM ROCKET.

18.8 KG OF TNT HURTLES TOWARDS THE ONCOMING DANISH TANKS.
FZZZ

ANOTHER MISS!
DET VAR FOR TOET!*
*THAT WAS A CLOSE ONE!

THE LEOPARD SLAMS A DEVASTATING VOLLEY OF 120 MM HIGH EXPLOSIVE SHELLS INTO THE TALIBAN POSITIONS.
NICE SHOT, LEOPARD 47! RIGHT ON TARGET.

THE INFANTRY APPROACH THE COMPOUND.
LOOKS LIKE THEY'RE ALL DEAD OR THEY'VE LEGGED IT.
ALL CLEAR!
DON'T BLAME THEM. I WOULDN'T FANCY BEING ON THE WRONG END OF THAT TANK GUN.

THE FOLLOWING MORNING THE TROOPS SUSPEND THEIR ATTACKS FOR TWO DAYS OUT OF RESPECT FOR THE MUSLIM RELIGIOUS FESTIVAL OF EID AL-ADHA. ACROSS THE REGION, THE MUSLIM FAITHFUL COMMEMORATE IBRAHIM'S WILLINGNESS TO SACRIFICE HIS SON, ISMAEL, ACCORDING TO GOD'S WILL.
THE TROOPS, MEANWHILE, ENJOY THE SUDDEN CALM. THEY KNOW IT WON'T LAST.

WITH THE GUNS SILENT, THE UK FORCES USE THE TIME TO PREPARE FOR THEIR NEXT MISSION.
STRANGE SEEING IT ALL SO QUIET... I WONDER WHAT IT MUST HAVE BEEN LIKE HERE BEFORE ALL THIS...

I DON'T MIND TELLING YOU, I'M NOT SORRY WE'VE GOT A CHANCE FOR A BIT OF A BREATHER.
YEAH, THAT WAS A REAL BLOWER LAST NIGHT. I'M GOING TO GET MY NUT DOWN IN A MINUTE, I'M TOTALLY KNACKERED.

BUT IT ISN'T LONG BEFORE THE CALL TO ACTION COMES THROUGH ONCE MORE.

ON THE NIGHT OF 11 DECEMBER, 42 COMMANDO GROUP, ROYAL MARINES, LAUNCH A HELICOPTER ASSAULT. OPERATION 'RED DAGGER' IS NOW WELL AND TRULY UNDERWAY...

AS THE HEAVY CHINOOKS POUND THROUGH THE DARKENED SKY, A GROUND ATTACK NORTH WEST OF LASHKAR GĀH IS LAUNCHED.

KEEP CLOSE TOGETHER, LADS!

OVERHEAD, NATO AIRCRAFT AND APACHE ATTACK HELICOPTERS MAINTAIN A THREATENING PRESENCE.
THIS IS UGLY 27, I HAVE YOUR MEN IN SIGHT. HORIZON LOOKS CLEAR.
ROGER THAT, UGLY 27.

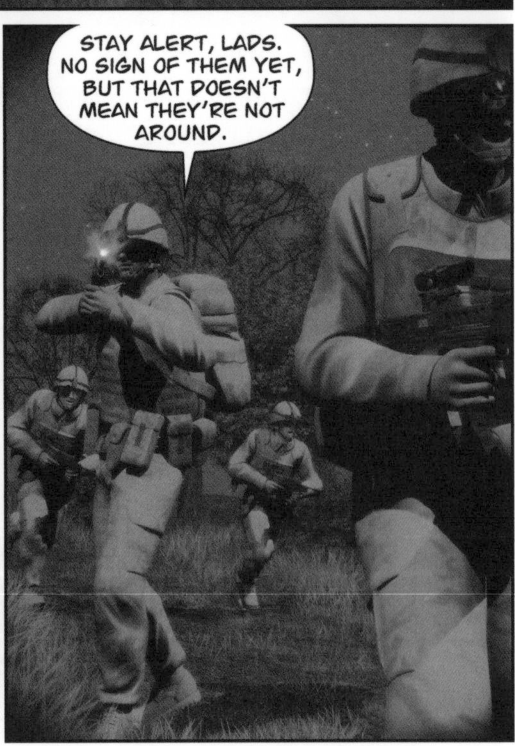

STAY ALERT, LADS. NO SIGN OF THEM YET, BUT THAT DOESN'T MEAN THEY'RE NOT AROUND.

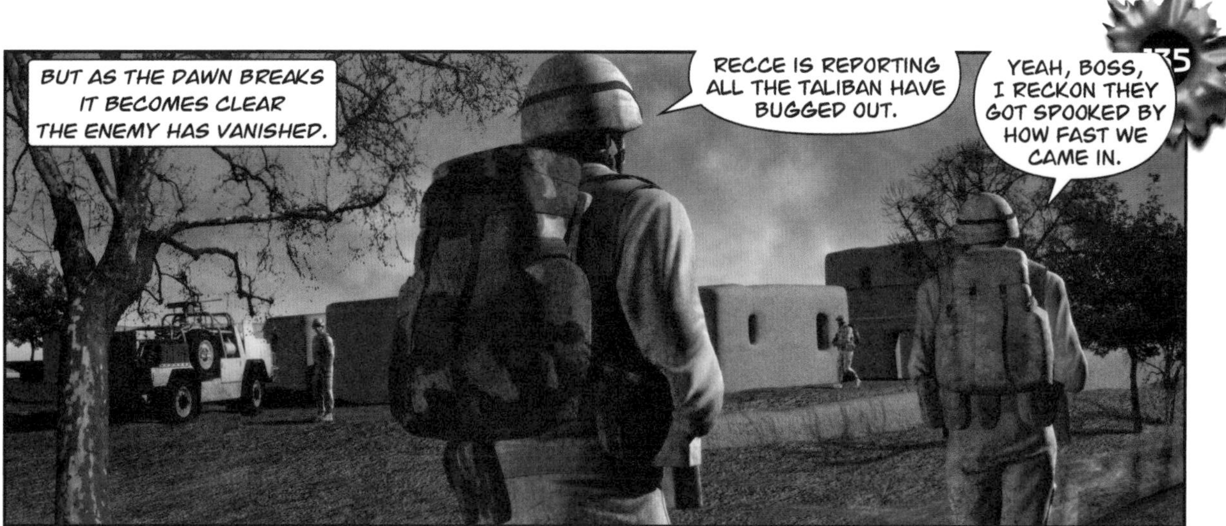
BUT AS THE DAWN BREAKS IT BECOMES CLEAR THE ENEMY HAS VANISHED.
RECCE IS REPORTING ALL THE TALIBAN HAVE BUGGED OUT.
YEAH, BOSS, I RECKON THEY GOT SPOOKED BY HOW FAST WE CAME IN.

EAGER TO MAINTAIN THE ADVANTAGE, THE TROOPS PRESS ON. THERE ARE A FEW FRANTIC POT-SHOTS FROM THE RETREATING TALIBAN...
LOOK OUT! INCOMING FIRE FROM THE WADI! TAKE COVER!
I'M ON HIM...
COME ON, MEN, WE'VE GOT THEM ON THE BACKFOOT.

...BUT THE ADVANCE IS TOO FAST AND THE ENEMY HAVE NO TIME TO SET UP DEFENCES.
GOT HIM! LOOKS LIKE IT WAS JUST THE ONE...

HOW LONG D'YOU RECKON WE'VE GOT BEFORE THEY RETALIATE?
NOT LONG, I RECKON. THEY'RE NOT GOING TO LIKE US SETTING UP CAMP, THAT'S FOR SURE.
OK LADS, WE'LL SET UP A PERIMETER HERE, THE ENGINEERS ARE AN HOUR BEHIND US. LET'S HAVE EVERYTHING NICE AND READY FOR THEM, EH? PUSH RIGHT OUT AND COVER YOUR ARCS.

THAT NIGHT THE SKIES OPEN AND THE RAIN POUNDS DOWN.
BLOODY RAIN...BLOODY MUD...BLOODY MISERABLE!
AH, STOW IT, JONESY. LET'S JUST GET THE DAMN THING UP.
THE DIRT COMPOUND THE TROOPS HAVE CHOSEN AS AN FOB* IS SOON LITTLE MORE THAN A MUDDY PIT.
*FORWARD OPERATING BASE

THE TALIBAN ATTACK AGAIN AND AGAIN, DESPERATE TO STOP THE BASE BEING BUILT.
INCOMING!

BLOODY HELL, NOT AGAIN! BOSS, WE'VE GOT CONTACT IN THE GREEN ZONE - AGAIN!

IN RECORD TIME, THE HESCO WALLS GO UP. BUT EVEN WITH THE THICK PROTECTIVE BARRIER IN PLACE, THE TALIBAN PERSIST...

CONTACT! TAKE COVER! BASE, THIS IS 5 PLATOON – WE'RE TAKING HEAVY FIRE!
BLOODY HELL, THAT'S THE THIRD ATTACK THIS MORNING! THEY REALLY WANT THIS GROUND BACK.
HNH-!

RIGHT, WE'RE GOING IN, LADS. BASE, I NEED 3 PLATOON UP HERE!
BETTER GET 'EM HERE QUICK, BOSS. I CAN SEE MORE OF THEM UNDER THE TREES.

AS THE RAIN PICKS UP ONCE MORE, THE TROOPS RUSH OUT, FORCING THE TALIBAN AWAY FROM THE BASE.

THE DOWNPOUR LETS UP...
KEEP IT UP LADS, WE'VE GOT TO KEEP THEM ON THE BACK FOOT.

...BUT NOT FOR LONG. AS NIGHT FALLS, THE HEAVENS OPEN ONCE MORE. GRIMLY, THE TROOPS PRESS ON.
GOOD THING WE DID ALL THAT DESERT TRAINING, EH BAZ?!

IT'S MORE LIKE BLOODY WALES THAN WHAT I EXPECTED IN AFGHANISTAN.
TOO RIGHT. I CAN'T SEE A THING IN THIS MESS.
HANG IN THERE, LADS!

THE BANTER KEEPS THEIR SPIRITS UP AS THE WEATHER WORSENS AND THE MEN, THEIR BOOTS CAKED IN HEAVY MUD, TRUDGE ON.

REST STOPS ARE FEW AND FAR BETWEEN. WHEN THEY DO PAUSE FOR A MOMENT, THE TROOPS SLEEP WHERE THEY FALL - IN THE MUD OF FLEA-RIDDEN COMPOUNDS AND SOGGY DITCHES THAT OFFER LITTLE COVER FROM EITHER ELEMENTS OR THE ENEMY.

OK LADS, I KNOW YOU'VE ONLY HAD HALF AN HOUR'S REST, BUT WE'RE MOVING OUT.
GROAN. ALREADY?

WITH THE FIRST LIGHT OF DAY, A BREAK IN THE WEATHER HERALDS A FRESH ATTACK.
KEEP AS LOW AS YOU CAN, LADS! THOSE BULLETS ARE COMING IN CLOSE.
HUH, HUH!

$@?*! THAT MISSED YOU BY INCHES, BOSS! WHEN THE HELL DID THEIR FIRE GET SO ACCURATE?!

THERE THEY ARE! EYES ON THE ENEMY AT TWO HUNDRED METRES! GET SOME FIRE DOWN!

JIM, KEEP ENGAGING THEM FROM HERE. THE REST OF YOU, WE'RE GOING RIGHT, FLANKING UP THIS DITCH.
GOT YOU, SIR!

FOLLOW ME! KEEP LOW! MORTARS, YOU KNOW WHAT TO DO. GIVE THEM SOMETHING TO THINK ABOUT AND KEEP US COVERED!

A NEARBY MORTAR TEAM LOADS A MORTAR AND...
FIRE!

...MORTAR SHELLS EXPLODE OVER ONE OF THE TALIBAN GROUPS, FLINGING SHARDS OF RED-HOT SHRAPNEL IN EVERY DIRECTION.
DIRECT HIT! GOOD SHOT, DAVEY!

THAT'S TWO DOWN, BUT THEY'RE BLOODY EVERYWHERE!
SCAN YOUR ARCS, LADS! WE NEED TO SPOT THESE GUYS FAST.
BUT FOR EVERY ENEMY FIGHTER WHO FALLS, TWO MORE SPRING UP.

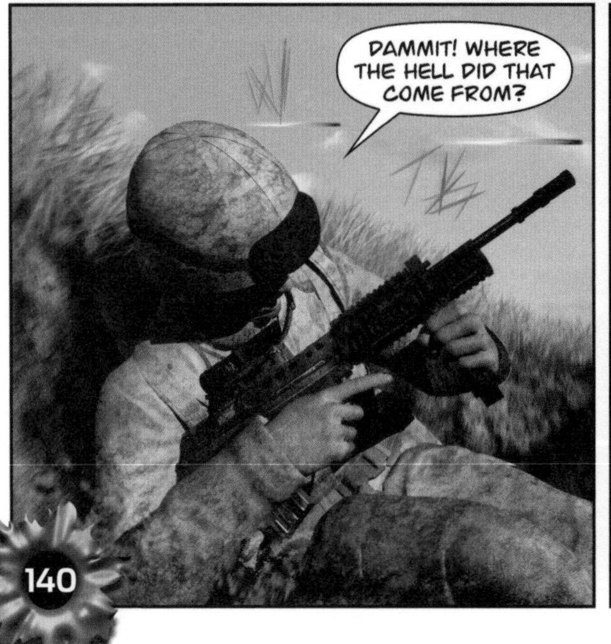
DAMMIT! WHERE THE HELL DID THAT COME FROM?

RAPID FIRE, LADS, THEY'RE ATTACKING FROM EVERY DIRECTION!
HQ, THIS IS 5 PLATOON, WE NEED BACKUP NOW! THEY'VE GOT US PINNED!

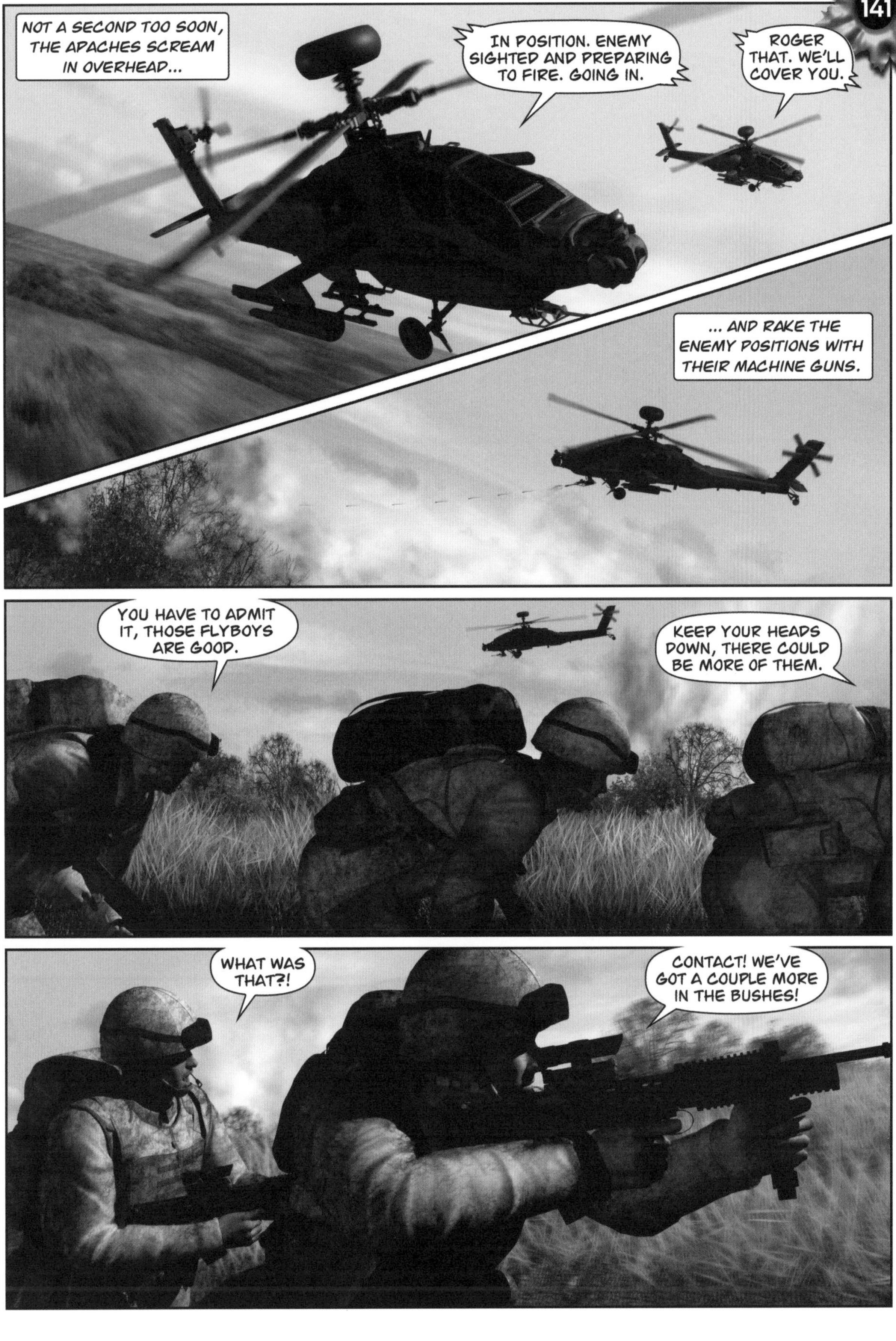

NOT A SECOND TOO SOON, THE APACHES SCREAM IN OVERHEAD...

IN POSITION. ENEMY SIGHTED AND PREPARING TO FIRE. GOING IN.

ROGER THAT. WE'LL COVER YOU.

... AND RAKE THE ENEMY POSITIONS WITH THEIR MACHINE GUNS.

CLOSE IN AND GET DOWN!
I DON'T BELIEVE IT, THESE GUYS JUST KEEP COMING!
DAVEY, GET THAT APACHE BACK HERE!

THERE THEY ARE...
BLOODY HELL, BOSS, THEY'RE CLOSE!

DELTA FIRE TEAM, ENGAGE FROM HERE. CHARLIE FIRE TEAM, PEEL OFF AND ASSAULT FROM THE RIGHT. GOT IT?
GOT IT!

AARGH!
KEEP LAYING THAT FIRE DOWN! GO! GO!

WE'LL KEEP THEM BUSY - GO! GO!
COME ON LADS, WE'VE GOT TO MOVE ROUND FAST AND ASSAULT THEM!

FOCUSED ON THE BATTLE IN FRONT OF THEM, THE TALIBAN FAIL TO NOTICE THE TROOPS FLANKING THEM UNTIL...

ATTACK!

RAAGH!
FIRE!

GOT THEM!
HNH-!
UGH-!

THE SURVIVING TALIBAN TRY TO ESCAPE - BUT ARE CUT DOWN BY THE FIERCE FIREPOWER OF THE APACHE.
OH NO YOU BLOODY DON'T... YOU'RE NOT GOING ANYWHERE!

WEEKS AFTER THE INITIAL ASSAULT, EARLY ON CHRISTMAS MORNING, THE KEY TALIBAN STRONGHOLD OF CHAH-E-ANJIR FALLS TO BRITISH FORCES.
WE'RE IN! WELL DONE MEN.

ELSEWHERE, TROOPS CAPTURE FOUR OTHER TALIBAN SAFE HAVENS.
WHAT A WAY TO SPEND CHRISTMAS!
YEAH, I CAN THINK OF A FEW BETTER THINGS TO DO, NO QUESTION.

MISSION ACCOMPLISHED, LADS, WE DID IT.

IT'S WITH MIXED FEELINGS THAT THE TROOPS HEAD BACK TO BASE AT LASHKAR GĀH – 'LASH VEGAS'. THEY HAVE WON AN IMPORTANT VICTORY: 180 SQUARE KILOMETRES CLEARED OF TALIBAN IN TWO WEEKS OF HARD FIGHTING. THE LOCAL PEOPLE WILL LIVE MORE SAFELY, BUT VICTORY CAME AT A COST. FIVE MARINES WERE KILLED DURING THE OPERATION.

AS THE SUN SETS ON CHRISTMAS DAY, THE TROOPS WHO FOUGHT IN **RED DAGGER** HAVE MUCH TO BE THANKFUL FOR – AND MUCH TO REMEMBER IN THE FIVE COMRADES WHO NEVER MADE IT BACK.

THE REAL DOGS OF WAR

Sometimes the most courageous soldiers of all aren't even human. Occasionally it's man's brave best friend who steps into the fray to serve and protect. Throughout history, dogs, cats, horses, and even pigeons, have played an important part in military campaigns across the globe, boosting front-line morale and saving the lives of troops.

Take **Treo**, for example. A seven-year-old black Labrador, Treo is regarded as one of the most exceptional Arms Explosive Search Dogs ever to serve in the British Army.

Deployed with other dogs to Afghanistan in March, he was the quickest to adapt to the extreme temperatures and was immediately sent forward to Sangin to join the troops of the 2nd Battalion, the Parachute Regiment, patrolling the hazardous Helmand Province badlands.

Treo made several significant finds of Taliban explosives, including a 'daisy chain' series of hidden bombs which would have killed or maimed many soldiers if it had been left undetected.

And Treo's not the only one. In the perilous battlefields of Afghanistan, five-year-old springer spaniel **Pip** is always leading from the front.

Pip and his handler, Lance Corporal Debbie Caffull, are often the first into a danger zone, searching for the hidden explosive devices that haunt British Army patrols.

When five thousand troops supported a hazardous mission in August 2008 to transport a massive turbine through bandit country to the Kajakī Dam in Helmand, Pip was once more at the forefront, checking the route. Major Chris Ham said: 'They were in the convoy for twelve [hours] solid, in the vehicles … and right at the front of the [convoy] looking for IEDs.'

Another amazing animal assisting on the front line is sniffer dog **Jamie**, who fought the Taliban for almost three years, nearly triple the time of his longest-serving human comrades.

The nine-year-old springer spaniel became a legend among British soldiers in Helmand, as he used his ultra-powerful nose to search over eighty lorries a day for hidden weapons and explosives.

Handler Lance Corporal Jim Wilkinson said: 'Jamie's awesome – the best dog I've ever worked with. Even after three years he [was] so enthusiastic, which makes him a dream to work with. It takes everything I've got to slow him down. His service has been outstanding. He's a true credit to the Army.'

Jamie was recruited after being dumped at a rescue centre as a pup. Also a veteran of Iraq, Northern Ireland and Kosovo, he has now retired from active service – and is helping teach other pooches his skills.

By Tom Newton Dunn

PROUD POOCH

A heroic pooch won an animal Victoria Cross for sniffing out a hidden terrorist bomb, then sitting by it until help arrived.

Black Labrador **Sadie** saved scores of troops by finding the primed package in Kabul. The bomb was planted as a secondary device to maim and kill rescue workers and troops at the scene of an earlier blast.

Animal charity PDSA (People's Dispensary for Sick Animals) nominated Sadie for the Dickin Medal. It is only the sixty-first time the highest gong for non-humans has been awarded since its creation in 1943.

The medal is recognized as the animals' equivalent of the Victoria Cross.

By Tom Newton Dunn

Corporal Dave Heyhoe and Treo, LEFT, at work with other members of the Working Dog Support Unit.

The War on Drugs

By Patrick Bishop

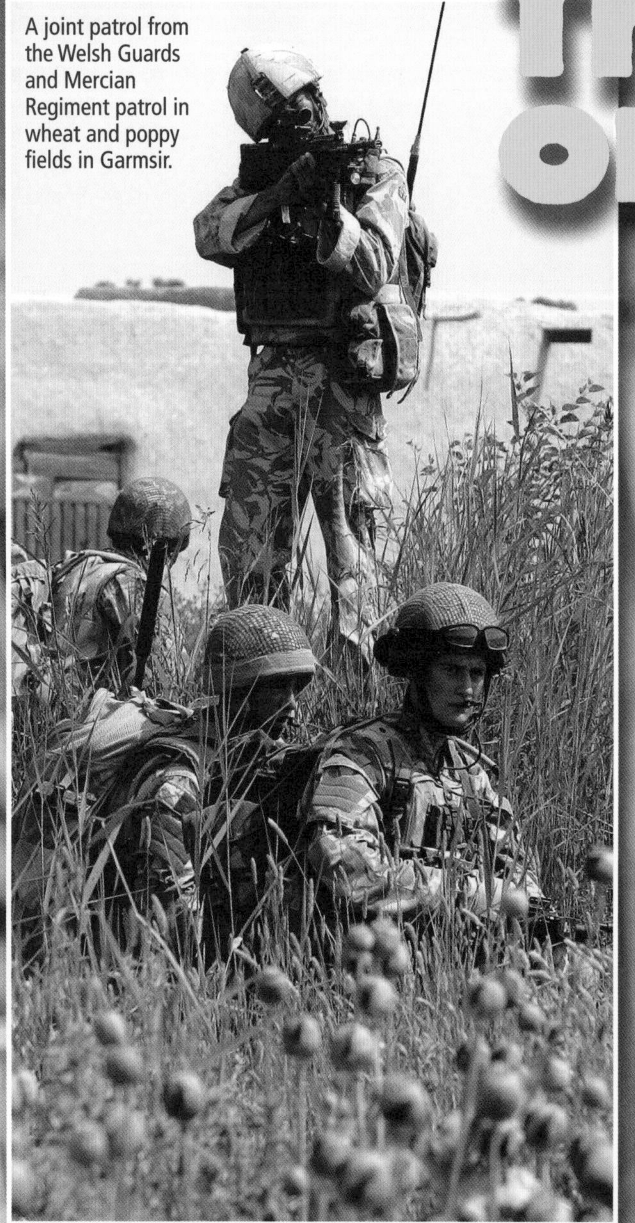

A joint patrol from the Welsh Guards and Mercian Regiment patrol in wheat and poppy fields in Garmsir.

An Afghan National policeman looks on while a drugs stash is destroyed.

When British troops were sent to Helmand Province in 2006, one of the many tasks set for them was to help stamp out the thriving drugs trade. It was clear from the outset that this would be easier said than done. The province was poor and many farmers grew opium poppies to earn money to feed their families. The purpose of the military operation was to win the support of the local people. Destroying their crops seemed like a sure recipe for turning them against the soldiers, who had arrived claiming that they had come to improve the farmers' lives. At meetings (*shuras*) with local leaders, the soldiers stressed that they were not planning to take away locals' livelihoods. In any case, the small number of troops were too busy fighting off constant Taliban attacks to deal with the drugs problem.

The result was that British soldiers found themselves patrolling through fields of multicoloured poppies while men, women and children busily scraped away the resin that would eventually end up as heroin on the streets of cities around the globe.

However, it was clear that sooner or later the opium trade would have to be tackled. Afghanistan is by far the world's largest supplier of heroin. It is estimated that 93 per cent of the heroin that reaches Britain comes from Afghan poppy fields. In addition, the profits made from drug trafficking are powering the insurgency. The Taliban are intimately involved in every stage of the business, which was estimated to be worth £2 billion in 2008. With this money, the Taliban buy weapons and vehicles and recruit gunmen from the local communities to fight alongside them for £6 a day – a good wage in a poor country. This money is also used to bribe politicians, judges and policemen to leave the Taliban alone. One of the biggest problems of the war on drugs is that many Afghan officials are themselves heavily involved.

Ultimately, it is up to the Afghans themselves to wipe out the drugs trade. In the meantime, though, British troops have been busy targeting the drug manufacturers and dealers rather than the farmers. In February 2009 the Royal Marines launched Operation Diesel to smash the Taliban drug set-up in Helmand's Upper Sangin Valley. The wave of helicopter assaults took the insurgents completely by surprise.

'The Taliban were confused and completely overmatched by our tactics,' said Sergeant Tony Dryden of Lima Company, 42 Commando Group. 'Our scheme of manoueuvre was completely fantastic. I have never seen anything like it, as they were on the back foot and unable to cope throughout.' The soldiers discovered more than 1,230 kilograms of raw opium and dismantled a big laboratory being used to turn it into heroin. Many more labs were also destroyed.

A collection of heroin, snagged in a counter-narcotics raid.

A soldier from 2 Para patrols through a flowering poppy field.

At the same time, British soldiers have been involved in the drive to get farmers to turn to legal crops. They helped the Afghan Army distribute 3,200 tonnes of wheat seed for planting. The result has been that poppy cultivation has fallen by more than one-third in the province.

There remain no easy victories in the fight against drugs. As opium production fell in Helmand, it was increasing by the same amount in neighbouring Kandahār Province. There is still a very long way to go before Afghanistan is free from the grip of drugs.

Patrick Bishop is the bestselling author of *3 Para* and *Ground Truth*. Find out more at www. patrickbishop.net.

'WE WALK TEN FEET TALL'

Leading the Army for the past three years has been a great honour, both inspiring and humbling.

We have achieved much on operations – which has, tragically, come at a high price.

When our soldiers return, it fills me with pride to see crowds lining streets across the country to welcome them home.

In times of intensive fighting in Afghanistan, this support for our troops is vital – particularly for those who return injured.

I have seen for myself the excellent job that military and NHS medics are doing at Selly Oak Hospital in Birmingham and at our rehabilitation centre at Headley Court in Surrey.

But charities like Help for Heroes, SSAFA (Soldiers, Sailors, Airmen and Families Association), the Royal British Legion and the Army Benevolent Fund give us the opportunity to make the best even better.

I have now left the Army after forty years serving the Queen, and General Sir David Richards has replaced me as head of the Army.

I know the Army serving in difficult places overseas is in excellent hands and our soldiers are in the thoughts and prayers of everyone back home.

Everyone in the Army walks ten feet tall when they come home, knowing they have your support.

By General Sir Richard Dannatt

'With our Forces fighting far from home – out of sight and, I fear, too often out of mind – sometimes it is not until they return home in flag-draped coffins that we become truly aware of all that we are asking of them.' PRINCE CHARLES

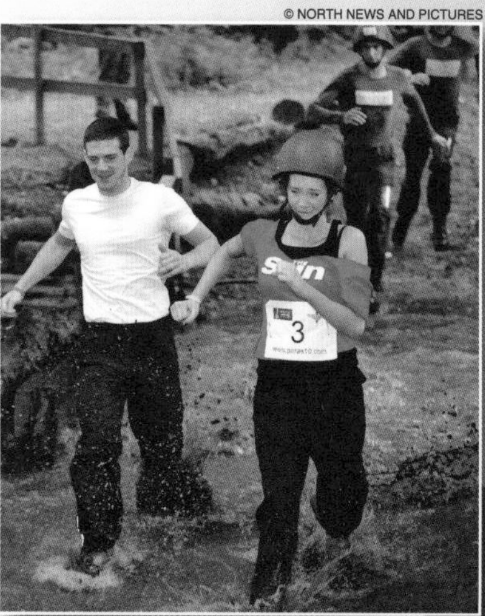

Above: Pegasus Company – better known as P Company – is the name for the punishing selection process for the elite Parachute Regiment, designed to push recruits to their absolute limit. After giving it a go, Peta said: 'I have never been so tired, but it was a great eye-opener….The Paras really are cut from a different cloth.'

Left: 'The lads had such a great sense of humour about the whole thing, which really took my mind off the agony of my blisters.'

'Whether it is cheering them on during a homecoming parade, solemnly lining the route of a funeral cortège, donating to Service charities or simply buying a soldier a pint in the pub, this support is noticed and greatly appreciated.' PRINCE CHARLES

IT'S AN HONOUR TO KNOW THEM

In just six months, she has leapt from a plane at 4,000 metres, trained with the Paras and travelled to the dangerous deserts of Afghanistan.

These aren't typical diary dates for a model – but this is no ordinary model, this is Peta Todd.

Peta has spent the past year working tirelessly to raise money and awareness for British troops injured in conflicts in Iraq and Afghanistan.

Since being moved to tears after meeting wounded servicemen and women at Army hospital Headley Court in Surrey in 2007, Peta has made it her mission to help.

Peta said: 'When I first visited, I treated it as another job. But when I saw them, it broke my heart. I thought, "Why don't I know about this?" If *I* didn't know, then other people didn't, either. I was in a room full of lads my age – or even younger – all of them just back from fighting and with bad injuries. I felt really humbled.'

Main picture: Rounding off her P Company experience, Peta travelled to Brize Norton military base in Oxfordshire for a tandem jump with the Parachute Regiment's elite display team, the Red Devils. She said: 'It was the most awesome experience of my life and I'm so glad I got to do it with the Red Devils. They're the best in the world.'

Peta became a patron of Help for Heroes after she wowed the organizers by cycling 565 kilometres across Europe to raise cash for the charity in June 2008. Her sponsorship alone raised £3,000 – and Peta managed to raise a further £4,000 by auctioning off her bike and cycling shorts on the last day of the ride.

Peta said of the troops she met on her travels: 'These lads are doing an amazing thing, but they don't get the credit they deserve. It takes very little to make a big difference. They don't want sympathy from anyone – just some recognition for what they are doing out there in the war zones. People are always so quick to slag off the youth of today, but there's an awful lot of Britain's youth who are brave, honourable and prepared to make the ultimate sacrifice. It's an honour just to know them.'

By Nick Francis

BRITISH ARMED FORCES AWARDS

Gallantry and bravery awards for active operations

Victoria Cross

Distinguished Service Order | **Conspicuous Gallantry Cross**

Distinguished Service Cross | **Military Cross** | **Distinguished Flying Cross**

Mention in Despatches

The **Distinguished Service Order**, or DSO, is awarded for highly successful command and leadership of troops during active operations.

It was originally created to reward junior officers in the Army for distinguished service or acts of bravery against the enemy. Previously, the Order of the Bath had been available for senior officers and the Distinguished Conduct Medal was available for the other ranks, but no award below the level of the Victoria Cross had existed for junior officers. It is now available to all ranks and all services.

The medal is a gold, curved-edge cross, overlaid in white enamel. At the centre of the cross is a raised laurel wreath, in green enamel, surrounding the Imperial Crown in gold on a red enamelled background. The back of the medal has a similar raised centre with the laurel wreath surrounding the Royal Cypher 'VRI'. The suspender is also decorated with laurel leaves, and a bar showing the same design is at the top of the ribbon.

The **Victoria Cross**, or VC, is the top award for gallantry. It may be awarded to all ranks of the Armed Services, as well as to civilians, for gallantry in the presence of the enemy. The award may be given posthumously.

Instituted by Queen Victoria to cover all military campaigns since the start of the Crimean War in 1854, the Victoria Cross has been awarded 1,356 times. It is made from the bronze of Russian guns that were captured at Sebastopol.

The most recent recipient was Corporal Bryan Budd, of the 3rd Battalion, the Parachute Regiment, who was posthumously awarded the VC for his acts of 'inspirational leadership and the greatest valour' in Afghanistan in 2006.

The medal is a bronze cross showing a lion atop the royal crown, with a semicircular scroll bearing the words 'FOR VALOUR'. A large circular panel is on the back of the medal, inside which is engraved the date of the act for which the award was given. The reverse of the suspender is engraved with the recipient's rank and name, as well as their ship, regiment or squadron.

The **Conspicuous Gallantry Cross**, or CGC, is awarded to all ranks of the Royal Navy, Royal Marines, Army and Royal Air Force to recognize acts of conspicuous bravery during active operations against the enemy.

The medal is a cross pattée (a type of cross that has arms which are narrow at the centre, and broader at the perimeter) in silver, which sits on top of a wreath of laurel leaves. The medal shows a circular medallion in the centre, featuring St Edward's crown. The back of the medal simply lists the recipient's rank, name and unit, as well as the date of the award.

The **Military Cross**, or MC, was set up in 1914 and is awarded to all ranks of the Royal Navy, Royal Marines, Army and Royal Air Force in recognition of outstanding bravery during active operations against the enemy on land. The medal is a silver cross, with straight arms that end with decorations of the Imperial Crowns. At the centre of the cross is the Royal Cypher. The back of the cross is plain, although sometimes the year of the award is engraved.

The **Distinguished Service Cross**, or DSC, is awarded to all ranks of the Royal Navy, Royal Marines, Army and Royal Air Force in recognition of outstanding bravery during active operations against the enemy at sea.

The medal is a silver cross with rounded edges, showing the Royal Cypher in the centre, with the Imperial Crown on top. The back of the medal is plain, but from 1940, the year of the award has been engraved on the bottom of the cross. The ribbon has a central white stripe with equal stripes of dark blue on each side.

The **Distinguished Flying Cross**, or DFC, was set up in 1918 and is awarded to all ranks of the Royal Navy, Royal Marines, Army and Royal Air Force in recognition of outstanding bravery during active operations against the enemy in the air.

The medal consists of a silver cross flory (similar to a fleur-de-lys). The horizontal and base bars end in bombs and the upper bar ends in a rose. This cross has another cross on top, made up of aeroplane propellers, and the centre has a roundel within a laurel leaf. The Royal Air Force monogram is at the centre, with the Imperial Crown on top. The back of the cross has an encircled Royal Cypher above '1918'.

The **George Cross**, or GC, is the highest bravery award for civilians. It can also be awarded to military personnel for acts for which military honours would not normally be given, such as acts of bravery not in the presence of the enemy.

After Britain came under severe air attacks during the summer of 1940, Prime Minister Winston Churchill believed that a new medal should be created to recognize the brave acts being performed by civilians. Although awards to recognize courageous civilians already existed, none of them held the prestige of the equivalent award for bravery in battle, the Victoria Cross.

The King agreed with Churchill, and in January 1941 the George Cross was established. Holders of the Empire Gallantry Medal, the Albert Medal and the Edward Medal were all allowed to trade their awards for the GC.

In total, one hundred and fifty-seven GCs have been awarded directly. Many recent GC recipients have been members of the Army serving in Afghanistan and Iraq. Corporal Mark Wright was recognized posthumously for bravery displayed both before and after sustaining fatal wounds when entering a minefield in Afghanistan. Lance Corporal Matthew Croucher was awarded the GC for smothering a grenade with his body and kit in Afghanistan.

The medal is a plain, silver, bordered cross, showing a circular medallion with St George and the Dragon surrounded by the words 'FOR GALLANTRY'. Between each arm of the cross is the Royal Cypher 'GVI'. The back of the medal is plain, listing the recipient's rank, name and service, or description. The date of notification of the award in the *London Gazette*, rather than the date of the act itself, is also engraved.

The **Elizabeth Cross and Memorial Scroll** is a new award that has been created to recognize the sacrifice made by families of Armed Forces personnel who have died during operations or as a result of an act of terrorism.

The Elizabeth Crosses and Memorial Scrolls were first awarded on 1 August 2009 and will be retrospective to the end of the Second World War.

The **Elizabeth Cross** is a hallmarked silver cross, with a laurel wreath woven between the arms of the cross. The arms show a rose (to represent England), a thistle (to represent Scotland), a shamrock (to represent Ireland) and a daffodil (to represent Wales). A crowned cypher of the Queen is at the centre. The back of the medal is engraved with the name of the serviceperson in whose memory the cross is awarded.

The **Memorial Scroll** is printed on parchment-style paper and is decorated with the Royal Coat of Arms and the words 'This Scroll Commemorates … who gave his/her life for Queen and Country on …'. The Scroll also bears the signature of the Queen in the top left-hand corner.

Gallantry and bravery awards for non-active operations

George Cross

George Medal

Queen's Gallantry Medal | **Air Force Cross**

Queen's Commendation for Bravery | **Queen's Commendation for Bravery in the Air**

The **George Medal**, or GM, is awarded to civilians for acts that are extremely brave, but not outstanding enough to be considered for the George Cross. The GM can also be given to military personnel for acts for which military honours would not normally be granted, such as acts of great bravery not in the presence of the enemy. It was introduced in 1941, at the same time as the GC.

The medal is silver and circular. It shows the crowned figure of the current British monarch (this example shows King George, who reigned from 1936 to 1952). The back of the medal shows St George on horseback slaying the Dragon, surrounded by the words 'The George Medal'.

PANTHER'S CLAW

IN JULY 2009, COALITION FORCES IN AFGHANISTAN LAUNCHED THEIR BIGGEST OPERATION YET - **PANTHER'S CLAW**. ITS AIM: TO DRIVE THE TALIBAN OUT OF THE BABAJI REGION AND SO ALLOW LOCAL PEOPLE THE CHANCE TO VOTE IN THE NATIONAL PRESIDENTIAL ELECTIONS, WITHOUT FEAR OF HARASSMENT.

THE TROOPS - ALL 3,000 OF THEM - ARE TASKED WITH SECURING A SERIES OF CANALS AND RIVER CROSSINGS TO BLOCK THE MOVEMENT OF TALIBAN FIGHTERS. THE REGION IS POUNDED BY APACHES, HARRIERS AND TORNADOS IN A DEVASTATING DEMONSTRATION OF AERIAL MIGHT. IN **PHASE I** OF THE OPERATION FOUR BRITISH BATTLEGROUPS MOVE IN: THE WELSH GUARDS, THE LIGHT DRAGOONS, THE 3RD BATTALION, ROYAL REGIMENT OF SCOTLAND AND THE 2ND BATTALION, MERCIAN REGIMENT. ON THEIR SHOULDERS RESTS NOT JUST THE SUCCESS OF THE OPERATION, BUT THE LEGITIMACY OF THE ELECTIONS TO COME AND OF THE AFGHAN GOVERNMENT THEY HAVE SWORN TO SUPPORT...

OK LADS, THE FLYBOYS HAVE DONE THEIR BIT. NOW LET'S MOVE IN AND DO THE REST...
RIGHT YOU ARE, BOSS.
PHASE I

LIEUTENANT DANNY WRIGHT IS AMONG MORE THAN 350 SOLDIERS DEPLOYED FROM THE SCOTS BATTLEGROUP.
YOU GOT ME COVERED, PETE?
YEAH, YOU'RE GOOD, WRIGHTY - I'VE GOT YOU.
BEFORE THE MAIN THRUST OF THE OPERATION, THE SMALL VILLAGES IN THE AREA WILL NEED TO BE CLEARED AND CHECKPOINTS ESTABLISHED. DANNY AND HIS TEAM ARE SENT IN AS AN ADVANCE PATROL.

OK, LET'S SET UP A CHECKPOINT PAST THIS CORNER. THAT SHOULD GIVE US GOOD CONTROL OVER THE ROAD.
I'M ON IT...
LOOKS LIKE THE LOCALS HAVE BUGGED OUT... GUESS THEY HAVE A GOOD IDEA OF WHAT'S COMING.

THAT NIGHT, THE OPERATION BEGINS IN EARNEST. THE BULKY CHINOOKS SWAY THROUGH THE SKIES, THEIR CARGO HOLDS FULL OF TROOPS. APACHES HOVER PROTECTIVELY AT THEIR SIDES, READY TO DISSUADE ANY TALIBAN FIGHTERS EAGER TO DOWN ONE OF THE 'COWS'.

THIS IS CHARLIE 3, COMING IN FOR LANDING. UGLY 22, CONFIRM THAT WE ARE COVERED TO LAND?

AFFIRMATIVE CHARLIE 3, WE GOT YOU COVERED.

AS THE INFANTRY RACE FROM THE HELICOPTERS, THE GROUND FORCES MOVE IN. MIGHTY JACKALS AND MASTIFF ARMOURED VEHICLES RUMBLE ACROSS THE DUSTY LANDSCAPE.

HQ, THIS IS GROUND FORCE – WE ARE ON ROUTE AND ON SCHEDULE.

AS THE HEAVY CHINOOKS HEAVE THEMSELVES INTO THE AIR...
COME ON, LADS, LET'S MOVE IT! WE DON'T WANT TO HANG AROUND THE CHINOOKS A SECOND MORE THAN WE NEED. THEY'RE REAL BULLET MAGNETS!
YES, SIR, RIGHT BEHIND YOU, SIR!

THE TROOPS HAVE MUCH TO ACCOMPLISH – AND LITTLE TIME BEFORE THE SUN COMES UP AND THEIR POSITIONS BECOME PAINFULLY VISIBLE TO THE ENEMY.
ALRIGHT PRIVATE, YOU KNOW WHAT TO DO! GET DOWN THERE FAST AND COVER US FORWARD!
YOU GOT IT, BOSS!

OVERHEAD, THE ENORMOUS HARRIER JUMP JET CUTS THROUGH THE SKY - ONE OF THE MOST NIMBLE VEHICLES IN THE AIR FLEET, IT IS POISED FOR BATTLE, AND A HEFTY DETERRENT TO ANY OVEREAGER ENEMY.
GROUND FORCE, THIS IS WIZARD. I'M IN POSITION.
WIZARD, THIS IS EAGLE 3. I'M RIGHT HERE BESIDE YOU, BUDDY.
THE AMERICAN AC-130H 'SPECTRE' GUNSHIP KEEPS THE HARRIER COMPANY. ITS AWESOME ARRAY OF FIREPOWER INCLUDES SIDE-FIRING 105 MM HOWITZERS, WHICH THE TALIBAN WOULD BE WISE TO AVOID.
THE FAMILIAR SILHOUETTE OF THE DEADLY APACHE DARTS ALONG BESIDE THE LARGER AIRCRAFT, ITS MULTIPLE DETECTION SYSTEMS FOCUSED ON ANY POTENTIAL DANGER TO THE GUYS ON THE GROUND.
THIS IS UGLY 22. LOOKS LIKE YOU MIGHT HAVE SOME COMPANY IN THE COMPOUND AHEAD, BOYS. KEEP YOUR EYES OPEN, AND WE'LL WATCH YOUR BACKS.
FEELS A LOT SAFER WITH ALL THE FIREPOWER UP THERE...
YEAH, THERE'S ENOUGH UP THERE TO TAKE OUT HALF OF HELMAND - NEVER MIND A SINGLE COMPOUND.
WE'VE STILL GOT TO GET IN THERE AND TAKE 'EM ON, LADS, SO DON'T GO GETTING TOO RELAXED.

BUT AS THE MEN APPROACH THE COMPOUND...
CONTACT! DAMMIT, THEY'VE SPOTTED US. KEEP YOUR HEADS DOWN, LADS!
I CAN SEE THREE, MAYBE FOUR OF THEM! THEY'VE GOT AK-47S BUT I CAN'T SEE ANY RPGS!
HNH--!

THEY'RE NOT LETTING UP! WE'RE GOING TO HAVE TO BLAST THEM OUT! DANNY, CHUCK IN YOUR GRENADE!
OK BOSS, I GOT IT. LOOK OUT, LADS, I NEED SOME SPACE!

UGH--!
GRENADE.
THE LIVE GRENADE SOARS THROUGH THE AIR AND...

... A MIGHTY EXPLOSION!
BOOM!
IT'S ALL THE SIGNAL THE GUYS ON THE GROUND NEED. THEY CHARGE AS ONE!
ASSAULT TEAM, FOLLOW ME! WE'RE GOING IN!
IT IS THE FIRST OF MANY SHORT, SHARP SKIRMISHES THAT LEAVE THE TROOPS IN COMMAND OF VITAL POSITIONS.

PHASE II
AS ANOTHER AFGHAN MORNING DAWNS, THE COMPOUND AND THREE SIGNIFICANT CROSSINGS HAVE BEEN SECURED. AS THE DUST BEGINS TO SETTLE, PHASE II OF PANTHER'S CLAW SWINGS INTO ACTION AS THE TROOPS PREPARE TO FIGHT THEIR WAY UP THE KEY SHAMALAN CANAL.
RIGHT, LADS, I KNOW YOU'RE TIRED AFTER LAST NIGHT BUT WE NEED TO PUSH UP TO THE CANAL. DANNY, ROUND UP YOUR GUYS AND LET'S GET MOVING.
OK, BOSS. I THINK MOST OF THEM HAVE HAD AT LEAST A BIT OF A KIP – SHOULDN'T BE TOO HARD TO GET THEM ON THEIR FEET AGAIN.

IN THE POUNDING HEAT OF THE FULL SUN, WITH THE SHOUTS OF LAST NIGHT'S BATTLE STILL RINGING IN THEIR EARS, THE MEN PRESS ON.
BLOODY HELL, IT DOESN'T TAKE LONG TO HEAT UP, DOES IT? WE'RE GOING TO HAVE TO BE CAREFUL WITH OUR WATER.

A VIKING TANK RUMBLES BEHIND THEM, READY TO PROVIDE DEVASTATING FIREPOWER IN CASE OF CONTACT.
MATE, IF YOU THINK IT'S HOT OUT HERE, IMAGINE WHAT IT'S LIKE INSIDE THAT TIN CAN BEHIND US. I DON'T ENVY THOSE GUYS, I TELL YOU.

YOU HOLD THAT POSITION. WE'LL GET SOME MORE MEN ALONG TO COVER THE CROSSING.
OK, WRIGHTY, I'VE GOT IT. DOESN'T LOOK LIKE THERE'S ANYTHING MOVING OUT THERE...
THE CANAL CUTS A BLUE STREAK THROUGH THE ARID LANDSCAPE. AS THE TROOPS SET UP TO SECURE THE POSITION, THEY KNOW THEY'VE BEEN LUCKY TO MAKE IT THIS FAR WITHOUT AN ENEMY CONTACT – BUT THE MISSION'S NOT OVER YET...

THE CROSSING SECURED - FOR THE TIME BEING, AT LEAST - THE ROYAL ENGINEERS MOVE IN ON ARMOURED TRACTORS. THEIR ROLE: TO CONSTRUCT PERMANENT CHECKPOINTS THAT WILL ALLOW TROOPS TO CONTROL MOVEMENT IN THE AREA.

THE INFANTRY ARE MUSTERED TO HELP WITH THE BUILDING WORK.
WHO NEEDS A GYM WHEN YOU'VE GOT BLOODY GREAT BEAMS TO LUG BACK AND FORTH, EH WRIGHTY?
YOU'RE NOT FAR WRONG, MATE. THIS THING WEIGHS A TON. I'M SWEATING BULLETS HERE.

SO FAR, THE TALIBAN HAVE KEPT THEIR DISTANCE...
OK, MATE, I'LL TAKE OVER, GO AND MAKE YOURSELF A BREW.
AYE, ALL RIGHT THEN. I WON'T MIND GETTING OUT OF THIS HEAT, I'LL TELL YOU THAT MUCH.

...BUT PEACE IN HELMAND PROVINCE RARELY LASTS.
CONTACT! THIS IS SANGAR 3, WE HAVE ENEMY CONTACT TO THE SOUTH-WEST!
I CAN SEE THEM, BOSS! THEY'RE FIRING FROM THAT COMPOUND. I'M ENGAGING!

A SKIRMISH - THE FIRST OF MANY, AS THE TALIBAN THROW THEMSELVES AGAIN AND AGAIN AT THE BRITISH FORTIFICATIONS.
BLOODY HELL, THEY DON'T LET UP, DO THEY?
YEAH, I KNEW THAT CALM PATCH WAS TOO GOOD TO LAST.

AS THE TROOPS SETTLE INTO A GRUELLING GROUND OFFENSIVE, WITH EACH INCH OF LAND HARD-FOUGHT, THE AIR SUPPORT ON WHICH THEY RELY IS NEVER FAR AWAY. HARRIERS, BLACK HAWKS, UAVS AND THE FEARSOME APACHES ARE ALWAYS READY TO RACE IN WHEN THE FIGHTING GETS PARTICULARLY FIERCE.

UGLY 83, WHERE ARE YOU?! WE'RE TAKING HEAVY FIRE HERE – WE NEED IMMEDIATE AIR SUPPORT!

ROGER THAT, 2 PLATOON. GIVE ME TWO MINUTES AND I'LL BE RIGHT ON TOP OF YOU.

THE APACHE'S SOPHISTICATED IMAGING SYSTEMS ZOOM IN ON THE INSURGENTS...

I HAVE THE ENEMY IN SIGHT...

... AS THE GUNNER RELEASES A DEVASTATING HELLFIRE MISSILE – 20 LB OF HIGH EXPLOSIVES, PACKING A 10 MILLION-POUND-PER-SQUARE-INCH PUNCH.

GOT 'EM! 2 PLATOON, THE ENEMY HAS BEEN ELIMINATED. YOU ARE CLEAR TO PROCEED.

WHAT A HIT! YOU'VE ALMOST GOT TO FEEL SORRY FOR THEM – NOTHING'S GOING TO SURVIVE THAT KIND OF A BLAST...

ELSEWHERE, THOUGH, THE BATTLE STILL RAGES.
WE'VE GOT INCOMING! EYES ON THREE ENEMY FIGHTERS AT 10 O'CLOCK – TWO RIFLES, ONE RPG!
DON'T LET THEM FIRE THAT RPG! WE'RE WELL WITHIN RANGE – TAKE IT OUT!

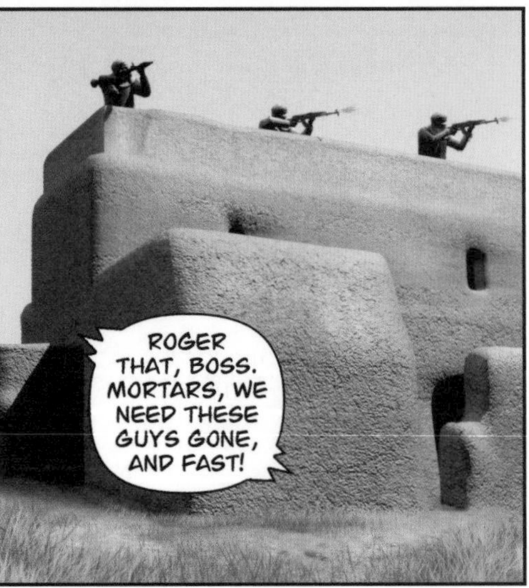

ROGER THAT, BOSS. MORTARS, WE NEED THESE GUYS GONE, AND FAST!

THE TRUSTY MORTARS PLAY A VITAL ROLE IN POUNDING THE ENEMY INTO SUBMISSION.
LOADING!
HANG ON, 7 PLATOON. WE'VE GOT YOU COVERED.

A FLASH OF LIGHT AND A DEAFENING EXPLOSION...
FIRE!

...AND THE TALIBAN POSITIONS ARE REDUCED TO RUBBLE.
DIRECT HIT! 7 PLATOON, ADVANCE!

THE TROOPS ON THE GROUND ARE QUICK TO TAKE ADVANTAGE OF THE AFTERSHOCK...
COME ON, LADS, WE'RE IN!

...RACING THROUGH THE SWIRLING DUST AND SMOKE TO ASSAULT THE ENEMY POSITION.
GO, GO, GO!
KEEP EACH OTHER COVERED! THERE MAY BE MORE!

ONCE INSIDE THE COMPOUND THE SOLDIERS' MONTHS OF TRAINING TAKE OVER AS, HEARTS POUNDING, THEY DUCK FOR COVER.
£*?$%, THAT WAS A BULLET! HEADS DOWN, LADS, WE'VE GOT MORE COMPANY!
SOME OF THEM MUST HAVE ESCAPED... YOU OK TO KEEP THEM BUSY FOR A FEW MINUTES, WRIGHTY?

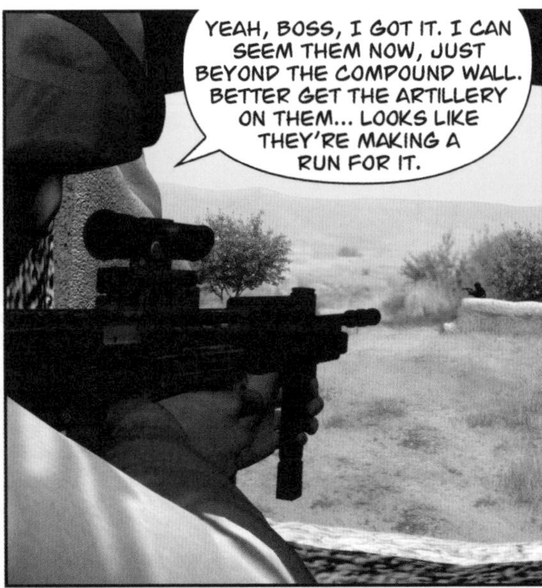
YEAH, BOSS, I GOT IT. I CAN SEEM THEM NOW, JUST BEYOND THE COMPOUND WALL. BETTER GET THE ARTILLERY ON THEM... LOOKS LIKE THEY'RE MAKING A RUN FOR IT.

THE FIRE SUPPORT GROUP GETS WORD OF THE SITUATION...
ARTILLERY, THIS IS FSG. WE'VE GOT A COUPLE OF ENEMY NORTH OF THE COMPOUND WHO ARE KEEPING OUR GUYS PINNED DOWN WHILE THEY MAKE A BREAK FOR IT. TAKE 'EM OUT!

YOU GOT IT, SIR – WE'RE ON IT. **FIRE!**
BOUM!
THE MIGHTY 105 MM FIELD GUN LETS LOOSE WITH A DEAFENING ROAR...

IT'S A BRUTAL ONSLAUGHT – AND ONE THAT SILENCES THE ENEMY'S GUNS FOR GOOD.
BLOODY HELL, THOSE THINGS PACK A HELL OF A WALLOP, DON'T THEY?
RIGHT ENOUGH. GLAD I'M NOT UNDER THAT LOT, I CAN TELL YOU.

WHEN THE DUST CLEARS, THE TROOPS MOVE IN TO THE NOW EMPTY COMPOUND. THE ENEMY HAVE TAKEN A BRUTAL BATTERING. THOSE THAT WEREN'T KILLED HAVE FLED, AND THE VITAL POSITION IS SAFE IN THE HANDS OF THE COALITION FORCES - UNTIL THE NEXT ATTACK.
4 PLATOON, CHECK THE PERIMETER. I PLATOON, TAKE THE EAST WALL AND MAKE SURE WE'VE GOT THE WADI COVERED - WE DON'T WANT ANYONE CREEPING BACK IN UNDER COVER OF THE GREEN ZONE.
THE REST OF YOU LOT, GET A BREW ON. WE'VE GOT AN HOUR BEFORE WE MOVE OUT AGAIN.
YOU GOT IT, BOSS.

IN AND OUT, I GUESS, EH WRIGHTY?
YEAH, I RECKON SO. NO REST FOR THE WICKED...

IN A LAND WHERE GUNS RARELY FALL SILENT, THERE IS LITTLE TIME TO CELEBRATE THE RECENT VICTORY.

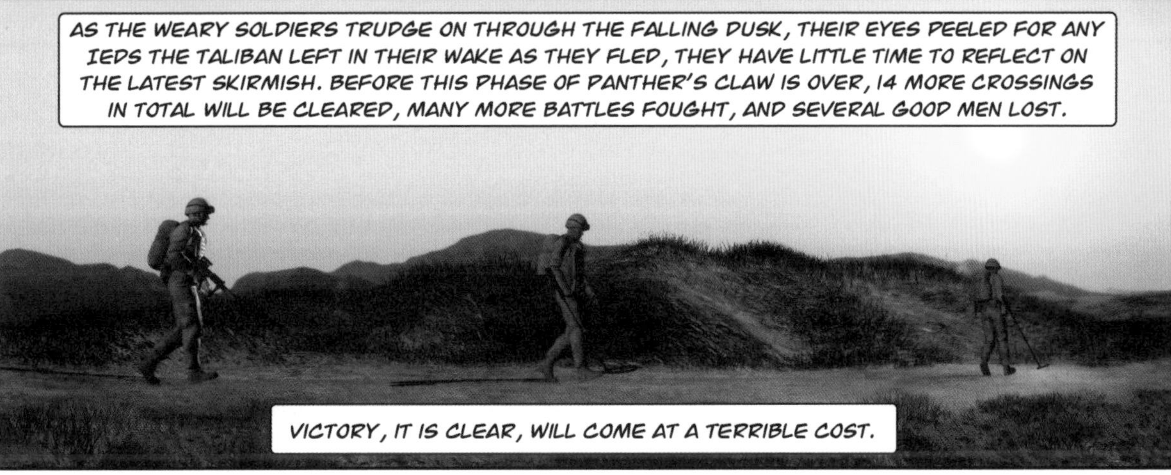
AS THE WEARY SOLDIERS TRUDGE ON THROUGH THE FALLING DUSK, THEIR EYES PEELED FOR ANY IEDS THE TALIBAN LEFT IN THEIR WAKE AS THEY FLED, THEY HAVE LITTLE TIME TO REFLECT ON THE LATEST SKIRMISH. BEFORE THIS PHASE OF PANTHER'S CLAW IS OVER, 14 MORE CROSSINGS IN TOTAL WILL BE CLEARED, MANY MORE BATTLES FOUGHT, AND SEVERAL GOOD MEN LOST.
VICTORY, IT IS CLEAR, WILL COME AT A TERRIBLE COST.

AS THE SUN BREAKS OVER THE HORIZON ON THE MORNING OF FRIDAY, 3 JULY, TASK FORCE HELMAND UNLEASHES **PHASE III** OF PANTHER'S CLAW.

WITH THE ENEMY THROWN OFF BALANCE FROM RECENT INITIATIVES, THERE IS NO TIME TO LOSE. THE LIGHT DRAGOONS BATTLEGROUP, THE 2ND MERCIANS AND THE AFGHAN NATIONAL ARMY PUSH OUT ACROSS BABAJI. THERE ARE OVER 750 TROOPS IN TOTAL – SOME ON FOOT, OTHERS ABOARD SCIMITAR TANKS AND HEAVILY ARMOURED JACKALS AND MASTIFFS. WITH ATTACK HELICOPTERS HOVERING OVERHEAD, THEY SWEEP THROUGH THE REGION, CLEARING ANY REMAINING TALIBAN FROM THEIR COMPOUNDS AND STRONG POINTS.

RIGHT, LADS, THIS IS IT... YOU ALL KNOW WHAT TO DO. JUST STICK TOGETHER AND KEEP EACH OTHER COVERED.

JUST THIS OTHER SIDE OF THE CANAL...
WITH THE RISING SUN COMES THE KILLING HEAT. THE SOLDIERS LABOUR ACROSS THE SCORCHED LANDSCAPE UNDER 80 LB BERGEN BACKPACKS AND HEAVY BODY ARMOUR.
NEARLY THERE, MATE. JUST A FEW MORE METRES. ANYTHING TO GET OUT OF THIS SUN AND INTO SOME SHADE...
DON'T PLAN ON GETTING TOO COMFY, MATE. I RECKON WE'LL HAVE ABOUT THREE MINUTES BEFORE FIRST CONTACT, AND THEN ALL HELL WILL BREAK LOOSE.

THE TROOPS CREEP INTO POSITION, CROUCHING IN THE SHELTER OF THE HIGH CROPS AND IRRIGATION DITCHES THAT CRISSCROSS THE LANDSCAPE.
OK, LADS, 2 PLATOON ARE COVERING US FROM THE WEST...
...SO ON MY SIGNAL PUSH UP ONTO THE HIGH GROUND, GO FIRM AT THE BASE OF THE HILL AND COVER ANY APPROACHES FROM THE EAST. GOT IT?
GOT IT. JUST SAY THE WORD, BOSS.

HEADS, DOWN, LADS - DON'T GIVE THEM ANYTHING TO SHOOT A–
SLOWLY, THE MEN INCH THEIR WAY UPWARDS UNDER THE SWELTERING SUN...

A BULLET CUTS THROUGH THE WARNING AND SLAPS INTO THE GROUND IN FRONT OF THE STARTLED TROOPS!
AMBUSH! TAKE COVER, TAKE COVER! GO, RUN!

TWO TALIBAN FIGHTERS SPRING UP FROM A NEARBY DITCH AND OPEN FIRE, THEIR AK-47S GLINTING IN THE HARSH SUN.
%?$&@! THEY'RE RIGHT ON TOP OF US!

BUT AS THE TROOPS DIVE DESPERATELY FOR COVER, THEY ARE AMAZED TO SEE BOTH FIGHTERS KEEL OVER...
HNH--!
UGH--!

...CUT DOWN BY AN EAGLE-EYED SNIPER KEEPING WATCH OVER THE ADVANCING TROOPS – A DEADLY GUARDIAN ANGEL.
GOT YOU! LET'S HOPE FOR THEIR SAKES YOU DON'T HAVE ANY OTHER FRIENDS IN THE NEIGHBOURHOOD – OR AT LEAST NONE STUPID ENOUGH TO POP THEIR HEADS UP WHERE I CAN SEE THEM.

WITH THE GROUND TROOPS IN POSITION, SCIMITAR TRACKED VEHICLES THUNDER IN TO PROVIDE SUPPORTING FIRE, THEIR 30 MM RARDEN CANNONS AND 7.62 MM TURRET MACHINE GUNS BLASTING ANY ENEMY IN THEIR WAY.
GO, GO, GO! KEEP THOSE GUNS TRAINED ON THE COMPOUND WALLS!

THERE AREN'T MANY THINGS THAT CAN STAND IN THE WAY OF A CHARGING SCIMITAR. WITH AN ANGRY ROAR, IT LOOSES A VOLLEY OF CANNON FIRE AND BLASTS ITS WAY INTO THE COMPOUND.
OK, WE'RE IN! COME ON, LADS, LET'S GET IN BEHIND THERE! DON'T GIVE ANYONE A CHANCE TO ESCAPE!

THE GROUND TROOPS RACE THROUGH IN THE TANK'S DUSTY WAKE, GUNS BLASTING IN ANTICIPATION OF RESISTANCE.
WE'VE GOT THEM ON THE RUN NOW! FOLLOW ME!
WITHIN MINUTES...

...IT'S ALL OVER.
I CAN'T BELIEVE THEY LEGGED IT...THOUGH I CAN'T SAY I'M SORRY. I'M SHATTERED.
WELL DONE, MEN.
YEAH, MATE, JUST BE THANKFUL WE CAME THROUGH IT OK.
DAYS AND WEEKS, OF FIERCE HAND-TO-HAND FIGHTING IN TEMPERATURES AS HIGH AS 55°C HAVE SAPPED THE TALIBAN'S STRENGTH. OUTMATCHED AND OVERWHELMED BY THE FORCE AND SPEED OF THE BRITISH ASSAULT, THEY HAVE WITHDRAWN.
TOO RIGHT. THERE WERE SOME PRETTY HAIRY MOMENTS IN THERE.

AS THE EVENTFUL DAY WINDS TO A CLOSE, THE EXHAUSTED SOLDIERS LEAN INTO THE SHADE CAST BY THE COMPOUND WALLS AND REST IN THE KNOWLEDGE THEIR MISSION IS ACCOMPLISHED.
THEIR COURAGE AND DETERMINATION HAS CLEARED THE WAY FOR A PERMANENT AFGHAN NATIONAL ARMY FORCE IN THE REGION - ONE THAT WILL HELP TO PROVIDE LONG-TERM SECURITY AND TO PROTECT THE 80,000 AFGHANS IN THE REGION FROM VIOLENT INTIMIDATION BY THE TALIBAN. IT IS A SIGNIFICANT VICTORY.
BUT EACH TRIUMPH COMES AT A COST. 10 BRITISH TROOPS LOST THEIR LIVES DURING PANTHER'S CLAW AND SEVERAL MORE WERE WOUNDED. THESE BRAVE MEN LEAVE BEHIND A LEGACY OF PROUD SERVICE - IT IS A SACRIFICE THAT NONE OF THEIR COMRADES, THEIR COUNTRYMEN OR THE PEOPLE OF AFGHANISTAN THEY FOUGHT TO PROTECT WILL SOON FORGET.

BIG GUNS

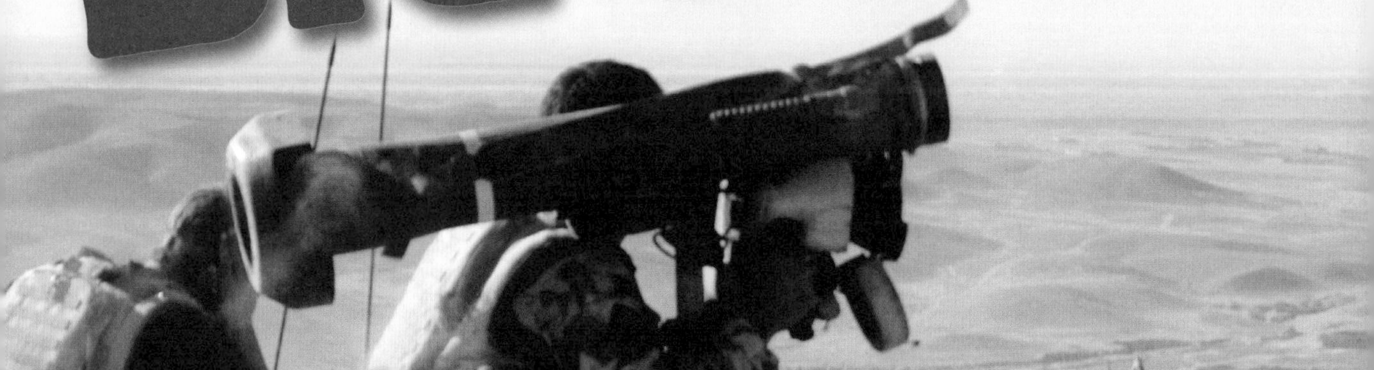

© EROS HOAGLAND – THE TIMES

JAVELIN MISSILE

Crew: 2
Weight: 22.3 kg
Length: 1.08 m
Diameter: 126 mm
Range: 2,500 m
Seeker: Imaging infrared, CMT, 64 x 64 staring focal plane array, 8–12 micron
Guidance: Lock-on before launch, automatic self-guidance

The javelin missile is a portable anti-tank weapon. It is fired from a resting position on the shoulder and can be installed on tracked, wheeled or amphibious vehicles.

The javelin missile system is usually carried by two people – a gunner and an ammunitions bearer. It is the gunner's job to aim and fire the missile, while the ammo bearer's task is to look for targets and threats, such as enemy vehicles and fighters. The javelin can be fired from within buildings, and it is deployed and ready to fire in under 30 seconds. Its reload time is less than 20 seconds.

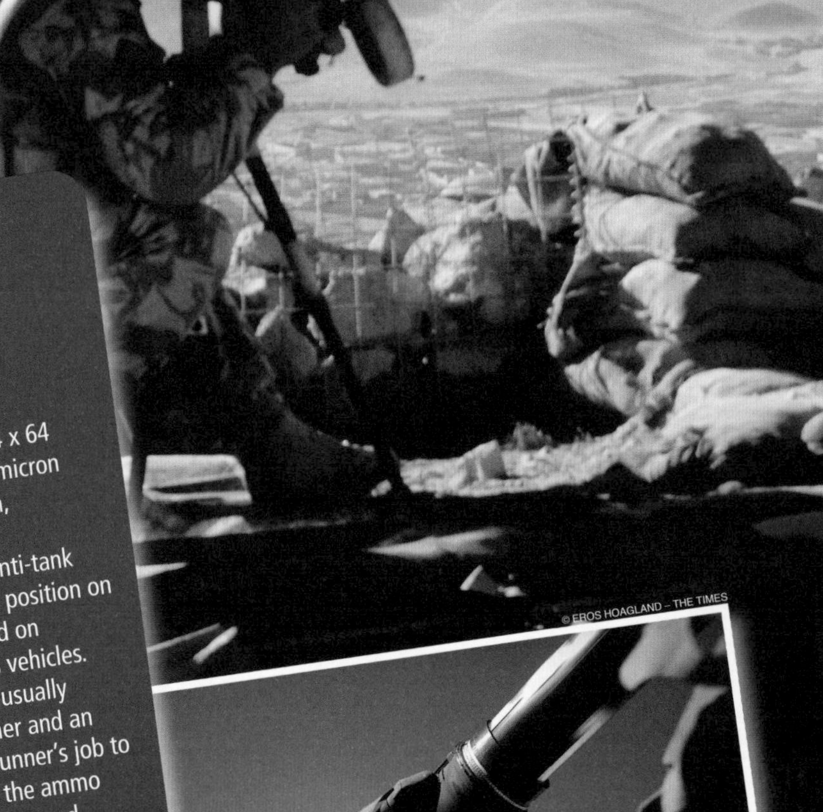

105 MM FIELD GUN / L118 LIGHT GUN

Crew: 6
Weight: 1,858 kg
Length: 8.8 m
Width: 1.78 m
Maximum range: 17.2 km
Anti-tank range: 800 m
Rate of fire: 6 rounds per minute

The 105 mm field gun/L118 light gun is a piece of artillery that first entered British Army service in the 1970s. It replaced its predecessor, the 105 mm Pack Howitzer, which, although compact and lightweight, lacked range.

The current light gun is heavier than the Pack Howitzer, however it can still be carried by both Puma and Chinook helicopters. A touch-screen display tells the gun controller when his or her gun is laid onto the correct target.

The light gun was used in the Falklands War, where it proved its worth. Since then it has seen operational service in Afghanistan, Iraq, Kuwait and Bosnia.

MORTARS

Calibre: 81 mm or 102 mm (the following details refer to the 81 mm)
Weight: 35.3 kg (in action)
Barrel length: 1.28 m
Muzzle velocity: 225 m/s
Maximum range: 5,650 m (HE)
Rate of fire: 15 rounds per minute
Bomb weight: 4.2 kg (HE L3682)

A mortar is a muzzle-loading, indirect-fire weapon – this means that it is loaded from the forward, or open end, of the gun's barrel. It fires shells at low velocities and short ranges and is relatively easy to operate. A mortar consists of three main parts – a barrel, base plate and bipod – and can be carried by one or more men or transported by vehicle. In order for a mortar to function, a gunner must drop a shell into the tube. At the bottom of the tube, a firing pin detonates the propellant and fires the shell.

APACHE PILOT

Q&A WITH APACHE PILOT ED MACY, MC

1. Name, age, rank, where you're from: Ed Macy, 43, WO1 (Weapons Officer), North-East

2. Time spent in the Armed Forces: 23 years, 5 months and 1 week. The five months was to complete an extra tour of Afghanistan; the week was time I had to repay after being in the 2 Para jail.

3. Previous conflicts involved in: School, Northern Ireland, Bosnia, Kosovo and Afghanistan

4. Where are you currently based? Wattisham, Suffolk (until I retire)

5. What does your job involve? What are your main areas of responsibility? Flying and commanding an Apache Attack Helicopter. I'm responsible to the Ground Commander and have to know exactly where his targets are, where he feels threatened and where all of his men are. Our pair of Apaches will then search for the enemy, using a 127x zoom TV camera and a thermal sight or radar, and warn the ground commander of any danger. If a threat decides to take on the ground troops, we will destroy it before it kills any of our soldiers.

6. What does your average day consist of? Apache pilots never have an average day, so I'll cover the Immediate Response Team. A day on IRT begins with sitting in the Operations Tent, listening to all the radios. When we hear that our troops are in

© GERBAN VAN ES

© ED MACY

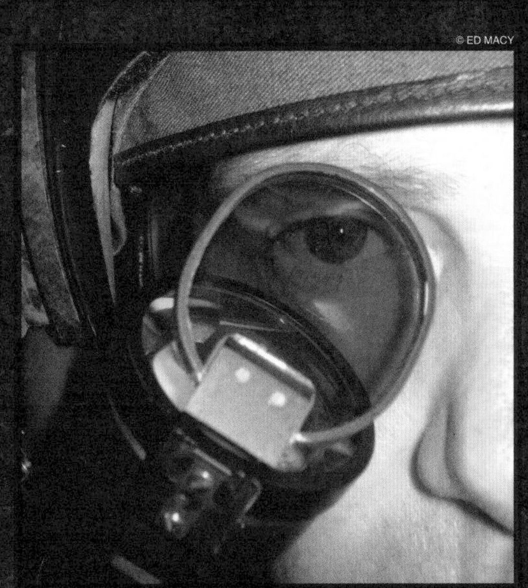

trouble, we run to the Apaches and fire them up. We fly directly to the action and engage with the enemy. Once the troops are clear of danger and happy, we fly back to camp or on to the next hotspot. This goes on twenty-four hours a day and has done since May 2006. Sometimes we can be in the aircraft for more than sixteen hours non-stop.

© SSGT CARL BIRD

7. Nickname? I've had a few. The Wizard, or Elton (Elton John sings 'Rocket Man', and I'm the Army Air Corps' rocket man).

8. Favourite football team/sport? Wreck-diving and climbing

9. Dream car? 1966 Volkswagen Beetle

10. Favourite film/book/holiday/food? Film – *Schindler's List*. Book – *Low Level Hell*. Holiday – diving anywhere. Food – bramble and apple pie.

11. Favourite bit of Army kit? I have two: the £43million Apache AH1 and the £4.30 Hexamine Stove.

THE APACHE IN ACTION

Landmines erupted in the dried-up riverbed, rocket-propelled grenades ripped across the sky and a steady flow of machine-gun bullets whizzed around their heads.

In the Nowzad district of Helmand, a British Army convoy led by Lieutenant Paul Hollingshead had driven into an ambush set up by twenty-five Taliban rebels.

They were in big trouble. The convoy of two British officers, twelve Gurkhas and eight Afghan policemen included two heavily armed WMIK open-topped Land Rovers. But as the convoy drove along the riverbed, the onslaught began.

Ambushers triggered home-made landmines and opened fire from a dug-in machine-gun position. Fighters in flanking positions in nearby houses joined in with AK-47s and grenades, causing mayhem.

Paul and his Gurkhas dived for cover. As they regrouped, Paul carefully chose four men and outlined the plan of action.

Screaming the war cry *'Ayo Gurkhali'* (The Gurkhas Are Upon You), they charged the machine-gun position, blasting it with grenade launchers as they fought their way forward.

Rifleman Kiran Yonzon shot the Taliban commander in the head. Rifleman Rupendra Rai leapt aboard a WMIK and pounded the rebels in the buildings with a .50-calibre machine gun, firing half-inch-wide bullets that can smash through walls and bodies with ease.

Paul called in an Apache attack helicopter. Within minutes it was pounding Taliban positions with 30 mm cannon shells. The soldiers were fighting back, hitting them with a deadly hail of lead.

Paul said: 'The Apache was directly over our heads and very low. A very brave pilot was taking a lot of fire but stuck at it.

'The spent brass shells from his cannon were clattering down all around us. At first I thought it was enemy fire, he was that close. But it really changed the battle.

'The Taliban hate Apaches and are genuinely scared of them. Even one flying overhead makes them go quiet, let alone attacking the hell out of them.

'The helicopter came under heavy fire but never pulled away. The lads were impressed.'

The battle won, Paul and his squad from 10 platoon, 2 Royal Gurkha Rifles, retrieved their vehicles and drove back to base.

'We presented the crew with a traditional kukri knife afterwards to say thank you.'

By Rob Kellaway

APACHE AH MK1

STARBOARD VIEW

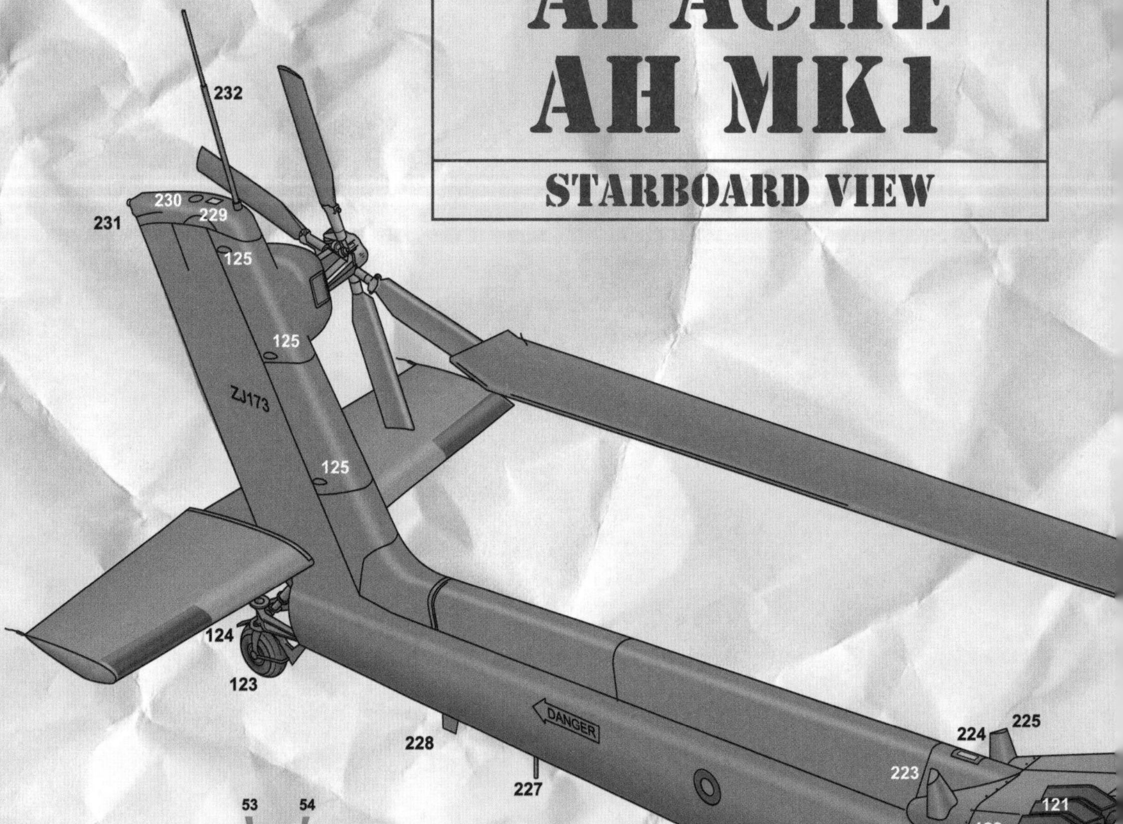

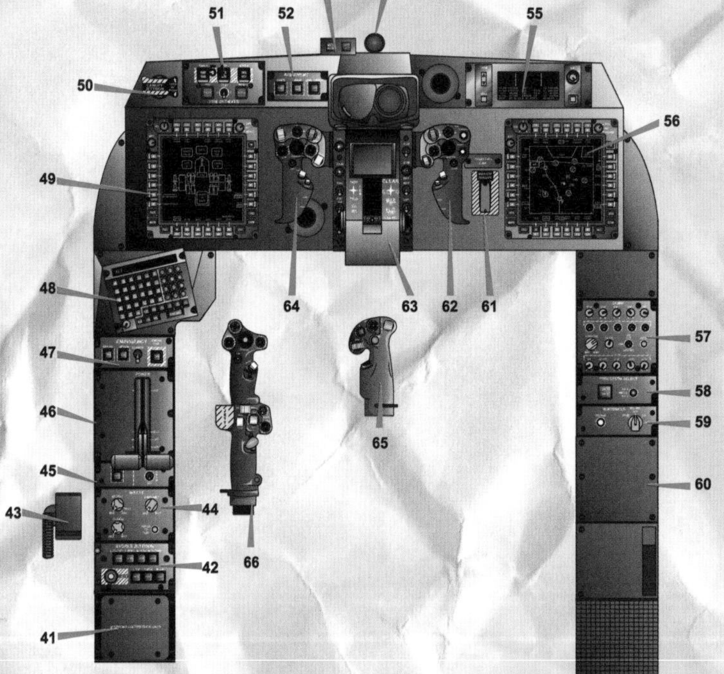

41. Lighting Distribution Unit
42. Stores Jettison Control Panel
43. Utility Light
44. Interior Lighting Control Panel
45. Tailwheel Lock / NVS Mode Panel
46. Power Control Lever Quadrant Panel
47. Emergency Panel
48. Keyboard Unit
49. Left Multi Purpose Display (MPD)
50. Canopy Jettison Handle
51. Fire Extinguisher Control Panel
52. Armament Panel
53. Master Warning / Caution / Light Push Buttons
54. Boresight Reticule Unit
55. Up Front Display
56. Right MPD
57. Communications Control Panel
58. System Processor Select Panel
59. Windshield Panel
60. Helmet Display Unit Stowage
61. Master Zeroize Switch
62. Optical Relay Tube (ORT) Right Hand Grip
63. ORT Assembly
64. ORT Left Hand Grip
65. Cyclic Grip
66. Collective Flight / Mission Grip

APACHE AH MK1 CO-PILOT GUNNER STATION

AIRFRAME

101. External Canopy Jettison Handle Access Panel
102. Right Fwd ECS Evaporator
103. Right ECS Compressor
104. Footstep
105. Fire Extinguisher
106. Right Extended Forward Avionics Bay (EFAB)
107. EFAB Stowage Bin (Open)
108. ECS Evaporator Bay Panel
109. Pressure Refuel Control Panel
110. Fwd Gravity Refuel Point
111. Pressure Refuel Manifold Panel
112. Servicing Access Panel
113. Main Gearbox Access Panel
114. Upper Fuselage Fairing
115. No.2 Engine Nacelle Servicing Platform
116. Aft Gravity Refuel Point
117. Battery/Charger and Radar Processor Panel
118. Aft ECS Condenser Bay
119. Auxiliary Fuel Tanks
120. Stowage Compartment
121. No.2 ECU Ducted Exhaust
122. Hydraulic Ground Servicing Supply Panel
123. Aircraft Towing Point
124. Tail Wheel Hyd/Manual Castor Lock
125. Extendable Foot/Hand Holds (Left and Right)

ARMAMENT

300. M230EI 30mm Gun Ammunition Side Loader

ELECTRICAL/AVIONIC

201. Front Right Missile Warning Sensor
202. Front Right RWR Quadrant Receiver
203. EFAB - Forward Right Avionics Bay
204. CTS GPS Antenna
205. Co-Pilot's Low Height Warning Indicator
206. Windscreen Wipers
207. Pilot's Low Height Warning Indicator
208. Ice Detector Sensor
209. IFF Upper Dipole
210. Right Pitot Tube
211. Right Wing Formation Light
212. VU1 & FM2 Full Band Antenna
213. Laser Warning Receiver Right Upper
214. Aft Right Avionics Bay with Cooling Grills
215. Nav. Light
216. Anti-Collision Strobe Light
217. Doppler Antenna
218. Right Side Airspeed and Direction Sensor
219. Right Flare Dispenser
220. VU2/UHF Blade Antenna
221. Laser Warning Receiver Right Rear
222. Safety Disarm Unit
223. Rear Right RWR Quadrant Receiver
224. Spine Formation Light
225. Rear Left RWR Quadrant Receiver
226. Right Aft MWS
227. IFF Lower Dipole Antenna
228. CTS UHF Antenna
229. Tail Formation Light
230. GPS Antenna
231. Tail Navigation Light and Bi Directional Radar Warning Receivers
232. VU2 & FM1 Whip Aerial

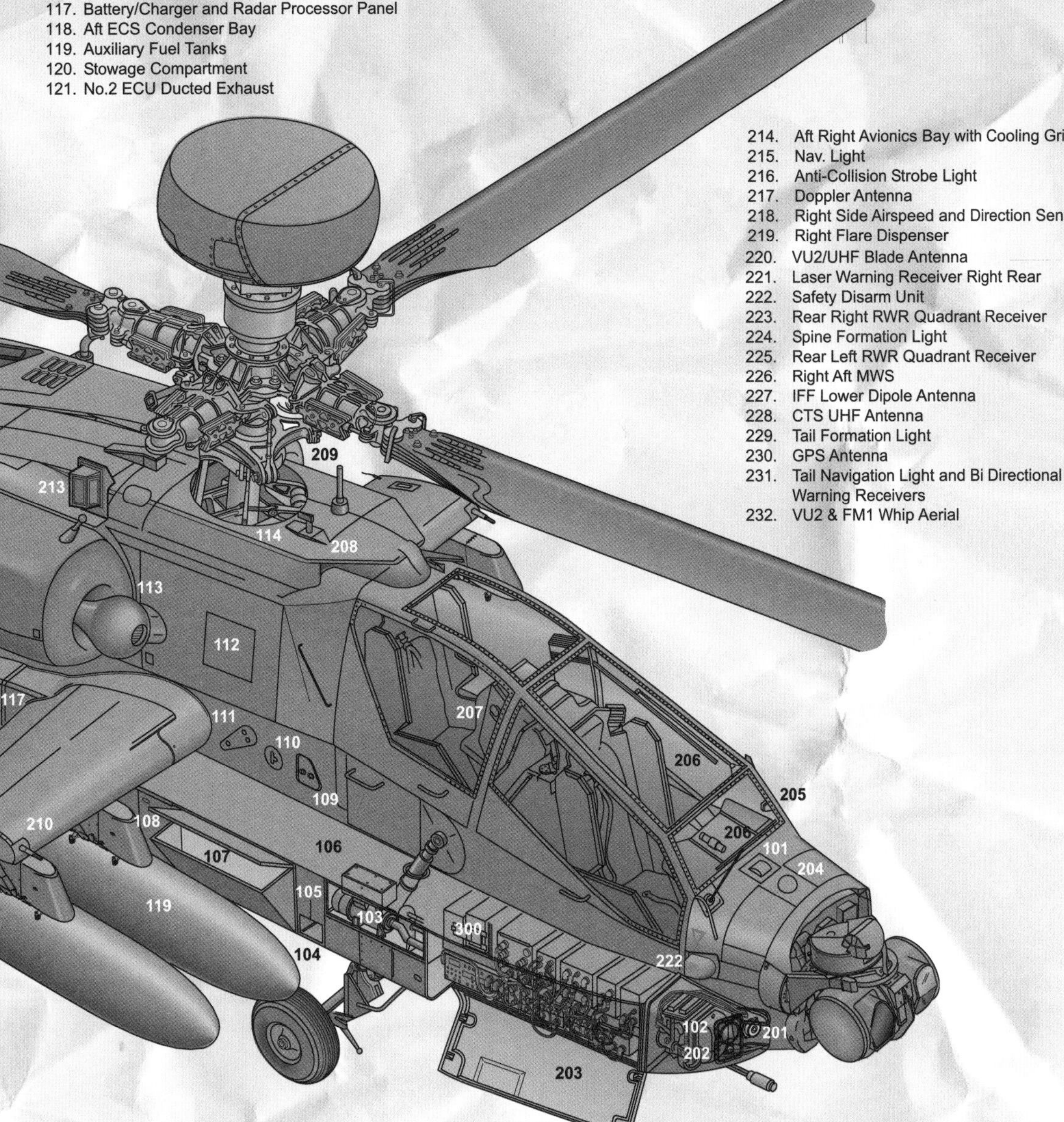

APACHE AH MK1

PORT VIEW

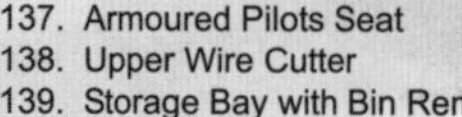

AIRFRAME

130. Left Environmental Control System (ECS) Evaporator
131. Left Main Landing Gear Wire Cutter
132. Main Wheel
133. Left ECS Compressor
134. Left Extended Forward Avionics Bay (EFAB)
135. Window Ejection Miniature Detonating Cord
136. Armoured Co-pilot Gunners Seat
137. Armoured Pilots Seat
138. Upper Wire Cutter
139. Storage Bay with Bin Removed
140. ECS Evaporator Bay Panel
141. Left Wing
142. Main Rotor Gearbox
143. No.1 Engine Nose Gearbox
144. No.1 Engine Bay - ECU Removed
145. Engine Nacelle in Servicing Position
146. Footsteps
147. Stowage Compartment
148. Rear Fuselage Footsteps
149. Castoring Tailwheel
150. Moving Horizontal Stabilator
151. Tail Rotor Hub
152. Tail Rotor Hydraulic Servo
153. Tail Rotor Gearbox
154. Intermediate Gearbox and Cooling Fan
155. Tail Drive Shafts
156. Main Rotor Blade
157. Catwalk Access Panel
158. Pre-cooler By-pass Exhaust
159. Catwalk Access Panels
160. Main Rotor Head
161. Integrated De-ice De-rotational Unit
162. MRB Strap Packs
163. Swash Plate Assembly and Scissor Links
164. Static Rotor Mast
165. Left Transmission Air Cooling Intake

ROLLS ROYCE/TURBOMECA RTM322 01/12 MK120

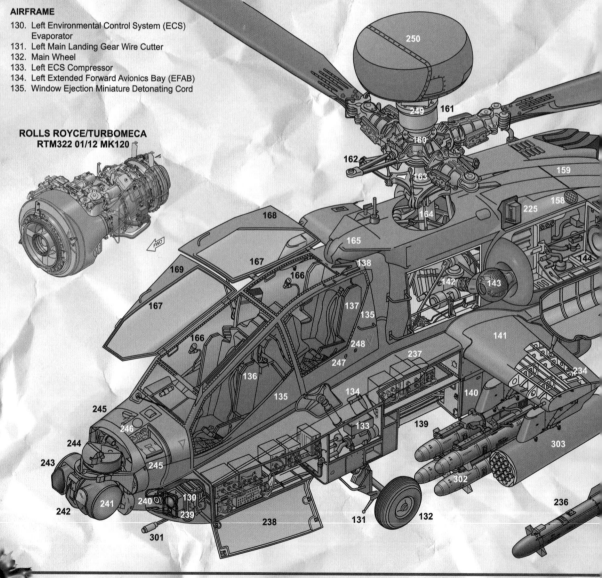

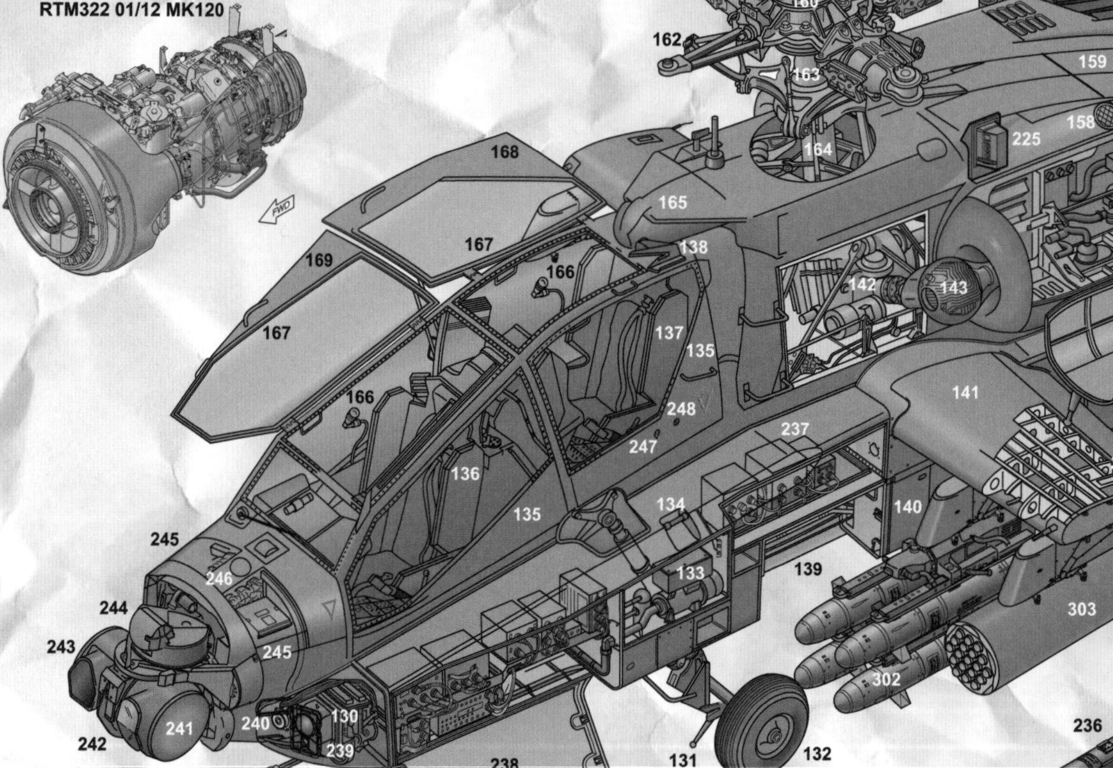

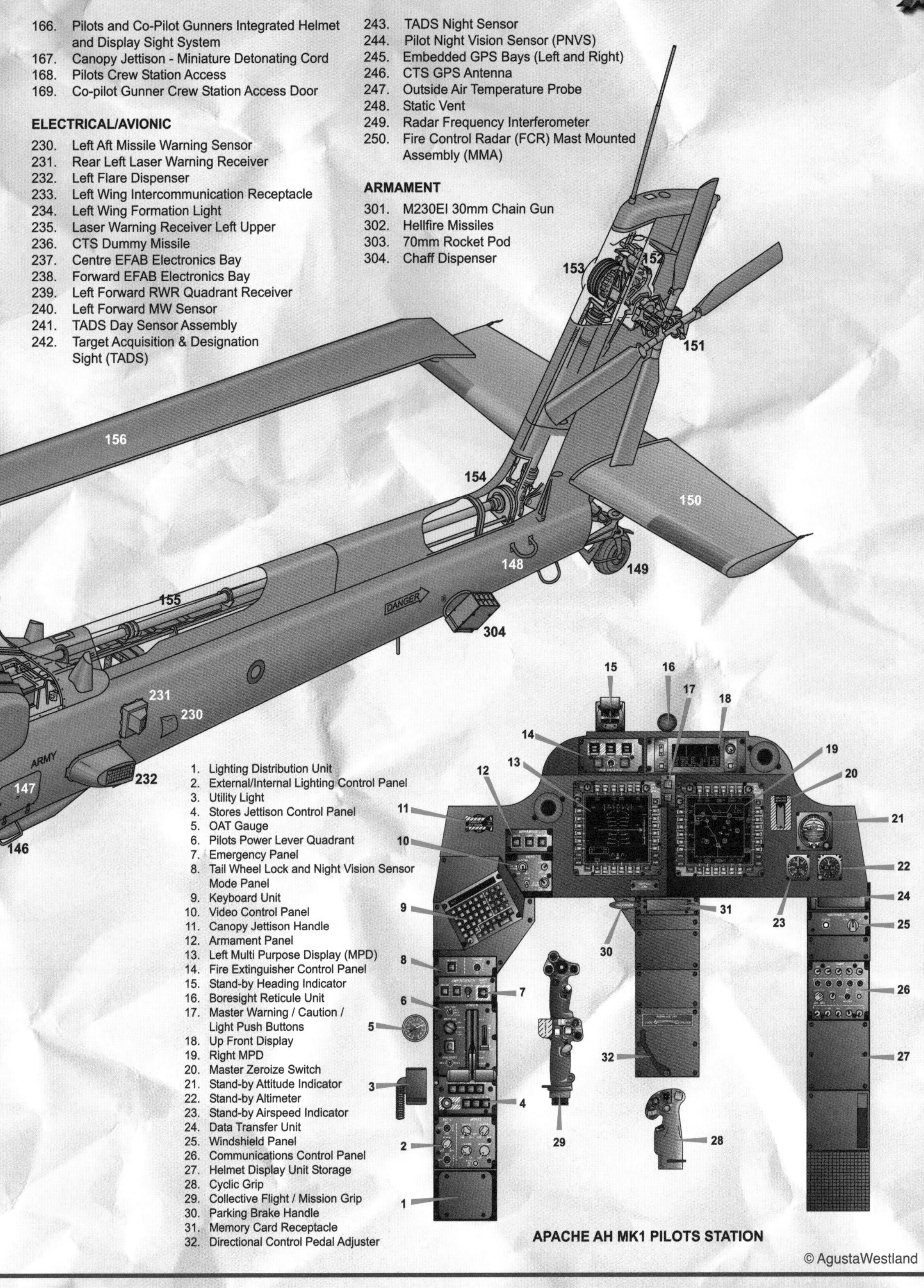

166. Pilots and Co-Pilot Gunners Integrated Helmet and Display Sight System
167. Canopy Jettison - Miniature Detonating Cord
168. Pilots Crew Station Access
169. Co-pilot Gunner Crew Station Access Door

ELECTRICAL/AVIONIC

230. Left Aft Missile Warning Sensor
231. Rear Left Laser Warning Receiver
232. Left Flare Dispenser
233. Left Wing Intercommunication Receptacle
234. Left Wing Formation Light
235. Laser Warning Receiver Left Upper
236. CTS Dummy Missile
237. Centre EFAB Electronics Bay
238. Forward EFAB Electronics Bay
239. Left Forward RWR Quadrant Receiver
240. Left Forward MW Sensor
241. TADS Day Sensor Assembly
242. Target Acquisition & Designation Sight (TADS)
243. TADS Night Sensor
244. Pilot Night Vision Sensor (PNVS)
245. Embedded GPS Bays (Left and Right)
246. CTS GPS Antenna
247. Outside Air Temperature Probe
248. Static Vent
249. Radar Frequency Interferometer
250. Fire Control Radar (FCR) Mast Mounted Assembly (MMA)

ARMAMENT

301. M230EI 30mm Chain Gun
302. Hellfire Missiles
303. 70mm Rocket Pod
304. Chaff Dispenser

1. Lighting Distribution Unit
2. External/Internal Lighting Control Panel
3. Utility Light
4. Stores Jettison Control Panel
5. OAT Gauge
6. Pilots Power Lever Quadrant
7. Emergency Panel
8. Tail Wheel Lock and Night Vision Sensor Mode Panel
9. Keyboard Unit
10. Video Control Panel
11. Canopy Jettison Handle
12. Armament Panel
13. Left Multi Purpose Display (MPD)
14. Fire Extinguisher Control Panel
15. Stand-by Heading Indicator
16. Boresight Reticule Unit
17. Master Warning / Caution / Light Push Buttons
18. Up Front Display
19. Right MPD
20. Master Zeroize Switch
21. Stand-by Attitude Indicator
22. Stand-by Altimeter
23. Stand-by Airspeed Indicator
24. Data Transfer Unit
25. Windshield Panel
26. Communications Control Panel
27. Helmet Display Unit Storage
28. Cyclic Grip
29. Collective Flight / Mission Grip
30. Parking Brake Handle
31. Memory Card Receptacle
32. Directional Control Pedal Adjuster

APACHE AH MK1 PILOTS STATION

THE GUYS ON THE GROUND

By Andy Crick

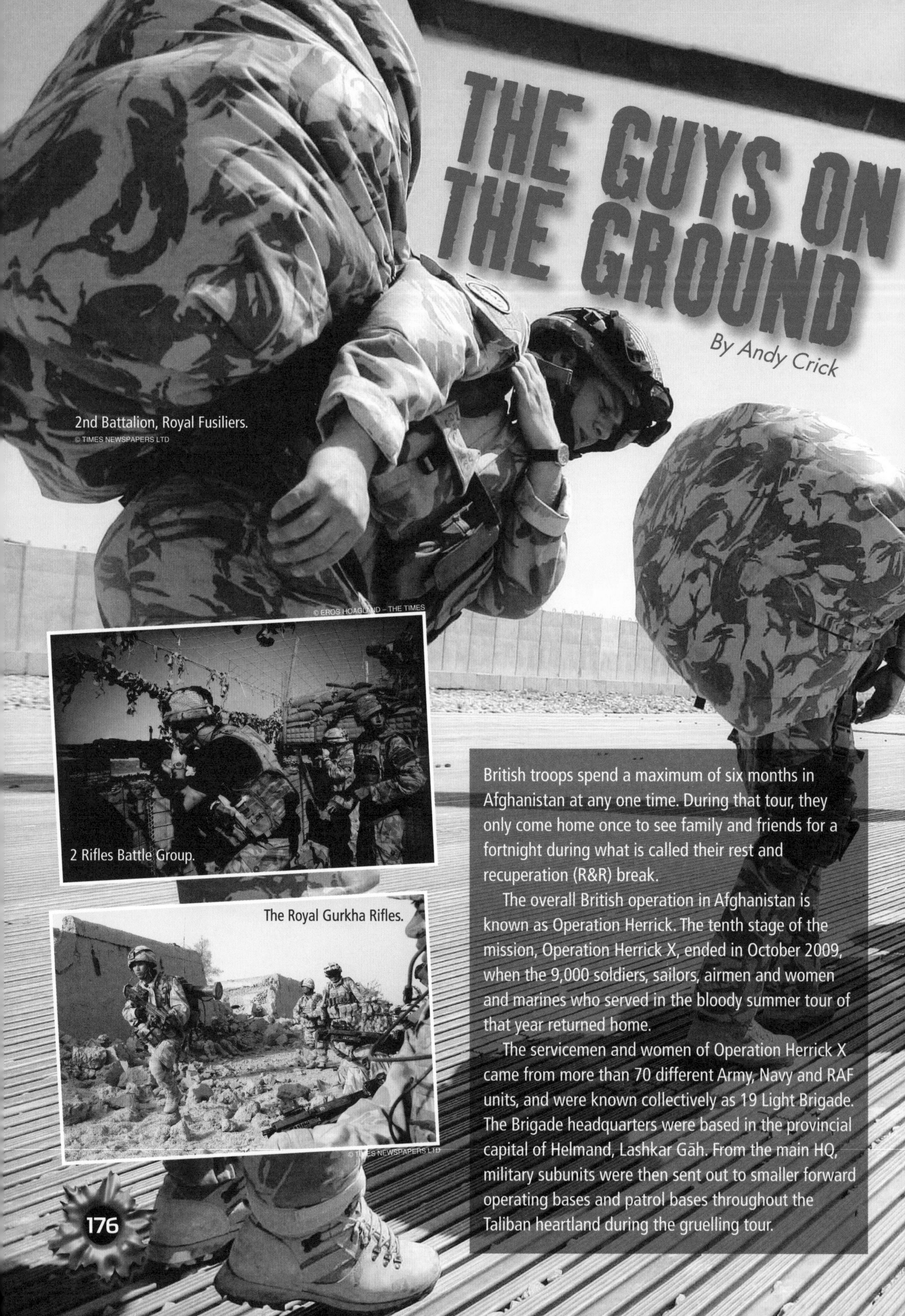

2nd Battalion, Royal Fusiliers.

© TIMES NEWSPAPERS LTD

© EROS HOAGLAND – THE TIMES

2 Rifles Battle Group.

The Royal Gurkha Rifles.

© TIMES NEWSPAPERS LTD

British troops spend a maximum of six months in Afghanistan at any one time. During that tour, they only come home once to see family and friends for a fortnight during what is called their rest and recuperation (R&R) break.

The overall British operation in Afghanistan is known as Operation Herrick. The tenth stage of the mission, Operation Herrick X, ended in October 2009, when the 9,000 soldiers, sailors, airmen and women and marines who served in the bloody summer tour of that year returned home.

The servicemen and women of Operation Herrick X came from more than 70 different Army, Navy and RAF units, and were known collectively as 19 Light Brigade. The Brigade headquarters were based in the provincial capital of Helmand, Lashkar Gāh. From the main HQ, military subunits were then sent out to smaller forward operating bases and patrol bases throughout the Taliban heartland during the gruelling tour.

Among the regiments who committed troops during 2009 were the 1st Battalion, the Welsh Guards, based near Lashkar Gāh. The infantry unit lost its battalion chief in the war when Commanding Officer Lieutenant Colonel Rupert Thorneloe was killed in an IED attack in July 2009. Colonel Thorneloe the most senior officer to die in combat since the Falklands War in 1982. The battalion was among the forces involved in Operation Panther's Claw, which aimed at clearing an area of Taliban fighters ahead of Afghan presidential elections.

Also taking part in the huge Panther's Claw mission were 300 soldiers from The Black Watch, 3rd Battalion, the Royal Regiment of Scotland. The Black Watch was additionally involved in smashing a Taliban drug factory in Howz-e-Maded, Zhari District in September 2009. This operation was crucial, as it helped to prevent insurgents from making and selling heroin – a vital step in cutting the cashflow that funds Taliban bombs and weapons.

Another front-line fighting unit in Helmand was the 2nd Battalion, the Rifles, who were based in the enemy stronghold region of Sangin in northern Helmand – one of the most dangerous places in Afghanistan. Among their achievements, 2 Rifles uncovered an enemy narcotics base in Ghorak district in September 2009. Sadly, 13 soldiers from the 600-strong battalion were killed and more than 70 wounded – a higher casualty rate than that of any other unit in a single tour.

But while the infantry troops take part in bloody battles, they couldn't do it without the support of back-up units. The additional fire power supplied by the mortars from the likes of 40 Regiment Royal Artillery and the fearsome might of armoured vehicles from regiments such as 2nd Royal Tank Regiment are absolutely vital.

When it comes to air support, the soldiers have relied on the fast Tornado GR4 fighter planes from the regiments such as 12 Squadron, Royal Air Force. These provide air cover and take out Taliban positions. The Navy's Sea King helicopters belonging to 845 Naval Air Squadron also played their part.

Bridges and camps wouldn't get built without the skill and determination of regiments like 38 Engineer Regiment. Equally significant, the supply networks operated by the Royal Logistics Corps provide the backbone for forces delivering food and equipment to the troops.

After their tough tour, the soldiers from 19 Light Brigade were replaced by 11 Light Brigade, made up of nearly 100 units, including:

1 Squadron, the Household Cavalry Regiment
1 Squadron, 1st Royal Tank Regiment
1st Battalion, Grenadier Guards
3rd Battalion, the Rifles
1st Battalion, the Royal Welsh (Royal Welch Fusiliers)
2nd Battalion, The Yorkshire Regiment (14th/ 15th, 19th & 33rd/76th Foot) (Green Howards)
1st Regiment, Royal Horse Artillery
28 Engineer Regiment, Royal Engineers
10 Queen's Own Gurkha Logistics Regiment
Signals Squadron, (261) Royal Corps of Signals
1 Battery, 5th Regiment, Royal Artillery
1st Battalion, the Royal Anglian Regiment

Their six-month mission, lasting until April 2010, is known as Operation Herrick XI.

Backup for 11 Light Brigade comes from the bomb-disposal experts of 33 Engineer Regiment, the four-legged forces' friends of 102 Military Working Dog Support Unit, who are providing their trained noses to sniff out Taliban bombs, and the double-rotor Chinooks from the RAF's 18 Squadron. The huge helicopters have had a continuous presence in Afghanistan, doing their bit again and again, by delivering troops and supplies, and extracting the wounded from war zones.

2nd Battalion, Royal Welsh, during 'Panther's Claw'.

Australian ISAF soldiers.
© AFP

A German ISAF vehicle.
© EPA

THE NATO COALITION

Britons aren't the only troops putting their lives on the line in Afghanistan. The following NATO nations have committed these troop numbers to help combat the Taliban threat, as of 1 October 2009:

Albania	250
Australia	1,200
Austria	4
Azerbaijan	90
Belgium	510
Bosnia & Herzegovina	2
Bulgaria	460
Canada	2,830
Croatia	290
Czech Republic	340
Denmark	700
Estonia	150
Finland	130
France	3070
Georgia	1
Germany	4,245
Greece	125
Hungary	310
Iceland	8
Ireland	7
Italy	2,795
Jordan	7
Latvia	165
Lithuania	250
Luxembourg	8
Netherlands, The	2,160
New Zealand	220
Norway	600
Poland	2,025
Portugal	105
Romania	990
Singapore	2
Slovakia	240
Slovenia	80
Spain	1,000
Sweden	430
The former Yugoslav Republic of Macedonia	185
Turkey	820
Ukraine	10
United Arab Emirates	25
UK	9,000
US	31,855
Total	**67,700 (approx.)**

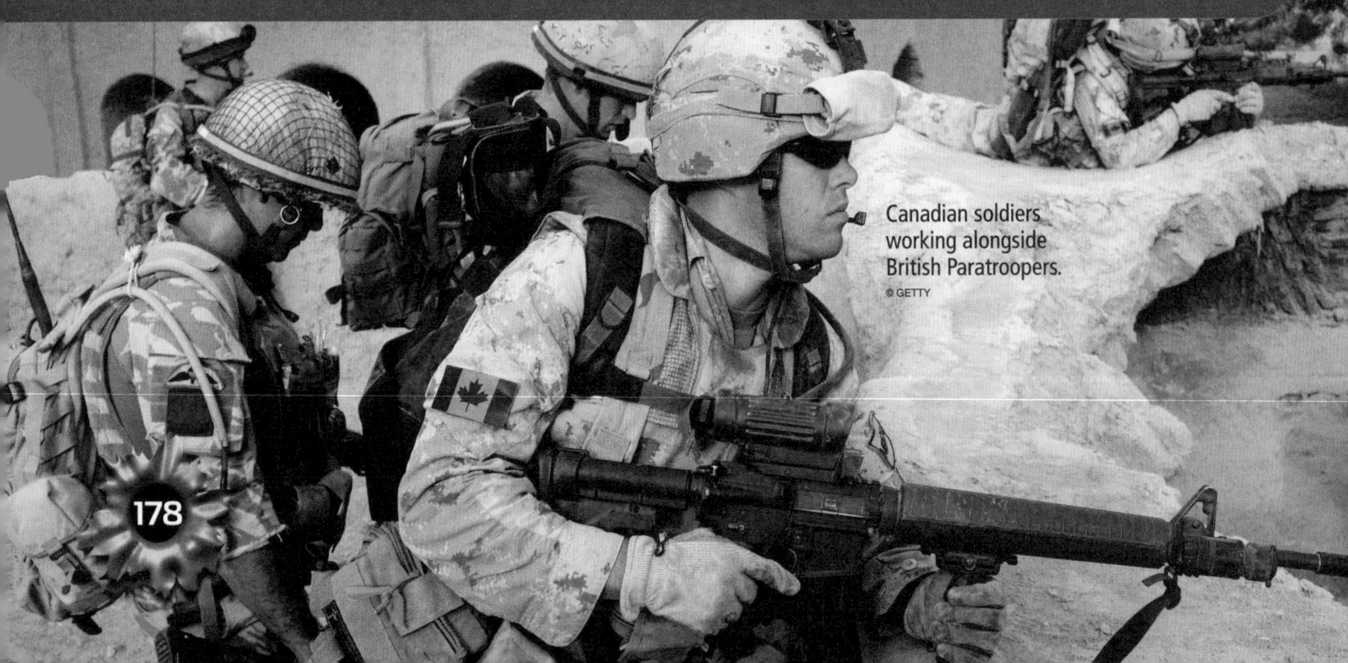

Canadian soldiers working alongside British Paratroopers.
© GETTY

A US Marine has a close call near Garmsir.
© REUTERS

Soldiers from the Danish Army.
© TIMES NEWSPAPERS LTD

The deployment is split across four main regions of Afghanistan. Australia, Canada, the UK, the US, Denmark, The Netherlands (acting as lead nation) and Romania are in Regional Command (RC) South, stretching from Nimroz Province in the west across Helmand Province, where British troops are stationed, to Zabul Province in the east. The US is the lead nation in Regional Command (RC) East, where France, Italy, New Zealand, Turkey and Poland are also deployed. This command area reaches from Bamyan and Ghazni Provinces in central Afghanistan to the troubled border with Pakistan in the east. Germany is the lead nation in Regional Command (RC) North, which also includes Sweden, Norway and Hungary. This area includes the strip of land across the north of the country, from Faryab Province in the west to Badakhshan Province on the Pakistani border in the east. Finally, Italy leads Spain and Lithuania in Regional Command (RC) West, covering Farah, Hirat, Badghis and Ghor Provinces.

These coalition forces work closely with approximately 93,980 members of the Afghan National Army on operations, training, development and by supplying crucial kit. NATO countries have contributed everything from mortars and ammunition to blankets and clothing, from helicopters to fire trucks, and from generators to helmets, in the hope of strengthening the Afghan National Army to protect its own nation.

THE PRICE THEY PAY

© LEWIS WHYLD/PA WI

HEROES COME HOME

One by one, they passed – eight hearses each carrying a coffin draped in the Union flag.

Four thousand people formed a corridor of tears through which the fallen soldiers were taken.

Some tossed flowers on the hearses. Some closed their eyes in silent prayer. Loved ones of the dead broke down, overwhelmed with grief.

And when the procession moved out of sight, the air was filled with the heavy sound of sobbing.

The scene could have been the recreation of a moving line written by the First World War poet Wilfred Owen in November 1917.

He wrote to give a voice to comrades with whom he served, saying: 'These men are worth your tears.' This slow parade was the largest single repatriation yet seen in Wootton Bassett, Wiltshire, the small town through which war victims pass from nearby RAF Lyneham on their way to a mortuary.

THANK YOU *By John Coles*

The British military staged a moving 'thank you' parade to a town that has honoured more than one hundred fallen service personnel.

Residents have lined the streets of Wootton Bassett every time a body has been flown home to nearby RAF Lyneham. Residents are now campaigning to rename the repatriation route 'Highway for Heroes'.

Now, the Army, Royal Air Force and Royal Navy were showing their appreciation – with a dramatic flyover by a Boeing C-17 Globemaster and a parade by bands from all forces.

The ceremony, organized by Mike Neville, Station Commander of nearby RAF Lyneham, saluted the 'outstanding efforts' of the town's 12,500 residents.

Mike explained: 'It never ceases to amaze me the contribution and respect shown by the people of North Wiltshire. I hope this parade will go some way towards recognizing that support.'

Wootton Bassett is the first town that the processions reach as they travel to the M4 en route to the John Radcliffe Hospital in Oxford, where postmortems are carried out.

Sir Richard Dannatt, former head of the British Armed Forces, said: 'It is the things that cost nothing that are the most important – a friendly greeting in the street, a prayer in church. And the gestures shown by the people of Wootton Bassett surpass these at every level.'

APOLOGIA PRO POEMATE MEO

By Wilfred Owen

I, too, saw God through mud—
The mud that cracked on cheeks when wretches smiled.
War brought more glory to their eyes than blood,
And gave their laughs more glee than shakes a child.

Merry it was to laugh there—
Where death becomes absurd and life absurder.
For power was on us as we slashed bones bare
Not to feel sickness or remorse of murder.

I, too, have dropped off fear—
Behind the barrage, dead as my platoon,
And sailed my spirit surging, light and clear,
Past the entanglement where hopes lie strewn;

And witnessed exultation—
Faces that used to curse me, scowl for scowl,
Shine and lift up with passion of oblation,
Seraphic for an hour, though they were foul.

I have made fellowships—
Untold of happy lovers in old song.
For love is not the binding of fair lips
With the soft silk of eyes that look and long.

By joy, whose ribbon slips,—
But wound with war's hard wire whose stakes are strong;
Bound with the bandage of the arm that drips;
Knit in the webbing of the rifle-thong.

I have perceived much beauty
In the hoarse oaths that kept our courage straight;
Heard music in the silentness of duty;
Found peace where shell-storms spouted reddest spate.

Nevertheless, except you share
With them in hell the sorrowful dark of hell,
Whose world is but a trembling of a flare
And heaven but a highway for a shell,

You shall not hear their mirth:
You shall not come to think them well content
By any jest of mine. These men are worth
Your tears: You are not worth their merriment.

The eight honoured soldiers were killed in three separate Taliban attacks. At noon on the day of the observance their bodies arrived at RAF Lyneham in a giant transporter aircraft. A sombre ceremony followed as each coffin was slowly unloaded and placed in a hearse.

The bell of St Bartholomew's Church began tolling at 4.36 p.m., heralding the arrival of the procession.

The crowd lining the street, ten deep in places, was made up of relatives, friends, service personnel and local residents eager to pay their respects. Applause showing pride and gratitude broke out as the hearses came into view.

Several soldiers from Rifles regiments – from which six of the victims came – lined the front of the crowd. They stood with heads bowed, struggling to contain their emotions.

Veterans from all over England massed with Royal British Legion flags, many with a black ribbon tied to the top.

Earlier, from Britain's Camp Bastion base in Afghanistan, the eight soldiers had been given an equally poignant send-off.

Teenagers just out of army training volunteered to carry the coffins to the aircraft. The procession's end was summed up by one squaddie's words on a web forum: 'Bugle Major Ben Budd played an immaculate Last Post to see the boys home.'

By John Coles

A memorial service held in Afghanistan.

IN JULY 2009, FIVE MEMBERS OF THE 2ND BATTALION, THE RIFLES, WERE KILLED IN A DEVASTATING DOUBLE IED ATTACK IN SANGIN. THE FIVE YOUNG MEN - THREE OF THEM ONLY 18 YEARS OLD - ALL DIED IN A SINGLE DAY, MAKING IT ONE OF THE WORST FOR THE ARMED FORCES SINCE THE AFGHAN CONFLICT BEGAN.

NO!

NOW, THE ARMY IS DETERMINED TO STOP THE IED MASTERMINDS FROM KILLING AND MAIMING AGAIN - AND TO HONOUR THE MEMORY OF THE FALLEN MEN.
PAYBACK

AS THE OPERATION SWINGS INTO ACTION, IN A QUIET HELMAND FIELD, TWO LOCAL TALIBAN FIGHTERS ARE GIVEN THEIR MARCHING ORDERS, UNAWARE THEIR EVERY MOVE IS BEING WATCHED.
HQ, THIS IS SIGNALS. WE'RE INTERCEPTING A MESSAGE – SOUNDS LIKE SOME KIND OF INSTRUCTION...

THEIR INSTRUCTIONS: TO LAY ANOTHER ROUND OF IEDS TO CATCH ONE OF THE BRITISH 'PORCUPINES'* AS IT PASSES BY ON PATROL.
THIS IS HQ. SIGNALS, CONFIRM LOCATION OF INTERCEPT. DEPLOY THE WATCHKEEPER.
* WMIKS

WHILE ONE MAN PROVIDES COVER IN CASE OF A SUDDEN ARRIVAL OF TROOPS, THE OTHER LAYS HIS LETHAL CHARGE.

THEY SMOOTH OVER THE EVIDENCE OF THEIR AMBUSH AND MAKE THEIR ESCAPE...
SHAABAAS!*
* WELL DONE!

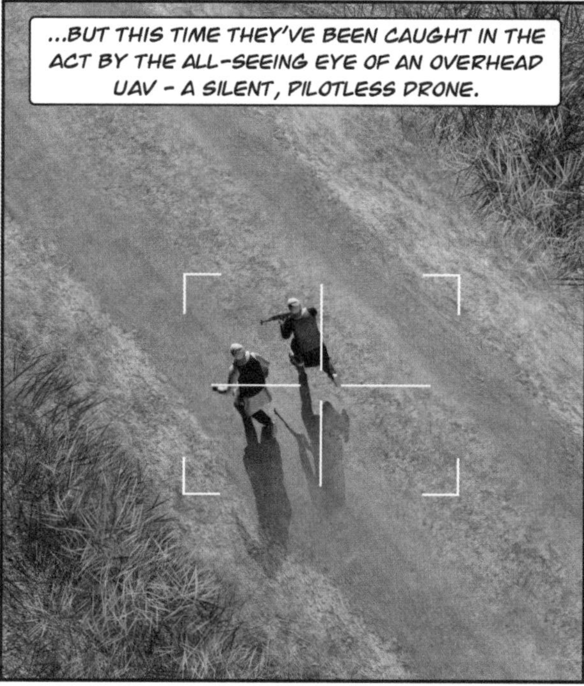
...BUT THIS TIME THEY'VE BEEN CAUGHT IN THE ACT BY THE ALL-SEEING EYE OF AN OVERHEAD UAV – A SILENT, PILOTLESS DRONE.

WATCHKEEPER
HQ, THIS IS GROUND CONTROL. WE HAVE A VISUAL, REPEAT, WE HAVE A VISUAL.

HUNDREDS OF FEET ABOVE THE GROUND, THE DRONE SILENTLY FOLLOWS THE BOMBERS TO A MEETING WITH OTHER INSURGENTS.
THE TARGET IS IN CONFERENCE. THERE ARE FOUR IN TOTAL. HQ, CONFIRM WE ARE TO MAINTAIN EYES ON?
ROGER THAT, GROUND CONTROL. AFFIRMATIVE MAINTAIN EYES ON. KEEP THEM IN YOUR SIGHTS.

AS THE FIGHTERS CONSULT, THE COMPOUND WHERE THEY MAKE THEIR BOMBS IS CLEARLY VISIBLE.
GROUND CONTROL TO HQ, WE HAVE A GRID REFERENCE FOR THE COMPOUND. BEGINNING TRANSMISSION OF COORDINATES.

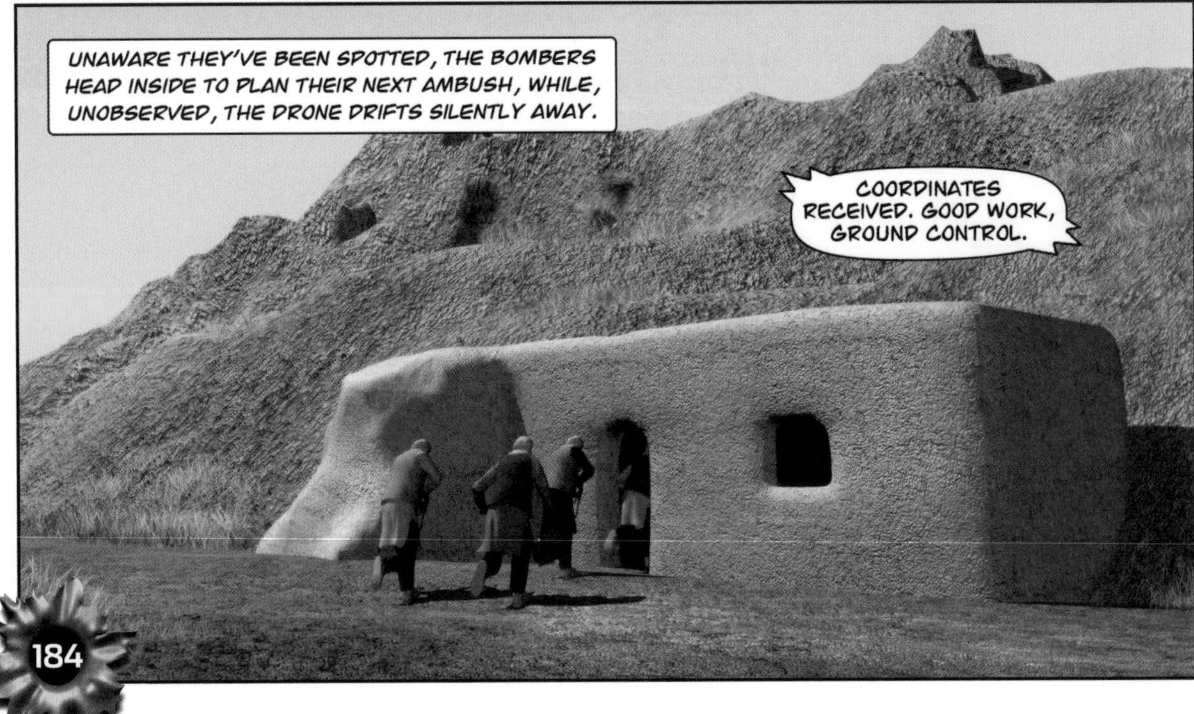
UNAWARE THEY'VE BEEN SPOTTED, THE BOMBERS HEAD INSIDE TO PLAN THEIR NEXT AMBUSH, WHILE, UNOBSERVED, THE DRONE DRIFTS SILENTLY AWAY.
COORDINATES RECEIVED. GOOD WORK, GROUND CONTROL.

THE NEXT DAY, THE BOMBERS MOVE OUT. SECRETS ARE HARD TO KEEP IN AFGHANISTAN AND THE TALIBAN KNOW THE ROUTES THE BRITISH FORCES ARE LIKELY TO TAKE. THE SMALL TEAM ARE PLANNING TO STUD A PATROL ROUTE WITH CRIPPLING IEDS.

BUT THIS TIME THE BRITISH FORCES ARE ONE STEP AHEAD. A SPECIAL RECONNAISSANCE UNIT, UNDER LIEUTENANT DANNY WRIGHT, HAS BEEN DEPLOYED TO COUNTER ANY IED ACTIVITY.
QUIETLY NOW, LADS. DON'T LET THEM SPOT YOU. AND NO COMMS – WE DON'T WANT TO GIVE THE GAME AWAY.

FROM A POSITION OF COVER, DANNY AND HIS TEAM WATCH AS THE TALIBAN LAY THE IED.
THERE IT GOES... RIGHT IN THE MIDDLE OF OUR PATROL ROUTE.
THAT WOULD DO SOME DAMAGE AND NO MISTAKE, EH BOSS?

ONCE THE TALIBAN HAVE LEFT, DANNY'S TEAM MOVES IN TO DISMANTLE THE DEVICE.
EEAAAASY DOES IT, PRIVATE, THAT THING LOOKS VICIOUS.
TOO RIGHT, SIR – THERE'S ENOUGH SHRAPNEL HERE TO TAKE OUT A FULL PLATOON.

WITH THE TROOPS A SAFE DISTANCE AWAY, THE MINES ARE DESTROYED. THAT'S ONE LESS IED TO WORRY ABOUT...
KABOUM?!
$%£*@! THAT WAS A BIG ONE.

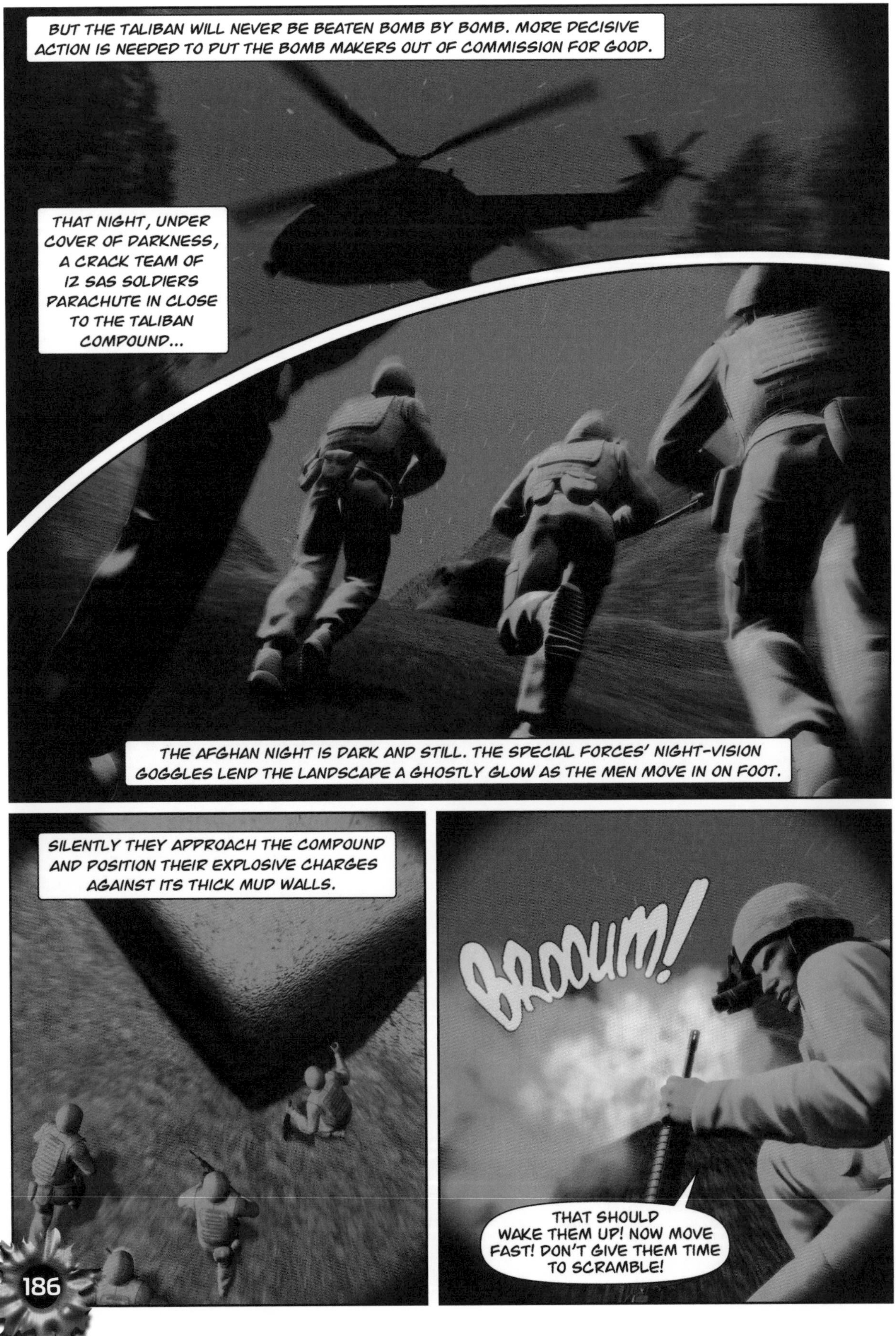

BUT THE TALIBAN WILL NEVER BE BEATEN BOMB BY BOMB. MORE DECISIVE ACTION IS NEEDED TO PUT THE BOMB MAKERS OUT OF COMMISSION FOR GOOD.

THAT NIGHT, UNDER COVER OF DARKNESS, A CRACK TEAM OF 12 SAS SOLDIERS PARACHUTE IN CLOSE TO THE TALIBAN COMPOUND...

THE AFGHAN NIGHT IS DARK AND STILL. THE SPECIAL FORCES' NIGHT-VISION GOGGLES LEND THE LANDSCAPE A GHOSTLY GLOW AS THE MEN MOVE IN ON FOOT.

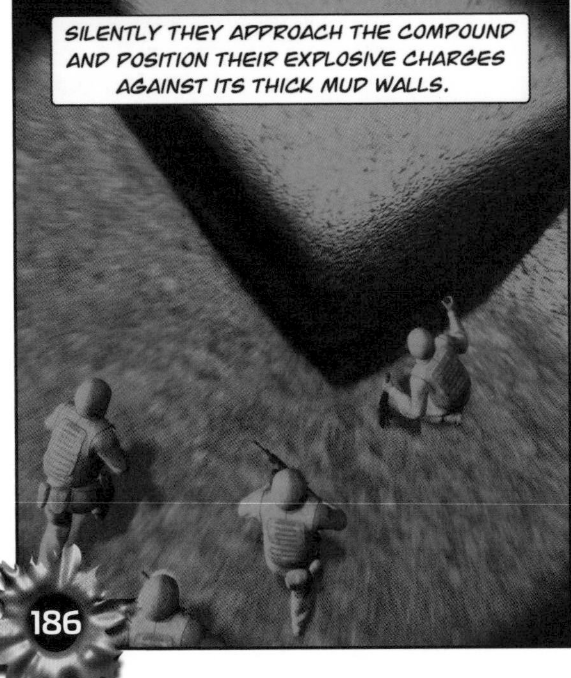

SILENTLY THEY APPROACH THE COMPOUND AND POSITION THEIR EXPLOSIVE CHARGES AGAINST ITS THICK MUD WALLS.

BROOUM!
THAT SHOULD WAKE THEM UP! NOW MOVE FAST! DON'T GIVE THEM TIME TO SCRAMBLE!

QUICK, STUN GRENADES! GET THEM IN THERE!

WHUMPH!
NOW MOVE IN, MOVE IN! GUNS AT THE READY!
WHUMPH!

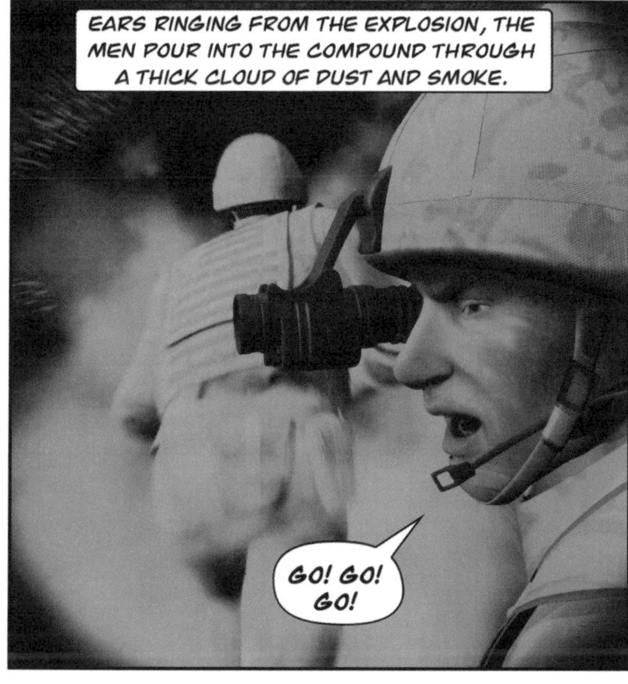
EARS RINGING FROM THE EXPLOSION, THE MEN POUR INTO THE COMPOUND THROUGH A THICK CLOUD OF DUST AND SMOKE.
GO! GO! GO!

I'VE GOT YOUR BACK! GO, GO!

AN APACHE, LOITERING OUT OF SIGHT AND SOUND, NOW SCREAMS IN OVERHEAD, READY TO UNLEASH A DEVASTATING BARRAGE IN SUPPORT OF THE GUYS ON THE GROUND.

THIS IS UGLY 57, WE HAVE YOU IN SIGHT! CANNON ARE LOCKED ON TARGET AND READY TO FIRE!

AS THE SOLDIERS BURST IN, THE DAZED TALIBAN ARE CAUGHT BY SURPRISE.

DROP YOUR WEAPONS OR WE WILL FIRE!

THEY'VE GOT GUNS! FIRE! ***FIRE!***

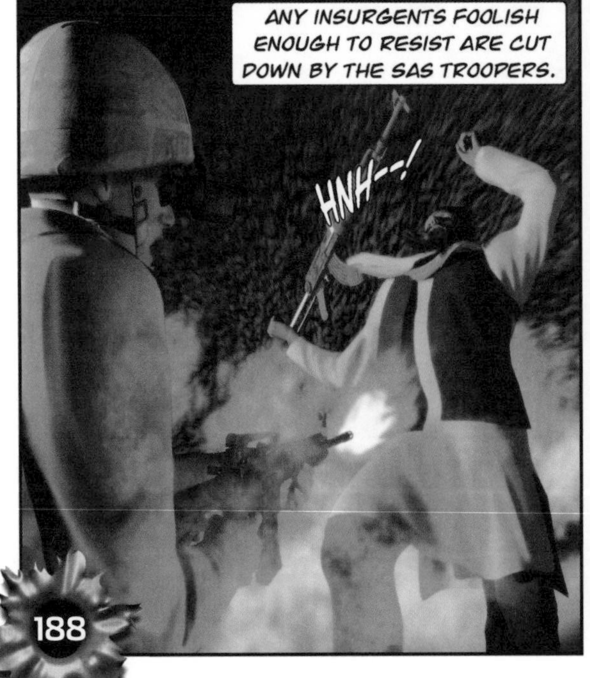

ANY INSURGENTS FOOLISH ENOUGH TO RESIST ARE CUT DOWN BY THE SAS TROOPERS.
HNH--!

IN A MATTER OF MINUTES, IT'S ALL OVER. THE BATTLE IS WON SO QUICKLY THAT SOME TALIBAN ARE STILL SHAKING THEMSELVES FROM SLEEP WHEN THE SHOOTING STOPS.
EH...?
WAKEY, WAKEY, MY FRIEND. YOU'RE HAVING A VERY BAD DREAM.

THERE'S NO QUESTION WHO HAS WON THE DAY. THE REMAINING TALIBAN SURRENDER QUICKLY AND ARE TAKEN PRISONER AS THE DUST SETTLES OVER THEIR SHATTERED COMPOUND.
HANDS ON YOUR HEAD! NO SUDDEN MOVES!
BOSS, I'VE GOT ANOTHER ONE!

DAYS OF CAREFUL SURVEILLANCE HAVE PAID OFF. THE SOLDIERS UNCOVER A CACHE OF HIGH-EXPLOSIVE SHELLS AND OTHER BOMB PARTS - PROOF POSITIVE THAT THESE WERE INDEED THE BOMBERS WHO KILLED THEIR COMRADES.

AS DAWN BREAKS, THE APACHE IS CALLED OFF TO ANOTHER CONTACT AND THE PRISONERS ARE ROUNDED UP. THEY WILL BE TAKEN BACK TO BASE FOR QUESTIONING. THE ENTIRE BOMBING TEAM HAS BEEN CAPTURED OR KILLED - A ROUSING SUCCESS FOR THE BRITISH FORCES. WHILE TOMORROW WILL BRING ANOTHER CHALLENGE, FOR TODAY, AT LEAST, THEY CAN REST EASY KNOWING THAT THEY'VE SAVED TROOPS FROM FURTHER IED ATTACKS.

POEM OF THE UNKNOWN SOLDIER

'Twas the night before Christmas,
He lived all alone,
In a one-bedroom house, made
Of plaster and stone.
I had come down the chimney,
With presents to give,
And to see just who
In this home did live.
I looked all about,
A strange sight I did see.
No tinsel, no presents,
Not even a tree.
No stocking by the mantle,
Just boots filled with sand,
On the wall hung pictures
Of far distant lands,
With medals and badges,
Awards of all kinds.
A sober thought
Came through my mind,
For this house was different,
It was dark and dreary.
I found the home of a soldier,
Once I could see clearly.
The soldier lay sleeping,
Silent, alone,
Curled up on the floor
In this one-bedroom home.
The face was so gentle,
The room in such disorder,
Not how I pictured
A lone British soldier.
Was this the hero
Of whom I'd just read?
Curled up on a poncho,
The floor for a bed?
I realized the families
That I saw this night
Owed their lives to these soldiers
Who were willing to fight.
Soon round the world
The children would play,
And grown-ups would celebrate
A bright Christmas Day.
They all enjoyed freedom
Each month of the year
Because of the soldiers,
Like the one lying here.
I couldn't help wonder
How many alone
On a cold Christmas Eve
In a land far from home.
The very thought brought
A tear to my eye,
I dropped to my knees,
And started to cry.
The soldier awakened
And I heard a rough voice:
'Santa, don't cry,
This life is my choice.
I fight for freedom
I don't ask for more
My life is my God,
My country, My corps.'
The soldier rolled over
And drifted to sleep,
I couldn't control it,
I continued to weep.
I kept watch for hours,
So silent and still,
And we both sat and shivered,
From the cold night's chill.
I didn't want to leave
On that cold, dark night,
This guardian of honour,
So willing to fight.
Then the soldier rolled over,
With a voice, soft and pure,
Whispered: 'Carry on, Santa,
It's Christmas Day, all is secure.'
One look at my watch,
And I knew he was right:
'Merry Christmas, my friend,
And to all a good night.'

WHERE WILL THEY BE FOR CHRISTMAS?

As families gather to celebrate Christmas, spare a thought for the thousands of British servicemen and women serving overseas.

From southern Iraq and the Persian Gulf to the Falklands and Kosovo, more than 14,000 British troops are far from home. In the Gulf of Aden and the Indian Ocean, the Royal Navy is conducting counter-piracy missions with Coalition Task Force (CTF) 151, while warships and aviation assets are committed to Op Atlanta off the coast of Somalia.

To the forces fighting for Britain overseas, 25 December is just like any other day on an operational tour of duty. Nevertheless, the holidays are especially tough for our soldiers on the front line in war-torn Helmand Province, Afghanistan. Over 220 British military personnel have died while serving in the country since October 2001.

Several hundred British Forces personnel are based in the strategically important Middle East area supporting operations in Afghanistan and the wider region on land and sea and in the air.

A combined force comprising members of the Army, Royal Air Force and Royal Navy are based on the Falkland Islands, where troops have been stationed since the war in 1981. Further troops are serving overseas in numerous UN and EU operational and training missions, including in Sierra Leone, the Democratic Republic of Congo, the Balkans and Oman.

Air Chief Marshal Sir Jock Stirrup has urged Brits to remember all those who have made a sacrifice for their country. He said: 'At this special time of year it is more than usually appropriate that we stop for a moment and think about all this. That we remember those we've lost and the families that will be facing, for the first time, a Christmas with an empty place at the table. That we remember those colleagues and families who are having to cope with painful and sometimes disabling injuries. That we think of those who are spending the holiday season far from home and loved ones, in the service of their country. Christmas is, above all, a time for remembering others.'

As the violence rages on around the world, the minds and hearts of British servicemen and women will be with their loved ones thousands of miles away.

By Oliver Harvey

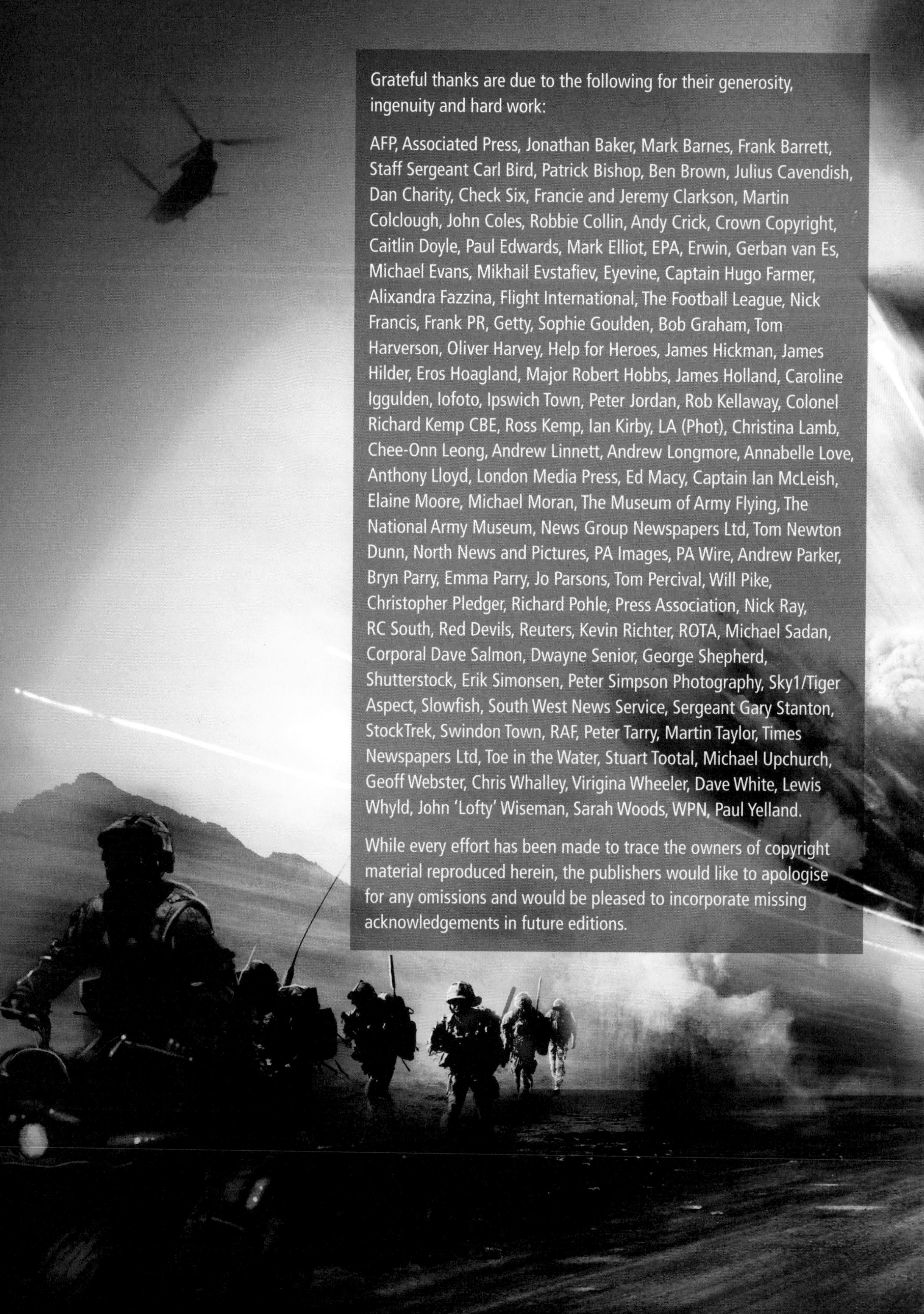

Grateful thanks are due to the following for their generosity, ingenuity and hard work:

AFP, Associated Press, Jonathan Baker, Mark Barnes, Frank Barrett, Staff Sergeant Carl Bird, Patrick Bishop, Ben Brown, Julius Cavendish, Dan Charity, Check Six, Francie and Jeremy Clarkson, Martin Colclough, John Coles, Robbie Collin, Andy Crick, Crown Copyright, Caitlin Doyle, Paul Edwards, Mark Elliot, EPA, Erwin, Gerban van Es, Michael Evans, Mikhail Evstafiev, Eyevine, Captain Hugo Farmer, Alixandra Fazzina, Flight International, The Football League, Nick Francis, Frank PR, Getty, Sophie Goulden, Bob Graham, Tom Harverson, Oliver Harvey, Help for Heroes, James Hickman, James Hilder, Eros Hoagland, Major Robert Hobbs, James Holland, Caroline Iggulden, Iofoto, Ipswich Town, Peter Jordan, Rob Kellaway, Colonel Richard Kemp CBE, Ross Kemp, Ian Kirby, LA (Phot), Christina Lamb, Chee-Onn Leong, Andrew Linnett, Andrew Longmore, Annabelle Love, Anthony Lloyd, London Media Press, Ed Macy, Captain Ian McLeish, Elaine Moore, Michael Moran, The Museum of Army Flying, The National Army Museum, News Group Newspapers Ltd, Tom Newton Dunn, North News and Pictures, PA Images, PA Wire, Andrew Parker, Bryn Parry, Emma Parry, Jo Parsons, Tom Percival, Will Pike, Christopher Pledger, Richard Pohle, Press Association, Nick Ray, RC South, Red Devils, Reuters, Kevin Richter, ROTA, Michael Sadan, Corporal Dave Salmon, Dwayne Senior, George Shepherd, Shutterstock, Erik Simonsen, Peter Simpson Photography, Sky1/Tiger Aspect, Slowfish, South West News Service, Sergeant Gary Stanton, StockTrek, Swindon Town, RAF, Peter Tarry, Martin Taylor, Times Newspapers Ltd, Toe in the Water, Stuart Tootal, Michael Upchurch, Geoff Webster, Chris Whalley, Virigina Wheeler, Dave White, Lewis Whyld, John 'Lofty' Wiseman, Sarah Woods, WPN, Paul Yelland.

While every effort has been made to trace the owners of copyright material reproduced herein, the publishers would like to apologise for any omissions and would be pleased to incorporate missing acknowledgements in future editions.

GENERAL

A General is the highest peacetime rank in the British Army and its logo is a crossed sword and baton, with a bath star and a crown. A General is a very senior commander. The equivalent rating in the Royal Navy and rank in the Royal Air Force are Admiral and Air Chief Marshal, respectively.

LIEUTENANT GENERAL

Lieutenant General is a senior rank in the British Army. It is above Major General but below full General. Its logo is a crown over a crossed sword and baton. The Royal Navy and Royal Air Force equivalents are Vice-Admiral and Air Marshal, respectively.

MAJOR GENERAL

Major General is a senior rank in the British Army. It falls below Lieutenant General and above Brigadier and its equivalents are the Rear-Admiral in the Royal Navy and the Air Vice-Marshal in the Royal Air Force. Its logo is a crossed sword and a baton, beneath a bath star.

BRIGADIER

A Brigadier is either the highest field rank or the most junior General appointment in the British Army. Falling below a Major General and above a Colonel, its equivalents in the Royal Navy and Royal Air Force are Commodore and Air Commodore, respectively. The Brigadier's insignia is made up of three diamond-shaped bath stars underneath a crown.

This rank was called Brigadier General until 1922. In addition to the British Army, the title of Brigadier is also used by the Royal Marines, the Australian Army, the New Zealand Army, the Indian Army, the Pakistani Army and the Sri Lankan Army.

MAJOR

The rank of Major falls below Lieutenant Colonel and above Captain in the British Army. The Royal Navy equivalent is the Lieutenant Commander and the Royal Air Force equivalent is the Squadron Leader. The rank logo is a crown.

CAPTAIN

A Captain is a junior officer rank of the British Army and falls below Major and above Lieutenant. The Royal Navy equivalent of Captain is Lieutenant and the Royal Air Force equivalent is Flight Lieutenant. The rating (in the case of the Navy) or rank of Captain does exist in both the Navy and the Air Force; however, its status is different to that of a Captain in the Army – a Royal Navy Captain is much more senior. The Army Captain's logo is three diamond-shaped bath stars.